The Making of Julia Gillard

Jacqueline Kent was born in Sydney and grew up there and in Adelaide. Originally trained as a radio journalist and broadcaster, she has also been a book editor and a reviewer for numerous publications, and has a Doctorate of Creative Arts from the University of Technology, Sydney. As well as biography and general social history, she has written fiction for young adults. *A Certain Style: Beatrice Davis, A Literary Life* won the 2002 National Biography Award and the Nita B. Kibble Award. *An Exacting Heart: The Story of Hephzibah Menuhin* won the 2009 Nita B. Kibble Award. She lives in Sydney with her partner, John Tuchin.

Also by Jacqueline Kent

NON-FICTION

An Exacting Heart: The Story of Hephzibah Menuhin

A Certain Style: Beatrice Davis, A Literary Life

In the Half Light: Life as a Child in Australia

Out of the Bakelite Box: The Heyday of Australian Radio

YOUNG ADULT FICTION

Angel Claws I Love You

Bad Behaviour (with Joanne Horniman)

The Making of JULIA GILLARD

JACQUELINE KENT

VIKING
an imprint of
PENGUIN BOOKS

VIKING

Published by the Penguin Group
Penguin Group (Australia)
250 Camberwell Road, Camberwell, Victoria 3124, Australia
(a division of Pearson Australia Group Pty Ltd)
Penguin Group (USA) Inc.
375 Hudson Street, New York, New York 10014, USA
Penguin Group (Canada)
90 Eglinton Avenue East, Suite 700, Toronto, Canada ON M4P 2Y3
(a division of Pearson Penguin Canada Inc.)
Penguin Books Ltd
80 Strand, London WC2R 0RL England
Penguin Ireland
25 St Stephen's Green, Dublin 2, Ireland
(a division of Penguin Books Ltd)
Penguin Books India Pvt Ltd
11 Community Centre, Panchsheel Park, New Delhi – 110 017, India
Penguin Group (NZ)
67 Apollo Drive, Rosedale, North Shore 0632, New Zealand
(a division of Pearson New Zealand Ltd)
Penguin Books (South Africa) (Pty) Ltd
24 Sturdee Avenue, Rosebank, Johannesburg 2196, South Africa

Penguin Books Ltd, Registered Offices: 80 Strand, London, WC2R 0RL, England

First published by Penguin Books Australia Ltd, 2009

3 5 7 9 10 8 6 4 2

Cover and text design by Cathy Larsen © Penguin Group (Australia)
Front cover photograph by Peter Brew-Bevan
Back cover photograph by Andrew Taylor/Fairfaxphotos.com
Typeset in 12 pt Adobe Garamond Pro by Post Pre-press Group, Brisbane, Queensland
Printed and bound in Australia by McPherson's Printing Group, Maryborough, Victoria

National Library of Australia Cataloguing-in-Publication data:

Kent, Jacqueline
The making of Julia Gillard / Jacqueline Kent.
Viking ed.
9780670073191 (pbk.)
Includes index.
Gillard, Julia.
Australian Labor Party – Biography.
Cabinet officers – Australia – Biography.
Political leadership – Australia.
Politicians – Australia – Biography.
Women politicians – Australia – Biography.
Australia – Politics and government – Biography.

324.29407092

penguin.com.au

For John,
whose calm and acuity are,
as always, indispensable

Contents

Our Julia

In a country where distrust of politicians is almost an article of faith, Julia Gillard is a political celebrity. Ever since Labor won the 2007 federal election, and she became deputy prime minister, scarcely a day seems to have gone by without a media story about her somewhere. She has smiled out of the pages of the glossy women's magazines, gazed thoughtfully into the distance for the broadsheet newspapers as a woman of destiny, laughed and joked on TV and radio, been photographed and quoted as she shreds the Opposition in Parliament. Type 'Julia Gillard' into Google and you come up with hundreds of thousands of entries, including opinions about her right across the political spectrum.

She is not universally loved. For everyone who cheers her on as she lobs verbal grenades in Parliament there will be someone who thinks she is too shrill, sarcastic or bitchy. Some Labor loyalists still dislike her for her role in toppling party leader Kim Beazley in 2006; others continue to be angry about the immigration policy she crafted for the ALP in the wake of the 2001 *Tampa* crisis. She has been criticised for her hairstyle, for her fashion sense, even for the way she speaks. But many people, men as well as women, will rush to her defence, condemning adverse comment about her voice as snobbish, asking why just because she is a politician she should not change her hairstyle, approving the gun-metal-coloured trouser suits and other no-fuss corporate clothes.

Julia Gillard tells this story: 'At a shopping centre in Hoppers Crossing I'm handing out stuff. I am standing next to a board with my photograph on it.

'This old guy comes out of the supermarket, looks at me, looks at the photo, looks at me, looks at the photo, then turns back to me and says, "Taken on a good day, wasn't it, love?"

'I said, "And you'd be bloody Robert Redford, would you, mate?"'

One of the obvious things about this revealing little anecdote is that the incident could have occurred only in Australia. Not too many British or US voters speak to their elected representatives as the 'old guy' speaks to Gillard. (And not just Gillard: one Australian voter even pinched the prime ministerial bottom.) Australian MPs are often bailed up in the street by voters intent on pointing out where they think their representative is going wrong. It is part of the 'I'm as good as you' ethos that we like to believe is part of our national identity.

There is no 'side' to Gillard, but as the story shows she is no pushover. She can give as good as she gets, and she manages to do it without offending someone or sounding in any way superior. There is clearly a payoff: in this case the man at Hoppers Crossing said he would vote for her.

She can have fun with her political celebrity. Adam Hills, the stand-up comedian and host of ABC-TV's music quiz show *Spicks and Specks*, recently told a story to Channel Ten's *Rove Live* of finding himself on the same plane as Gillard.

During the flight she came over and sat next to him, put a hand on his arm and said, 'I'm the acting prime minister, and so I can order you to do whatever I want. And I order you, now, to be very nice to my assistant, who fancies you.' ('What an abuse of power!' gasped Rove McManus.)

When Gillard and her entourage – including the bedazzled Adam Hills – got off the plane, the assistant said Gillard should be on *Spicks and Specks*.

'Oh no,' said Gillard. 'I'm really bad at music.'

'No problem,' said one of the accompanying security men. 'You take my earpiece and I'll feed you the answers.'

Women voters often identify with Julia Gillard, whatever their own circumstances. In May 2007 Liberal senator Bill Heffernan described her as unfit for leadership because she was unmarried and childless.

'People can be very generous during those times,' Gillard has said. 'I was walking in Altona and a woman went past in a car with a back seat full of kids. She wound her window down and called out, "If you want any kids, love, you can have mine!"'

A few years ago a journalist for *Vive* magazine wrote: 'There is something about Julia Gillard's public persona that is grounded and ordinary. The public's instinct is never to give her an honorific, nor is it hers to demand one. Julia Gillard comes across as absolutely one of the girls. You went to school with a Julia, you live next door to her, you work with her.'

This is a comment that has been echoed elsewhere. It is not as though the voting public is unaware of Gillard's extraordinary qualities, just that she is not seen as someone who is 'up herself'. We do not much like politicians who present themselves as cleverer than we are. Classical scholars or enthusiasts for Second Empire clocks are all very well in their place, we think, but we are a bit suspicious of them if they are heading our governments. Nor are we very keen on leaders like the Malcolms Fraser and Turnbull, who if not actually born with silver spoons in their mouths have certainly acquired them. We are much more at home with a John Howard or a Bob Hawke, blokes who look as if they are up for a beer and a yarn.

If Gillard's political style is to be compared with anyone's, it is probably Bob Hawke's, although the comparison should not be pushed too far, not least because their temperaments are so different. But both are extraordinary people who know the value of appearing ordinary. Both connect easily with the person in the street; both are generally friendly and approachable. There are other similarities: both are highly intelligent, legally trained clear thinkers, good at putting across complicated policy ideas in simple, accessible language. And, possibly coincidentally but probably not, both have broad Australian accents.

Bob Hawke is said to have deliberately set out to broaden his Australian accent when he decided on a public career. (At about the same time, Margaret Thatcher was working hard to eliminate all verbal traces of the provincial grocer's daughter.) When she is making a point in Parliament, Gillard's voice can be flat, her delivery aggressive. This is something women often do not much like about her, whether they approve of her or not. (Note: her male colleagues' voices and demeanour do not attract this kind of scrutiny.)

Gillard smiles or shrugs when asked about her voice, telling journalist Michael Duffy: 'As you can probably tell from my voice, I've never been involved in voice coaching, though there have been a number of people who have suggested that I ought to, and ought to do so immediately, and not utter another word until I had. So I'd have to say I think it's not exactly dulcet tones but I think I've got a pretty strong voice and I think I can hold my own in Parliament, no matter what the noise level, and on various occasions have had to . . . I think in a perfect world it wouldn't be like that, but in the world we inhabit it is, so having a somewhat gravelly voice helps.'

Gillard's refusal to take herself too seriously is one of her most effective ways of connecting with the public. Another is her empathy, which was fully displayed when she spoke to a parliamentary condolence motion on Monday 9 February 2009, in the aftermath of the appalling Victorian bushfires.

Very close to tears and, like other speakers, rejecting high-flown rhetoric, she simply told some of the stories of the people affected: 'Let me share some of the media reports with the House: the tragedy of Rebecca Buchanan, who lost her fifteen year old son Macca Mackenzie, nine year old daughter Neeve and her brother Danny Clark, who was thirty-seven years old. Two young girls from down the street also perished inside the house of Rebecca's mother, Jenny Clark. Jenny is seriously injured with burns to thirty per cent of her body after she desperately tried to save her grandchildren . . .

'There is the courage of Kinglake resident Karen Drenan and her son Jakob. Karen was lying in the bath with her son, neighbour and a dog when she realised the front door was on fire. She then put wet blankets over her ten year old son Jakob and told him to run to the other side of the road. His shoes had melted, so he grabbed a pair of high-heeled boots. She said of her son: "He was so brave, he did everything that was screamed at him to do. We called him the high-heel hero" . . .

'As a Melburnian and a Victorian, the reality of the loss took on a familiar face with the death of Brian Naylor and his wife Moiree at their Kinglake West home. I am one of the millions of Victorians who for years only got the news because "Brian told us". He was loved and trusted like a reliable uncle.'

It is a very powerful speech. Much of its force and emotion comes precisely from Gillard's perceived ordinariness: here she is speaking for all Australians.

Australian politics has always been, and to some extent still is, a boys' club. This is gradually changing. Crude attempts at gender politics, like those of Senator Heffernan, gain very little advantage these days. Gillard has certainly been fortunate in her time. Former senator Susan Ryan, who was minister for education in the Hawke Labor government in the late 1980s, has observed that Gillard benefits from not being burdened with the huge expectations of the 1970s feminist movement, as she felt she herself was. It is a view that former premier of Victoria Joan Kirner, a staunch Gillard supporter, disagrees with. 'A lot of women worked bloody hard to get her there,' Kirner says of Gillard. So did a number of men. Most of all, so did Gillard herself.

Sometimes politics, especially on the Labor side, can seem too complicated for its own good, or indeed anyone's. To those not actively involved, the distinctions between the various factions in the Right or the Left can be like the difference between C sharp and D flat in musical notation: both are the same pitch, but what they are called depends totally on context. Weaving one's way through the factional complexities, let alone prevailing against them, is not something for the faint of heart.

But as her story demonstrates, Julia Gillard is one of the most single-minded and determined realists in this or any other Australian government. These are qualities that have traditionally not been associated with women in politics. In the words of one Labor source, 'Julia Gillard knows how to play it as hard and as well as the blokes.'

She scoffs at the assumption that women are unsuited to the rough and tumble of politics. 'The kind of image that somehow we are too gentle for it, I resent that,' she has said.

She also rejects the idea that if there were more women in politics it would be a different, probably kinder, profession. 'Certainly five or ten years ago people would have [had] the view, if only there were more women in politics somehow it would be a less adversarial, more caring and sharing environment. I have always thought that was bloody nonsense. One of the things I have always wanted to show is that it doesn't matter whether you are a man or a woman, you can thrive in an adversarial environment.'

1

'Australia is my only reality'

I always knew growing up that we had chosen this place because it offered us opportunities beyond what our homeland could have delivered . . . My parents could muse on what life might have held for them in Wales. Frankly I cannot. Australia is and always has been my only reality.

In July 2005 Julia Gillard, Labor's shadow minister for health, launched *Ten Pound Poms: Australia's Invisible Migrants.* This book, by James Hammerton and Alistair Thomson, dealt with a subject very close to her heart. Although strictly speaking not a Pom at all – she has always insisted that her people are proudly Welsh – she had travelled with her family to Australia as a four-year-old, under the Australian government's assisted-passage migration scheme.

'This means the Australian taxpayer kindly paid the 120 or so pounds to get me here,' she told a large and appreciative audience at Melbourne's Immigration Museum. 'I hope you believe that Australia has broken even on the deal.'

Julia's father, John Oliver Gillard, comes from Cwmgwrach, a village in South Wales whose small houses cluster, as closely as the consonants in its name, around a crossroads en route to the steelworks town of Port Talbot. Born in August 1929 at the start of the Great Depression, John Gillard was one of seven children. As with most families in this part of the world, the Gillards' lives were shaped by the mining of coal. Two of John's brothers became miners; two of his sisters married miners. Most members of the Gillard family still live in or around Cwmgwrach, but John and a brother and sister left Wales to seek their fortunes. There are relatively few Welsh people in Australia. Although life in Wales has frequently been harsh and difficult, their numbers as immigrants reflect their proportion of the population in the United Kingdom.

When John was very young the family assumed that he would go down the coalmines, but from an early age he saw the possibilities for a different kind of life. A highly intelligent boy, he enjoyed studying and dreamed of a future filled with learning and books. At twelve he was reading the newspapers: 'I could give you the wartime cabinet in England,' he told an interviewer. He was one of the top three students in South Wales in his final year of primary school and the first member of his family to win a scholarship to grammar school. But it was World War II and times were bleak in the coalmining villages, so young John had to follow the rest of his family into work. He was fourteen. Giving up his education was the cruellest possible blow for a young boy with a probing, questioning mind and love of words and ideas.

Julia, who is close to her father and who bears an obvious physical resemblance to him, has often told this story. Journalists have commented – with obvious surprise because Gillard is usually such a controlled and measured media performer – that she talks about the injustice done to her father with real passion. Gillard repeatedly says that the main difference between herself and her parents is not that she is smarter, or that she has worked harder – it's that she had the chance for education and they did not. The forces of poverty and the British class system were just too great for them to overcome. She has repeatedly said that her role as minister for education in the Rudd Labor government is to ensure that no Australian child will ever have to endure what her father did.

John Gillard spent his teenage years doing a succession of unrewarding and mostly menial jobs, with a grocer, the Royal Air Force and the Coal Board. In his twenties he escaped into the police force, where his job included shining a torch on courting couples in a local lover's lane. His work took him to Barry, a coastal town 11 kilometres from Cardiff, on the northern side of the Bristol Channel. It was there that he met and married Moira Mackenzie, whose reddish blonde hair and fair skin proclaimed her Scottish and Irish ancestry. She was one of four children, two of whom had died in childhood. Like John, she had had little formal education. And like him, she was a great reader. Julia Gillard sees her parents as brought together by their shared high intelligence, sense of humour and love of books. There is, she says, a very strong intellectual and emotional bond between her parents; the warmth between them is obvious even now, after many years of marriage.

Another interest they shared was politics. True to their working-class background, John and Moira were both Labour supporters. John was a particularly keen admirer of Aneurin Bevan, the political leader whom working-class Welsh people claimed as their own. Born in South Wales of Nonconformist parents, Bevan had emerged as the leader of the region's miners during the 1926 General Strike. When minister for health in the Attlee Labour government after World War II, he was responsible for putting in place the new and comprehensive National Health Service, a free health service funded directly through government revenue, including increased taxes on the wealthy. John admired both Bevan's principled pragmatism and his oratory. He was also an admirer of Harold Wilson, Eleanor Roosevelt and, in particular, John F. Kennedy, whose words he liked to quote. John Gillard's children grew up with progressive politics as their birthright.

After John and Moira married, John left the police force and became a booking clerk for British Railways. In November 1958 Moira gave birth to the couple's first child, a daughter named Alison Mary, who had dark hair, a round face and blue eyes. Julia Eileen, Moira and John's second child, was born three years later, on 29 September 1961. With light hazel eyes and reddish hair, a long, narrow nose and wide mouth, she does not look very much like Alison, although both have the same fine, pale complexion. Julia's hair colour, as much as her political orientation, is part of her Welsh heritage.

Barry, the town where Julia spent the first four years of life, had been an important port in the 1880s, with railways bringing coal down to it from the valleys, and for a time after 1913 it was the largest coal-exporting port in the world – a fact still mentioned with pride on the town's website. These days Barry spruiks itself as a seaside resort, but in the 1960s when the Gillard family lived there it could accurately be described as a grimy industrial town, squatting under a freezing pall of coal dust for much of the year. (In 2005 part of Barry stood in for a World War II London bombsite in *Doctor Who,* and the town was pilloried as a bastion of provincialism in the hit BBC-TV comedy series *Gavin & Stacey.*)

Julia Gillard does not remember much about Barry. As a very young child she was plagued by respiratory problems, including a dose of pneumonia, which often kept her in bed. The family doctor told her parents that she was developing chronic lung problems, exacerbated by the cold winters and polluted air. If the Gillards stayed in Barry, he said, Julia would have to spend large parts of winter at home. Moira Gillard had had health problems herself as a child, and knew the difficulties of being forced to miss school. Julia would not recover, said the doctor, unless the family moved to a warmer place.

His advice became a factor in a decision that John and Moira were already considering. For a while they had been thinking of leaving Wales, of getting out of the United Kingdom altogether. Taxes and prices were high, wages low. John felt he was looking into a future of hard, grinding work, with no way of getting ahead. Life would surely be easier elsewhere. But could they abandon everyone and everything they had known to go to a foreign place, wherever that might be? John was keen; Moira hung back. She did not want to leave her mother. But the Gillards were a young and energetic couple in their early thirties: if they intended to pull up stakes, there would probably not be a better time.

For many families in the United Kingdom the time was right. Thanks to the Australian government's assisted-passage migration scheme, UK citizens could travel to Australia for as little as 10 pounds per head. The real cost of bringing a family of two adults and two children from Britain was closer to 600 pounds. Australia's immigration policy was still shaped by the idea that the country must 'populate or perish', and preference was given to citizens of the 'Mother Country'. Intending British immigrants had only to be white, in good health and younger than forty-five. They were expected to stay for at least two years; if they returned to Britain before then – and some did – they had to refund the balance of the full fare. The Australian government was also keen to offer citizenship to its settlers; and those who committed themselves to staying permanently could vote, move freely in and out of the country, and apply for some social security benefits. It was an almost ridiculously good deal, and UK citizens responded in large numbers. During the 1960s more than half a million came to settle in Australia: almost 47 per cent of the country's migrant intake for the decade.

John and Moira Gillard finally decided to make the move after Moira's mother died. Moira felt that her strongest link to Wales had been broken.

It became a Gillard family joke that when they told the family doctor they planned to go to Australia he was taken aback. 'Oh,' he said. 'When I was thinking of a warmer climate, I meant Cornwall.'

Early in February 1966 the Gillard family travelled to Southampton, where they boarded the Italian-owned Sitmar Line *Fairsky*, one of three former cargo ships bought to transport British migrants to their new home. The others were the *Fairsea* and the *Fairstar*, and the three names became fixtures in the shipping pages of Australian newspapers. They were more comfortable than the vessels bringing migrants to Australia from Europe – 'old' Britons were often treated better than 'New Australians'. The *Fairsky* had four upper decks, a swimming pool, courts for tennis and quoits, two bars and a cinema, and could take about 1400 passengers.

When Julia Gillard was launching *Ten Pound Poms* she shared some of her snapshot memories of the voyage. She remembered storms and seasickness and misadventures with toys. Every child on board was given a present to celebrate the ship's crossing of the Equator, and her sister scored a toy truck because the Italian crew thought Alison was a boy's name. Julia herself was inconsolable when she accidentally dropped a new toy koala over the side of the ship as they docked in Fremantle.

John and Moira Gillard had planned to travel on the *Fairsky* as far as Melbourne. They had no particular reason for choosing that city – they more or less picked the name off a map. But on the ship they made friends with the only other Welsh people, a couple with two daughters who were going to Adelaide. The thought of having friends in a strange city tipped the balance, and the Gillards changed destination. As they had turned their lives upside down already, a change of city was a comparatively small matter for John and Moira.

The Gillard family left the ship at Port Adelaide and were taken straight to Pennington Hostel in the nearby suburb of Finsbury Park. No doubt John and Moira had been told that new migrants to Australia were usually housed in hostels in the major population centres, and were hardly expecting a lavish reception. Even so Pennington – a collection of corrugated-iron army huts and tin sheds spread out across a flat, almost treeless landscape – must have been a shock.

Few who have stayed at Pennington have fond memories of the place, which was in operation for about thirty years from 1950 in the service of Australian migration. During the long, relentless Adelaide summers the heat in the huts was stifling, and in winter the iron roofs crackled with the cold. Every family was allocated a section of hut, separated by flimsy partitions, where they slept on iron bedsteads and thin mattresses. Families shared laundry facilities and bathrooms: every family was issued with a rubber plug for the bath. A cafeteria served stodgy, utilitarian food. It would be surprising if John and Moira had not wondered, at least briefly, why they had come to Australia.

Migrants were allowed to stay in Pennington for months, sometimes even years, but John Gillard had no intention of remaining a minute longer than necessary. As soon as he had found work, he and Moira began the search for a home of their own. The South Australian government was directing British migrants north of Adelaide to Elizabeth, the satellite town created a decade before, where there were new jobs and housing. General Motors had established a factory there, and it was also the headquarters of the Long Range Weapons Research Establishment. But the idea of settling in such a raw place did not appeal to John and Moira. If the government was herding people north, they would look south. Besides, they were able to afford something better, in a more salubrious suburb closer to the city. And so they found a small brick house in Kingswood, a suburb about 8 kilometres south-east of the city, in the Adelaide foothills. Their new address was 33 Truro Avenue: the closest the Gillard family came to living in Cornwall.

Like all new immigrants, the Gillards were sensitive to the immediate contrasts between their old country and their new home. Sometimes it was the small differences rather than the larger ones that struck them most forcibly. Skirts were longer, voices slower and flatter. The hard Adelaide water from the Murray River smelled of chlorine, and soap and shampoo did not lather readily under the shower. A swimming costume was *bathers*, a suitcase was a *port*, and for a while John and Moira were puzzled about what mysterious beast a *chook* might be. Strangers often gave friendly, matter-of-fact advice: one woman explained to Moira that even in the autumn sun fair-skinned young girls could be badly sunburned if they were not careful. And there were differences in manners. One night John Gillard came off shift work and caught the last bus home; when he arrived he announced to the family that the bus driver, who had said 'See ya later, mate', was about to drop round for a cup of tea.

John and Moira cemented their friendship with the Welsh couple they had met on the boat; Julia knew them as Uncle Frank and Aunty Glad all her childhood. The two families visited each other's houses often and were included in family celebrations. But finding other congenial people took time, especially for Moira Gillard, a reserved woman who relied heavily on her husband for companionship. One of their neighbours was a Baptist minister, whose church the family joined. The Gillards were not a particularly religious family, but church membership did increase their social circle.

At first John Gillard took whatever work he could find, starting in a cheese factory. As soon as he could, he began to study at night to make up for his lost education. Eventually he undertook three years' hospital training to become a psychiatric nurse. For many years afterwards he worked in a local hospital, often choosing to do night shifts because the money was better, and he even took a second job at one point. Moira worked just as hard. 'Our whole thrust was to earn the money, pay the mortgage, get the kids through uni. We both worked like Trojans,' John Gillard later said. Moira looked after a couple of young children and then, once her own girls had started school, took a part-time job as cook and assistant in an old people's home run by the Salvation Army. She worked from 1.30 to 6.30 every day, preparing meals for seventy to eighty women, which frequently meant lugging huge pots and pans around and cleaning up after the evening meal before going home to cook dinner for her own family.

Julia Gillard has often described how hard her parents worked, and she makes a point of observing how much she has been guided by their example. 'I had a sense that [my] parents had moved half-way round the world to give [us] a better life,' she says. 'There was an expectation you'd go as far as you could. It was in the ether.'

All the same, having parents who seemed always to be working must have been difficult for her and Alison when they were small. Julia recalls endless days when they had to whisper and tiptoe around the house because their father was studying or snatching some sleep before heading back to work. She and her sister spent a great deal of time with their mother because they could go to her work after school. Julia says she could count on the fingers of one hand the times she and Alison were left with babysitters.

The Gillards have remained a very close family, with their own jokes and teases, and they get together whenever possible. 'One of the many great things about family is that they have known you too long for you to be anything other than just you,' says Julia. 'I think that works for you in the best of times and probably in the worst of times as well.'

School holidays for Julia and Alison were typical of those many Australian children enjoyed in the 1960s: hanging out with friends; catching tadpoles in the creek; making sandwiches, packing a bag and setting out for a day exploring the local bush. They would often be gone for the whole day. Once they were caught in a bad thunder-storm and a passing motorist offered them a lift home, which they accepted without thinking twice. 'I'm not sure how that adds up in the city of the Beaumont children,' says Julia, recalling the famous 1966 case in which two young girls and a boy disappeared and have never been found. 'But it was a more innocent age.'

John and Moira bought a car as soon as they could afford it, and the family explored the Adelaide Hills and the fine-sanded, scrubby beaches that fringe the coastline not far from the city. Hectic work schedules meant that family holidays away were rare, but John spent his free time with the girls whenever he could.

Alison and Julia went to Mitcham Primary, the local state school. Both knew how to read and write before they started school: Moira used the British Dick and Dora books to teach them. 'Other women would tell her it was bad for the baby's brain, you'll do them damage, but she kept on with it,' said Julia later.

Alison, who had started school in Wales, was not altogether comfortable in her new surroundings at first: her accent marked her out as different from the other children at a time before Australian state schools were the towers of Babel they have since become. Quick, intuitively intelligent and sometimes rebellious, she was inclined to chafe against the strictures of the system.

Julia had an easier time, perhaps because she had known no other school or because of her temperament. 'She was a very calm child, never let things ruffle her too much,' Moira has said. The structured environment, a place where there were rules to follow, suited her. She plunged into school life, fitting in with the local kids from the first and quickly leaving behind the soft Welsh lilt that her parents have retained. She forged friendships readily. Because state schools in the South Australian education system were zoned, it was common for children to move from primary to secondary school with the same group.

'I've still got friends I went right through school with,' Julia says.

2

'I grew more confident in high school'

What sort of child was Julia Gillard? Her parents and sister Alison have said she was shy, even timid. 'Julia was always the good sister, the studious one – and very quiet,' says Alison. Julia herself says she was reserved, with a tendency to blush easily, and when she was very young she hated having attention drawn to her. So perhaps she was shy and a little cautious, but this is not the quality that shines through her youthful photographs. Julia Gillard aged ten, a freckle-faced child with her reddish hair in the regulation high pigtails, beams at the camera: she appears outgoing and friendly, although certainly not as if she is saying 'look at me'. Even when she is several years older and facing the uncertainties of adolescence, she looks a thoughtful, serious girl, but not awkward or lacking in assurance.

Julia went through with her group from primary school to Unley High School. Founded in 1910, Unley High was academically oriented and very large: in the early 1960s the baby boom after World War II, and the mass entry of students into secondary education, had swollen its population to a peak of over 2000 students. Julia thrived there, eventually becoming a prefect in what she later described as 'a muted form of democracy' in which students could vote for candidates preselected by the teachers. (It was possibly the easiest election victory she has ever had.) She was good at academic subjects, but less so at sport and art – or home economics.

Unley High, like other secondary schools of the time, insisted that girls in the junior years study this subject. Julia and her friends could not see why girls were stuck with cooking, laundry and sewing while the boys did woodwork and metalwork. They did not want to do woodwork and metalwork: it was just that they found home economics utterly boring. Not for the last time Julia, with her friends, decided to make a point by using ridicule. On one occasion they baked a cake with a cactus in it. Another time they put a whole packet of soap powder in a washing machine, then tried to pretend that the bubbles surging out of the drain had nothing to do with them. These days Gillard makes no bones about the fact that the domestic arts have never been high on her agenda.

The most important training for Julia's future career came not in class, but when she joined Unley High's debating group. As has happened several times in Gillard's career, this was not a decision she made on her own. One of her friends, Kathy Pilowsky, was involved in debating, and Julia became caught up in her enthusiasm. Once she started, however, she discovered that she was good at speaking in public and thinking on her feet. She found it nerve-racking at first to rebut points and to depend on little cue cards to build a case – but she also enjoyed the stimulation and the tension.

Before long she was a star, although the night her team was forced to argue that 'A Man Should Lead' was not one of her finest hours.

She took part in interschool debates, pitting her growing verbal and analytical skills against those of other students and developing a competitive streak. It is no coincidence that early debating talent is a thread that links many successful Australian politicians: Robert Menzies, John Howard, Susan Ryan, Kevin Rudd and Malcolm Turnbull among others.

When Julia was sixteen she told her mother she did not want to have children. She simply didn't see herself at home as a wife and mother. Her priority was to get as good an education as possible in order to have a career – even though she did not yet know what that career might be – and she did not see how marriage, a family and a demanding job could be combined. Julia has always said that her parents never brought their daughters up to believe that home and family would necessarily be their destiny. Nor was there any suggestion that boys were superior intellectual beings, with more options open to them. 'My parents believed that work was important, that career was important, and they encouraged us to dream bigger dreams if we wanted to,' says Gillard.

Julia Gillard was beginning to look outwards, longing for a wider world. South Australia had become a more interesting place, politically and culturally, during the years that the Gillards had been in Australia. For thirty-two almost unbroken years, the Liberal and Country League had ruled South Australia thanks to a persistent gerrymander, but in 1970 it was trounced by the Labor Party under Don Dunstan. His was a socially progressive government the like of which the state – and the nation – had never seen before. The Dunstan government came to office two years before the federal Labor administration of Gough Whitlam. It anticipated and exceeded some of the Whitlam administration's reforms and outlived it by four years – facts that are often forgotten when considering the seismic influence of the federal Labor government.

Don Dunstan was a fervent advocate of multiculturalism, Indigenous land rights and the abolition of the White Australia policy, and a crusader against discrimination who brought in legislation to protect the rights of women, homosexuals and Aborigines. Under his government, drinking laws were liberalised, police powers restricted and environmental programs introduced; censorship was relaxed and capital punishment abolished. Consumer protection laws, urban planning and the state education system were also reformed. The rest of Australia took particular notice of his cultural innovations: the establishment of the South Australian Film Corporation, which became a vital player in the 1970s Australian film revival, and the expansion of the Adelaide Festival of Arts. Adept at using the media, articulate, relaxed and unconventional – 'flamboyant' is always the adjective stapled to his name – Dunstan embodied the modern era he had ushered in.

While John Gillard cast a quizzical eye on Dunstan's wearing of hot-pink shorts to state Parliament, the apparent casualness and ease with which the Premier brought about some long-overdue social reforms must have impressed him. They showed that politics was so much more fluid, changes could be made so much more easily in this new country than in the often hidebound United Kingdom.

John Gillard was politically active in the affairs of his union at the hospital, although he was not a member of the Australian Labor Party. He was a keen observer, though, delighting in and embracing the rough and tumble, the unpredictability and vitality of politics in his chosen country. While the family watched television in the evening, he was more likely to be in the kitchen listening to federal Parliament on ABC Radio and could sometimes be heard interjecting during the rebroadcasts of Question Time.

Julia Gillard and her father both say that discussion of Labor politics was part of normal Gillard family conversation around the dinner table. 'We grew up in an environment where we were Labor by instinct,' says Julia. 'Dad was pro-Labor, Mum was pro-Labor, that's just who we were. That was our team.' However, Alison, who does not share this fascination with politics, has observed that her sister must have absorbed it by osmosis since she never seemed very interested in the subject while they were growing up.

Gough Whitlam, with his wit, erudition and knowledge of the classics, greatly appealed to John Gillard as a personality as well as a reforming prime minister. 'Our great Gough' or 'The Colossus' was a prime favourite in the Gillard household. When someone called out, 'Quick, Gough's on', the rest of the family would rush to the TV news. Whitlam's direct and confident appeal to the 'men and women of Australia' was immensely attractive to the Gillards, as were his government's social policies. The contrast to Britain at the time, with its strikes, unemployment, power cuts and general despair was very obvious. Although the Whitlam government was in office for only three years, from 1972 to 1975, its gift to its supporters was a sense of optimism that political action could bring a progressive agenda to fruition. Without being aware of it at the time, young Julia must have absorbed this from what she saw and read and her conversations with her father.

For the Gillards, and for thousands of families like them, the Whitlam government brought in two reforms of profound importance: the introduction of Medicare, which provided universal health care insurance, paid for out of general revenue, and ensured public patients free care in public hospitals; and the abolition of tertiary education fees and replacement of competitive entrance scholarships with the Tertiary Education Assistance Scheme, a needs-based grant intended to meet the basic requirements of full-time students studying for their first degree. It meant a great deal to John and Moira Gillard to know that their daughters would be able to go to university.

Julia Gillard says her first strong political memory was the shock and sense of instability caused by the sacking of the Whitlam government on 11 November 1975 – something that her father found equally devastating, as did thousands of others. She was fourteen, and although she did not race out and join the ALP at the time, many others did. An interesting subject for investigation would be the influence of the Whitlam dismissal in politicising members of the current Labor hierarchy, most of whom were teenagers or in their twenties when it happened. John Faulkner, now Labor's minister for defence, who was one year out of school, remembers hearing the news of the dismissal on his car radio. 'My reaction was immediate, white-hot anger,' he told the *Age* many years later. Straight away he drove to Canberra to join a demonstration against the sacking. He speaks for many Australians when he says, 'Gough Whitlam wasn't a mentor, but I think like many of my generation I found him a very inspirational political figure.'

Gillard has said little about the influence of the Whitlam government on her early political development. This may be because the dismissal is still a polarising episode in our history, and because Gough Whitlam remains a controversial figure, even among Labor supporters. (Former senator Robert Ray has said that Labor voters became very familiar with the back sections of their newspapers during the last year of the Whitlam government: sports results were the only news they could bear to read.) But the Whitlam government's social democratic agenda must at some level have influenced the way she thought about the possibilities of politics.

In her final year of school Julia Gillard had to decide what her career would be. She intended to go to university, probably to study arts. Alison had just finished her third year at Flinders University without enjoying her time there, but Julia was looking forward to university. The standard bachelor of arts led to two obvious professions: librarianship and teaching. Because Julia had enjoyed her time at school and had developed a flair for public speaking, she thought of becoming a teacher. A factor in her decision might also have been that teachers' college scholarships gave a more generous living allowance than the government's allowance for university students. But as it happened, she took another path altogether.

Julia, Kathy Pilowsky and Kathy's twin sister, Lyn, had been friends ever since the three girls were in primary school. They had been in and out of each other's houses for many years, and they knew each other's families well. The twins' parents, Issie and Marlene Pilowsky, were Jewish and liberal. They had migrated to Australia from South Africa to escape having to live with apartheid. Issie was professor of psychiatry at the University of Adelaide. Marlene had challenged her traditional Jewish upbringing by first training to be a nurse, then completing a bachelor of arts degree with a major in anthropology, while bringing up four children, and eventually becoming a marriage guidance counsellor and a teacher of communications skills to occupational-health nurses.

Marlene Pilowsky was a large woman with black hair and olive skin who wore Indian caftans – which in suburban Adelaide, even in the late 1970s, made her exotic. Gillard describes her as 'very vibrant, larger than life, loud in a good way'. She was also strong, assertive, and demanding, again in a good way, and she expected great things of people. 'She would half-encourage, half-hector you into things,' says Gillard. Marlene and her children often had furious arguments about her plans for them, which Julia witnessed. However much they mutinied against their mother, the Pilowsky children evidently listened to her: Kathy became a dental specialist, Lyn a consultant psychiatrist in London, Paul a senior medical researcher and Marion an executive in a major film company.

When Julia told Marlene that she intended to become a teacher, Mrs Pilowsky said she wasn't aiming high enough. She should use her talents in a more focused way. She had done well at school, had an excellent memory for facts and a logical mind, knew how to work hard and was an excellent debater. She should study law.

Marlene Pilowsky was Julia Gillard's first mentor outside her immediate family – and, like all successful mentors, she provided the right advice at the right time. Julia had a few misgivings: she would be the only member of her school group who was going into law, as the other bright girls were heading for science or medicine. But Marlene was very persuasive. 'I started mulling over this thought of being a lawyer,' says Gillard, 'and put it down on my preference sheet during my matriculation year.' At the same time, she suspected that studying law by itself might be rather dull and decided to combine it with studies in arts, especially economics and English, two subjects in which she had excelled at school.

Julia Gillard achieved straight As in her matriculation exams. At the end of 1978, just before she started at the University of

Adelaide, the Gillard family returned to Wales for a holiday. John and Moira had planned the trip for years. It was the first time they had been back, although a few years earlier John had thought of making a quick trip by himself because his mother was ill. She recovered, and was in Cwmgwrach to greet John, Moira, Alison and Julia when they arrived there to stay with John's family.

There were so many Gillard relatives that a party was held in the Cwmgwrach village hall. 'The thing that amazed my sister and me was being in a room with fifty people and being related to all of them,' says Julia. 'We'd never had grandparents or cousins or uncles or aunts before: there had always just been the four of us.'

At one point during the reunion party, an uncle came up and spoke to Alison and Julia. They couldn't understand a word he was saying. 'He had this heavy accent, and we thought he was speaking Welsh,' says Julia. 'We were watching his mouth move, and it was just impossible. Finally Dad came up and translated.' It turned out that their uncle had been asking 'Are you courting?', meaning 'Do you have boyfriends?'

Since that first trip, Julia has been back to see family in Cwmgwrach several times. These days, indeed, she has more Gillards in her life than ever before. There has been quite a lot of publicity in Wales about her career, especially since she became deputy prime minister of Australia, and she figures prominently on at least one website headed 'Famous Welsh People'. Her Canberra office gets many emails from people, in Wales and elsewhere, who say their name is Gillard and that they must be related to her.

For John and Moira, the trip back to Wales was a mixed experience. They had thought about home so much, they had saved up for so long, that the return was bound to be a little disappointing.

Their Wales was frozen in time, and in the thirteen years since their departure for Australia Cwmgwrach had moved on: children had grown up and married, more people had cars and television sets, life seemed more prosperous. The Gillard family had come from a hot, dry South Australian summer to the damp and bleakness of winter in South Wales: the weather was one thing John and Moira did not remember with nostalgia. At last, and with some regret, they accepted that Wales was no longer really their home. For Julia it was different. Australia had been where she belonged from the moment she walked up the path to primary school.

3

'Student politics is a great way of building up your skills'

Julia Gillard started her Arts-Law course at the University of Adelaide in 1979. The main Adelaide campus was right in the centre of the city, alongside the art gallery, museum and state library: by the standards of Melbourne and Sydney universities, it could be described as cosy. It was not particularly intimidating for freshers, but like most first-year students Julia took time to find her feet.

Her main contacts were her friends from Unley High, whom she would meet for lunch or coffee in the student cafeteria or on the lawns in front of the Barr Smith Library. But as Julia was the only member of her school group who was studying law, the Unley High group began, inevitably, to fracture. As well, Julia was gradually getting to know other law students. By the end of her first year, she had respectable exam results and a much wider circle of friends, including Mandy Cornwall.

Mandy was the daughter of a prominent member of the Australian Labor Party who later became a state Cabinet minister, and she was very active in student politics. Her family connections might well have made her glamorous to someone brought up in a fervently Labor household. Mandy encouraged Julia to become a member of the university's Labor Club. She did, and it was then that she joined the ALP.

Campus activity and the Labor Club in particular brought Julia into contact with students who had views similar to her own – and into conflict with those who did not – as well as some with different life experiences. To a law student from a small, self-contained and work-focused family, this was all heady stuff. Julia joined the Labor Club at a time when ALP supporters were still maintaining the rage against Whitlam's dismissal, and there was widespread suspicion and dislike of Malcolm Fraser's conservative government.

At the time, Mandy was involved in a campaign to put more students on the council of the Adelaide University Union, and soon Julia was involved, too. The Union, supported by compulsory student fees, was the body responsible for running all the non-academic services on campus for students, such as the Union building, which housed the caf and various social and political clubs and organisations. Although all students were automatically members of the Union, most of the council members were appointed from the academic staff.

Julia quickly became a leader of the small group pushing for fairer student representation on the Union council. The push was so successful that in 1981, early in her third year, she was elected as Adelaide University's first student president of the council.

It was Julia Gillard's first political success. In achieving it she had learned that an effective campaign required a clearly defined, justifiable objective, sustained organisation and lots of hard work – and that she had the skills needed. The victory marked her out in student circles, and not just at Adelaide University.

Across the country student activism was at a low ebb. Gone were the heady days of the early 1970s, when anti-Vietnam-War and anti-conscription protests had united students all over the country and influenced public opinion. There were still specific issues – East Timor's independence, for instance – that called out the demonstrators, but nothing that built into the huge, sustained participation of earlier days. By the beginning of the 1980s former student leaders were complaining that the current crop of students were parochial, apathetic and concerned only about getting degrees, not with what was happening in the wider world.

The peak body for the various tertiary student organisations was the Australian Union of Students. In the early 1970s it had been taken over by the radical Left. The success of the anti-Vietnam-War campaigns reinforced the far Left's belief that a righteous cause could ignite a mass movement and bring about radical social change. It found a new cause in the Palestinian struggle against Israel. The immediate reaction in some quarters was widespread outrage, notably among Jewish students and Labor members with strong links to the Jewish community, who began to regard AUS as little less than a branch member and financial supporter of the Palestine Liberation Organisation.

In 1977 a group of right-wing students that included a young Peter Costello, then at Monash University, and Tony Abbott, president of Sydney University's Students' Representative Council, capitalised on this perception to advance their own agenda against left-wing dominance of the campuses and AUS. Arguing that they should not be forced to pay compulsory student union fees to support an organisation whose policy they disagreed with, they combined with other disaffected students to drive a wedge into AUS.

The campaign had only a limited effect on voluntary student unionism, but under pressure from their student groups a significant number of campuses decided to disaffiliate from AUS, which was then faced with dwindling revenues and declining membership. But students such as Julia Gillard were convinced that AUS still had a vital role to play. There were specific and pressing issues affecting the whole student body that required a concerted national response, of which university education itself was one.

Since the Whitlam Labor government had abolished university fees and introduced the Tertiary Education Assistance Scheme, giving most of the student population living allowances, a greater proportion of less affluent students had enrolled. But when the Liberal Party came to federal office at the end of 1975, it began reducing expenditure on education. At a time of rising inflation and increasing unemployment, culminating in the recession of the early 1980s, the Fraser government's view was that institutions of higher education had too many students and were being managed inefficiently.

Over Fraser's three terms the focus of TEAS was changed. It became a complicated scheme to give a small amount of supplementary income to those who were financially disadvantaged, and the maximum TEAS fell from 67.5 per cent of the amount considered to be on the poverty line to 56.5 per cent. As the means test cut-off declined relative to the average wage, student numbers declined. In 1981 a parliamentary committee, quickly dubbed the Razor Gang, recommended in its *Review of Commonwealth Functions* that full fees be reinstated for second and higher degrees.

Considering the rehabilitation of Malcolm Fraser's reputation over the years, it is instructive to be reminded of the almost visceral hatred that Whitlam supporters, including students, felt for the government he led. As they saw it, here was a patrician grazier at the head of a government that had gained power by illegitimate means, a man who had never had to struggle in his life, bent on destroying public tertiary education as fast as he could.

'We thought it was a complete outrage,' says Gillard, and when the Australian Union of Students undertook a campaign against the education cuts, using as its theme 'The Union Strikes Back' (the second part of the original *Star Wars* trilogy had recently been released), she was one of the chief organisers.

Michael O'Connor, then a student at the University of Melbourne, remembers her from those years: 'Probably the first time I met Julia was in the early 80s when hundreds of students would come from around the country [to AUS conferences]. She was representing Adelaide University students' union. There's no doubt she was really articulate and had a really strong intellect about her in arguing a case.'

Julia found the nationwide campaign against the Fraser education cuts an exhilarating experience: 'There were some very public parts of it, but I remember more than anything else having to be logistically organised. If you were doing a leaflet you had to get someone to operate the Gestetner machine, which broke down every ten minutes, and then you'd get things typeset and lay them out on the lightbox. The actual marshalling of the labour was also a real challenge, getting students to physically be present instead of sleeping in till three-thirty in the afternoon and using other student excuses.'

Even though she sometimes railed against ten-hour meetings in which nothing was actually done, she says on the whole it was 'a lot of hard work, teamwork', with 'a sense of common endeavour'. 'And there was also a kind of enjoyment in working for six hours on the Gestetner with four or five other very motivated people. There was a great sense of energy.'

The 1981 Fight Back campaign raised about $150 000 to run ads against the cuts, and there were big rallies on campuses Australia-wide, with an estimated 60 000 students involved. Gillard spoke at some of the meetings and demonstrations. She was still a slightly nervous public speaker, but she was learning a lot about building a case and presenting it effectively in a public forum.

In the end the Senate defeated the Razor Gang's cost-cutting proposals. AUS was jubilant, and Gillard was given a lot of the credit for the campaign's success. After that, she was noted around AUS as one of its leading lights. 'I think the fact that the first big campaign I was involved in ended up making a difference reinforced a sense that this was a good thing to be doing,' she says.

Julia Gillard had come quite a way from the Unley High student with a talent for debating. By the end of her third year at Adelaide University she was something of a student personality in certain circles and a significant member of the Labor Club group within AUS. She had left home and moved into a student share house, supporting herself by doing the usual part-time jobs such as waitressing, with a little help from her parents.

The neatly dressed uni fresher no longer existed. She now got around in jeans and T-shirts and boots, and like most students she did a lot of her shopping at army disposal stores. 'We all tended to look a bit like unemployed soldiers,' she says. She drove a large, ageing Chrysler, which she had taken over when her parents changed cars, and she had learned to sink the odd beer at the Adelaide Uni bar.

At the end of 1981 she was asked to run for the job of AUS education vice president. 'She would have been twenty-one [actually just twenty],' says Ken McAlpine, who knew Gillard at Adelaide University and AUS. 'She was one of the smartest people in the ALP Club, though that didn't take very much. And she was an accomplished public speaker, compared with the rest of the student politicians.

'Education vice president was regarded as the most important job in the union, because you'd be dealing with the government. It was seen as the main lobbying position. It was considered unusual to have somebody that young in such a senior role. I was twenty-four, which was a big difference in skills and life experience. The fact that she was put forward at that time was an indication of her skills and how widely recognised they were. She was from Adelaide, which was not perceived as a heavyweight in Labor politics. So the offer [was based] on her ability.'

To McAlpine's surprise Julia Gillard took a lot of convincing. 'I remember sitting down with her and others at the bar at Adelaide Uni, saying, "You should do this." She said that she just wanted to be a lawyer in Adelaide. At that stage she had no burning ambition for a political career.'

But lack of ambition was not the reason Gillard hesitated. By 1981 student politics had become all-consuming in her life, with law studies a very poor second. 'When I did Contract Law, I went to the first lecture and none of the others and basically turned up for the exam and had a go, which wasn't all that smart,' she says. Her sister Alison had left university without completing a degree, and Julia knew her parents were worried that she herself would be sidetracked, never come back and fail to graduate. Julia understood how important it was to her parents that she concentrate on finishing her studies.

On the other hand she was involved in something she found satisfying and exciting, and she knew she was good at it. The AUS secretariat was in Melbourne, but she would be able to support herself because the job of education vice president paid a basic wage. She would be able to run other effective student campaigns, too: the AUS budget, although not lavish, would certainly allow for that. It was a fulltime position, but she would be able to transfer her Arts-Law degree across to Melbourne University and complete it in due course.

After some persuasion Gillard became convinced she should give it a try, and put her name forward. It was by no means a foregone conclusion that she would be successful – most Australian universities still had vocal radical Left contingents and Julia, being an ALP member, was considered somewhat to the right – but in the end the various Left groups across the spectrum more or less united in her favour, and she won. And so in 1982, as the newly elected education vice president of the Australian Union of Students, she packed her share-house belongings into the Chrysler and moved to Melbourne.

4

'It's like compressing ten years of Parliament into one'

It is no accident that some of this country's most prominent politicians – Peter Costello and Tony Abbott, Lindsay Tanner, Anthony Albanese and Tanya Plibersek, as well as Julia Gillard – cut their teeth in student politics. Gillard says: 'When you come out of it, if you get the difference between long-term politics and the flashpoints of student politics, it's a great experience.' Also, she says, an exhilarating one: 'I don't think there's much that's more irrationally passionate. It's a heady cocktail, you really get into it.'

When Julia Gillard went to work at the head office of the Australian Union of Students early in 1982, she was already on the way to being a seasoned student politician. Having attended AUS conferences for the last couple of years, she had met many of the other movers and shakers in the organisation. As a South Australian representative, she had also visited Melbourne for meetings of the national education action committee, and so she was well known. But although many people found her impressive, she was not yet considered a force to be reckoned with.

Andrew Scott, who was studying Arts-Law at the University of Melbourne at the time, says: 'A number of other people were seen as potential future leaders in that AUS group. I remember at one student conference someone saying, "Well, if you look round the room it is obvious that there is a future Cabinet minister here. Paul Carrick!" Somebody else said, "No, it's not, it's Lindsay Tanner." Nobody said Julia.'

She was establishing a reputation as a moderate; some would have said a conservative. 'Student politics had been skewed well to the extreme ultra-left during the 1970s,' Gillard has said. 'Being a Labor student you were viewed as a right-winger. I mean, we didn't really have that many Liberals to create that right-wing pole, so most in [the Left of] student politics thought the Labor students were the enemy for being too right-wing.'

By the time Julia Gillard became education vice president, Peter Costello and his group from the Right had largely moved on – in his case into the law – leaving the destabilised AUS behind them. Although the erosion of AUS had been reversed for a couple of years by an alliance between Labor Left and Communist Party of Australia members and the consequent success of the education Fight Back campaign, essentially the organisation was locked in a stalemate. The national union could not convince the disaffiliated campuses to rejoin, but the far Right had insufficient support to kill off AUS on the campuses that remained affiliated.

There were still passionate debates about the position of AUS and its role in student life, and a group of non-Labor Left students, mostly from the smaller campuses, remained reluctant to abandon their commitment to radical causes. 'There was always the big search for the new galvanising issue that would have students on the streets and prepared to go to gaol,' says Gillard. 'But though there were lots of failed attempts to find such an issue, it didn't exist.'

It's a statement supported by Andrew Scott, who remembers a student conference in Canberra during 1982: 'Some group announced that the Malaysian government was going to execute some students the next day, and they should all march to the Malaysian embassy and protest. The motion was carried in a surge of high emotion, and we all marched over there. It was three o'clock in the morning.'

Gillard's argument was always that AUS shouldn't bother with world issues it could not influence, but instead concentrate on matters that directly concerned students. As education vice president her job was to lobby state and federal education ministers in order to get more money for student allowances, scholarships and better facilities for students on campus.

Says Dr Nick Economou, senior lecturer in politics at Monash University: 'AUS used to be the place where ideologues could go and make great speeches and pass motions supporting the PLO or the IRA or wars of national liberation. [The Gillard group] said, Forget all that, we should restrict our gaze to education policy on behalf of students. Let's jettison the radical element and concentrate on student unionism as a form of activism in an institutionalised way.'

Gillard and her AUS executive colleagues – that year's president, Paul Carrick, Candy Broad and Michael O'Connor – decided that the old left–right divisions had hardly served the organisation well. They realised that their first responsibility was to bring disaffected students back into the fold. This meant maintaining alliances across the spectrum of the Left, even though student political alliances were notoriously fluid and quick changing. There were roughly three Left groups affiliated to AUS during the 1970s and early 1980s. They are worth delineating here because echoes of their various beliefs and policies continued to influence Gillard's career for some time to come.

Moving rightwards from the far Left, there were first the Trotskyites, some of whom were ready, as a contemporary of Gillard dryly observed, to die in a ditch for Palestinian human rights, no matter what effect their policy had on AUS. Then there were those allied to the Communist Party of Australia who were turning away from Soviet orthodoxy towards a democratic socialism based on the Eurocommunism adopted by some Western European parties; they believed that members should embrace new social movements such as feminism and gay liberation and work within democratic institutions. Finally there were the centrists, with whom Gillard and the rest of the AUS executive allied themselves and who were generally cautious about direct action and confrontational tactics, preferring negotiation and lobbying as a means of operation.

Paul Carrick and the executive thought that it was possible for most of the members to find common cause for the benefit of the Australian student body as a whole – even if, as one colleague pointed out, they simply joined in hating the Trots – and to prevail against the conservatives who had supported voluntary student unionism.

Gillard's own instinct in dealing with the student body was to focus the progressive forces on working together towards a common position. There were some very fiery debates with the far Left over the direction AUS should take, during which Gillard impressed some of her colleagues with her firmness and clarity of argument, but she tended to adopt a conciliatory approach – more conciliatory than that of Paul Carrick.

There were other potentially separatist issues, one of which was radical feminism. Being naturally drawn towards making strategic alliances and not necessarily seeing men as the enemy, Gillard was never a part of the separatist feminist group, although she naturally supported equality for women. She had generally good relations with student feminists across the board but did not use the women's movement as a platform for promoting herself or for her advancement, perhaps because she found the debate too restricting.

Although issues were taken very seriously in AUS, there were light-hearted times as well. The secretariat was housed in a two-storeyed house on the corner of Grattan and Lygon streets in the inner Melbourne suburb of Carlton. Those students who were involved in AUS projects frequently dossed down in the building overnight, and illegal substances were available more often than not. It was a little world of its own, recalled by several people interviewed for this book with a certain rueful nostalgia.

Any image of Julia Gillard as a young woman whose entire life was consumed by student politics would be wide of the mark. She was certainly focused on the job at hand, but she also knew how to enjoy herself (although without the aid of the illegal substances). Like her colleagues she was a regular at the University Hotel opposite AUS headquarters. 'She had a great sense of humour and wouldn't say no to a gin and tonic,' says Andrew Scott, 'though she wasn't as great a partygoer as some of us in those days.' She was generous – Scott remembers that she lent him her law notes – and usually quite open, but she also had a reserved side. 'In some ways she could be a bit detached socially,' he says. 'But I think she opened up much more to those who were close to her.'

Gillard was forming friendships that have remained close to this day. One of her most significant was with Michael O'Connor, who was the AUS organiser in Victoria when she was education vice president. They were together for a couple of years, and shared a flat. Competition was part of their dynamic: both were very bright, both expected to succeed Paul Carrick as AUS president in 1983. O'Connor says: 'You didn't really want to be arguing a point of view against [Julia] if you could avoid it. She was very serious about winning it.' But at the same time their relationship was very important to them both. These days they are reluctant to talk about it in any detail. 'You always feel like you're intruding on the privacy of others when you're in public life,' says Gillard.

According to people who know them both, they differed strongly in temperament. Gillard, although warm and responsive, was not inclined to allow her emotions to hold sway. Michael, under a tough-guy exterior, was probably more volatile, perhaps less resilient.

By all accounts it was Julia who eventually broke off the relationship and moved out. 'Michael and I were young,' she has said. 'You know, university, all that sort of stuff, so I suspect as much as anything else it wasn't the right stage of life.' Their break-up was serious and sad for both of them. But they have remained friends as well as each other's loyally supportive ally.

Gillard paid special tribute to Michael when she first entered federal Parliament: '[F]riends from university have remained my comrades since the early 1980s,' she said in her maiden speech.

'Today I pay tribute to them and especially to the most committed of them all, Michael O'Connor, who has been my closest confidant since those heady days.'

Julia Gillard continued to be driven by a wish to make education as widely available as possible. As well as being education vice president of AUS, she was on an educational advocacy committee called Let's Develop Education. It included members of the national teachers' union, the vice-chancellors' committee, academic unions and other bodies that were vitally involved in improving Australian education. This was Gillard's first exposure to the wider education bureaucracy, and in view of her later career proved an invaluable learning experience.

Throughout 1982 Gillard saw her primary focus as the urgent issue of student participation. During the year Gillard ran several campaigns designed to encourage student bodies to reaffiliate with AUS. These were aimed at major campuses such as the University of Sydney and Macquarie University in Sydney, and RMIT in Melbourne, but they all rejected reaffiliation more decisively than they had done earlier. In some ways Gillard had taken on a lost cause. The issue of voluntary student unionism had deeply divided the organisation, and both the Left and Right were too fragmented to forge a strong AUS.

Gillard's centrist approach to reinvigorating and uniting AUS might have failed, but most observers felt that she had managed to avoid becoming a divisive figure herself. A forceful and effective debater in forums, she was calm, competent and pleasant to deal with behind the scenes – an unusual combination. She put her hand up to be president of AUS in 1983 and, to the surprise of some, was given Paul Carrick's imprimatur. She was only the second woman to fill that job. Many had expected Michael O'Connor to take the position, but in fact he generously supported Gillard.

This was the year that the ALP regained power federally, under Bob Hawke – to the great joy and satisfaction of Gillard and her Labor Club colleagues. And it was during this year that John Dawkins, the minister for education, contacted her.

They had already dealt together when he had been shadow minister, but now he needed to gauge AUS support for a policy he really wanted to push: the possibility of giving low-interest loans to students, which they would pay back at the end of their course. The scheme was to be called the Higher Education Contribution Scheme. AUS could see the attractiveness of HECS, for it would mean that students who had not been able to afford university education now could. All the same, any plan that moved away from the ideal of free education was something that AUS members, including Gillard, instinctively resisted. There was also the danger that the government would gradually decrease the amount of money available, just as the Fraser Razor Gang had done. As a result of that experience, AUS was under no illusion that education was a protected area when it came to government cutbacks.

There was a lot of agonising about the subject, but in the end AUS said it would not support the idea of HECS. Within the federal party itself Dawkins had evidently failed to make a policy case, for he shelved the idea for the time being. These days, as minister for education, Gillard looks back on the episode with a certain wry amusement. 'Now I'm dealing with the National Union of

Students, and they submit requests for funding and I have to say, "Yes, that's very interesting but it's all about the money",' she says.

By 1983 it was clear that AUS in its current form was becoming unviable. Those involved in student politics at the time agree about this. There were too many disaffiliations, and not enough cash to make the organisation work. The long-running right-wing smear campaign, based on AUS's previous support for the PLO under the far Left, was still proving effective. The education Fight Back campaign had been the organisation's last hurrah.

'It's so ironic that my student activism has been used in election campaigns as part of my so-called madcap Left past,' says Gillard. 'Because we were the ones who were trying to reform the organisation and take it away from the far Left.' Michael O'Connor succeeded Gillard as AUS president in 1984. By then the organisation was more or less unsalvageable, and he made the decision to kill it off in its current form. It was reformed, with major differences and under the name of National Union of Students, in 1987.

The issue of voluntary student unionism has continued to bubble away under the surface ever since the debates of the mid-1970s. In December 2005 the Liberal – National Party Coalition government under John Howard passed the Higher Education Support Amendment (Abolition of Compulsory Up-front Student Union Fees) Bill, abolishing compulsory payment of student fees to student unions. Many student organisations opposed the Voluntary Student Unionism Bill, as it was called, concerned about the ability of a university to provide non-academic services for students without a guaranteed income. Some National Party MPs were also unhappy about the VSU Bill, fearing that it would mean a reduction of services to students on rural campuses.

At the time sections of the media were inclined to treat the issue lightly, regarding it as another example of the Howard government's hostility to unions in any form – even those that had nothing to do with trade unions. But it is an issue that has continued to resonate inside and outside student organisations, especially among conservatives. As well as Peter Costello and Tony Abbott, other former conservative university students, later conservative MPs, who have supported VSU include John Howard, Sophie Mirabella and David Kemp (a minister for education under Howard). Now that Julia Gillard is minister for education, it will be interesting to see how this issue plays out.

Gillard's AUS activism was very important to her – and it is highly significant for understanding the way she has developed as a politician. Several people who worked with Gillard in the ensuing years were struck by the weight she placed on that time. Josh Bornstein, a friend and former colleague, observes: '[She] gave me the impression that it was a seminal moment, a formative experience in her life, when she was moderating between two fairly intractable factions . . . I have the impression that that sort of experience shaped who she is.'

Student activism also helped mature Gillard intellectually. 'Just being in that environment enabled me to start thinking about politics in a broad way,' she says now. 'I was able to direct and evaluate my political instincts. I wasn't studying politics or reading about it. But I was meeting people who were intrigued by ideas, not just in the ALP but in the peace movement – they were talking about things like the theories of Gramsci, solidarity wages policy, universal welfare provision versus targeted provision, changing family structures – and all of this helped in my political education.'

It was with AUS that she developed her skills as a networker, her instinct to keep supporters close and loyal, a reluctance to back away from fights and yet a willingness to find common ground – to evaluate issues pragmatically, discover a way through and try to make policies work by taking a centrist position. These are still at the heart of the way she operates, the way she handles her portfolios. As Josh Bornstein says, 'You see her now, she's able to forge compromise relentlessly.'

But the words Gillard chooses to describe the 'irrationally passionate' and 'heady cocktail' of her AUS experience suggest a strong emotional undertow, too. People in politics often talk about the adrenaline rush, the sense of control and possibility that comes from the exercise of power. For certain people that sense is irresistible: it is the 'high' that keeps them going even when things are running against them.

At those times what is also needed is the toughness and determination to, in Bornstein's words, 'keep going, keep going and keep going, while people are throwing things at each other'. The resilience Gillard developed as a student politician taking on the big fights would prove essential for what followed.

5

Julia the red menace

In the lead-up to the 2007 federal election, when a Labor victory was looking more and more certain, there was in certain sections of the media a spate of solemn worrying about Julia Gillard's 'far Left' leanings, which had allegedly blossomed during her time at the University of Melbourne. 'Scrapping the ANZUS treaty, twinning Melbourne with Leningrad and introducing a super-tax on the rich were among radical policies devised or backed by Julia Gillard as a student activist', wrote one of several commentators, Lincoln Wright of the *Sunday Herald Sun*. 'Labor's deputy leader was a key figure in a socialist group that pushed radical policies and social agendas in the 1980s and early 90s.'

Wright also breathlessly announced that the *Sunday Herald Sun* had 'obtained access to papers' providing details about the organisation, including talks that Gillard had given on such topics as 'Being a Socialist Teacher', as well as a list of events, summer schools and conferences she had organised. She had not been telling the truth! She was still the radical she had been twenty-five years ago!

The implication was clear. Gillard might proclaim herself a moderate, but it was only in order to win government – leopards do not change their spots, especially socialist leopards. Arch-conservative newspaper columnist Andrew Bolt summed it up like this: 'The issue isn't just whether there's a Red under the bed, but a liar as well.'

Exhibit A for Gillard's dangerous socialistic tendencies was her former membership of the 'far Left' group called the Socialist Forum. As described by Andrew Bolt, 'Labor's deputy leader Julia Gillard has claimed she was just a "typist" in her "university days" to a mere "debating society" called the "Socialist Forum" and has really been a "fiscal conservative" all along.' (The double quotes are there in case the reader misses his point: *he is being sarcastic*.)

The story had some coverage on radio and television as well as in the press, with Peter Costello weighing in to describe the Socialist Forum as a radical left-wing group linked to the Communist Party. This prompted journalist Tony Jones to ask Gillard jokily on ABC-TV's *Lateline*, 'Are you now or have you ever been a member of the Communist Party?' Gillard turned the question aside with a quip of her own: 'I suspect in this interview probably the Howard Government would think you're the dangerous radical. After all, I'm only from the Labor Party, you're from the ABC.'

The conversation continued:

JONES What's the Socialist Forum? Were you an organiser for it? And when did that happen, if you were?

GILLARD [It] is more than 20 years ago when I was in my 20s. I was a full-time university student and I had a part-time job for an organisation called Socialist Forum, which was a sort of debating society. It ultimately amalgamated with the Fabian Society, which of course is a long-running ideas and debating group in Australian politics and indeed in British politics before Australian politics. I worked in the clerical and administrative area.

JONES It wasn't a front organisation for Communists?

GILLARD Certainly not. It was an organisation where people who identified themselves as progressives, some in the Labor Party, some outside the Labor Party, would come together and talk about ideas . . .

JONES So what are you saying? As a young woman you flirted with a radical fringe group, you then joined the left wing of the Labor Party? Before you knew it, you were the deputy leader of the Labor Party and now you want to be deputy prime minister?

GILLARD Tony, it's been a fair old journey since my 20s . . .

JONES It does point to a sort of vulnerability, though, that you – that Kevin Rudd even – and the whole front bench with the possible exception of Peter Garrett has, and that is that many voters don't really know that much about you, and your pasts.

GILLARD Well, I think Australian voters know this about [us]. We're out there putting fresh thinking and ideas for Australia's future . . .

At this point Gillard segued into the ALP pre-election message, and so the interview continued.

The Liberal government continued to keep up the pressure, saying that, far from Gillard's membership of the Socialist Forum being a relic of her youthful left-wing follies, the parliamentary register of interests stated she had remained a member until 2002, and on the management committee until at least 1994.

The accusations had very little traction in the longer term. It became obvious that the voting public wasn't particularly interested, and after a couple of weeks the commentariat, and the electorate, moved on. But the episode is worth revisiting for a couple of reasons. If Gillard was recalling her past, she was not the only one: Peter Costello had re-entered as scourge of the Left, resuming the role he had taken against the Australian Union of Students thirty years before.

Costello, of course, was also giving voice to a persistent feature of Australian conservative politics: the attempt to demonise the ALP as a party that was at least sympathetic to communism and perhaps even proto-communist. The 'reds under the bed' scares have waxed and waned during Australian election campaigns since the end of World War II. A 1949 Liberal Party advertisement showed Labor prime minister Ben Chifley and Joseph Stalin both puffing away on their pipes, their rising smoke joining in one sinister stream. However, the high points (or the low, depending on one's perspective) were probably the sensationalism of the 1954 Petrov affair and the ALP Split in 1955, when the party divided over the issue of Communist Party domination of some unions, and the strongly sectarian Democratic Labor Party was formed. During the 1983 federal election campaign, however, when Prime Minister Malcolm Fraser said people would be safer keeping their money under the mattress than entrusting it to Labor's management, Bob Hawke was secure enough to joke: 'He's getting a bit desperate, isn't he? You can't put your money under the bed because that's where the communists are . . .' It was an effective riposte.

The way Gillard spoke about her involvement with the Socialist Forum is interesting, however. She did not explain how the organisation came into being, or its relationship to the Victorian ALP – and the thought of a woman of her skills and talent being merely a typist and someone who ran off documents could, and did, sound rather disingenuous. In the context of the 2007 election campaign she naturally did not want to give oxygen to an issue that would deflect attention from the message the ALP was selling to the electorate.

Her slight vagueness was pounced on as being evasive, but there was another reason for it, one that anyone who has ever been involved with the Left will recognise: this is not a thirty-second soundbite kind of story. 'Like most things to do with the ALP,' says Gillard ruefully, 'it's a bit complicated.'

Julia Gillard's national organisation of students might have been moribund in 1984, but in the wider world large social issues still faced the Left. The 1980s – the time of economic rationalism, Thatcherism, Reaganomics – was a decade of underground rumblings for the Left. Few communists could have foreseen that it would end in the implosion of the Soviet bloc; few non-communist leftists could have predicted the transformation of old-style labour parties and their trade union base. There were straws in the wind, of course – always easier to see with the benefit of hindsight.

In Australia most of the executive of the Communist Party's Victorian branch walked out in 1984 to form the Socialist Forum. The disaffected CPA members were mainly Eurocommunists, who believed in working within existing democratic institutions to achieve socialist reforms. This group found common cause with a number of Labor Party members – including Julia Gillard, who had fought against the radical Left in AUS – and with those opposed to the hard Left in the trade union movement. All felt the time was right to form an independent organisation to discuss left-wing ideas: a meeting point for people who wanted to talk about socialist issues.

In Gillard's words of the time this was 'a non-party, non-factional group that would debate ideas and publish papers with a more Left edge than the Fabian Society'. In a pamphlet she wrote in 1985 she described its composition: 'The members of the forum are drawn from varied backgrounds. Around 45 of the forum's members left the Communist Party of Australia in the division of a year ago and about eighty are members of the ALP. The largest group are not members of any political party.'

The Forum's objectives were laid out in its 1985 Statement of Identity: 'Our commitment to a reshaped socialist objective and strategy arises from our firm belief in the need for a radically different society. We seek a socialist society which includes the realisation of feminist and environmental objectives and which is non-racist. We work for peace . . .' The statement continued: 'Democracy is central to our understanding of socialism . . . The Socialist Forum supports the election of Labor governments and works towards making them more responsive to their constituency . . .' However, the Forum emphasised that it held itself aloof from the ALP's organisational concerns, and declared itself 'consciously removed from the numbers games, the caucusing and factional struggles within political parties'. It was hardly the stuff of bomb-throwing anarchism, or even Hollywood-movie communism.

The Forum had inherited the funds of the Victorian CPA, which were substantial enough to employ one full-time and one part-time organiser. Mark Taft, son of Bernie Taft, a former leader of the Victorian CPA branch, was offered the fulltime job, Julia Gillard the other. It was good news for Julia, who was trying to support herself while she studied.

After her stint as AUS president she had been somewhat undecided about her future. Her instinct was to continue working in politics: she loved it, she was good at it. But she was not sure what the next step to a political career should be. She knew that she should complete her Arts-Law degree, but the thought of going into the law was not particularly appealing. She even considered giving up university altogether. But friends put pressure on her to finish, and Gillard allowed herself to be persuaded. Her wish not to disappoint her parents was undoubtedly a factor here.

At the Socialist Forum office in Fitzroy, Julia Gillard and Mark Taft were responsible for producing a monthly magazine and organising speakers for events – this is how she first met leading members of the Victorian Labor government such as the premier, John Cain, and Joan Kirner. (At the time she was living in a share house with Kirner's son David.) Most of her time at the Forum, from December 1984 until February 1987, was spent organising political discussions. She also wrote a number of papers about the organisation and its objectives.

The Forum, which relied on subscriptions and donations for its ongoing survival, had around 220 members at its peak. Its structure was based on a policy-setting annual conference, with an elected management committee responsible for administration and finances (of which Gillard was a member) and coopted interest groups to deal with such issues as education and the exchange of information.

Julia Gillard was considered a straight-up-and-down member of the ALP, with a very strong – some said too strong – streak of pragmatism, so there had been surprise in certain quarters when she agreed to take on the Socialist Forum job. (According to one source, however, she was chosen to give the Forum ALP credibility.) But Gillard found the Forum's organisation and beliefs congenial.

Her position was always clear: she had little, if any, patience with doctrinaire socialism. In 'Future Directions for the Left', a paper Gillard wrote for Forum members, she looked at the whole question of the Left's relationship to Labor in government. She argued that the Left's response had been 'profoundly inadequate' and often exacerbated by a deep sense of disillusionment with the actions of Labor governments:

> Having worked for the election of Labor governments, the tendency of many on the Left is to scream 'sell-out' when they fail to deliver the goods. The political constraints arising from the current nature of Australian society restricting the actions of Labor governments are ignored. This cycle of expectation and disappointment is fuelled by the Labor Party often promising the world when in opposition, whether or not the promises can be upheld in government, and the lack of political experience with and education about the realities of government.

She added that even if Labor governments were not able to deliver all they promised or what the Left might have hoped for, 'we need to recognise that the only possibility for major social change is under a long period of Labor administration', and that the Left must give Labor strategic support. The nature of that support, of course, was always open to discussion, and the Socialist Forum was intended to be part of that.

Even at this early stage, then, Julia Gillard brought a realist's eye to the possibilities of politics. The paper is probably as clear a statement of her basic political position as any she has made since.

The paper might have referred to Labor governments in the plural, but Gillard was undoubtedly thinking specifically of the recently elected federal one under the prime ministership of Bob Hawke.

The ALP had worked hard to get back into office in 1983 and to overcome the perception created by the Whitlam government – and fed by its conservative successor – that Labor governments were bad economic managers in thrall to the trade unions. The party was haunted by the spectre of a wage–price spiral and uncompetitive protected industries in a globalised economy. Hawke and his treasurer, Paul Keating, were determined that the Labor government would comprehensively reform the Australian economy, using the mechanisms of financial deregulation, competitive industries, a retreat from government ownership, low inflation and low interest rates to ensure economic growth.

For Hawke and Keating, the country's industrial relations were part of the problem. Some in the union movement agreed. Almost since Federation, Australia had lived with a state and national conciliation and arbitration system of tribunals and courts designed to regulate relationships between employers and employees; the concept of a basic wage, achieved through national wage cases, was regarded as sacrosanct.

Hawke – as a former president of the Australian Council of Trade Unions, an expansive personality with huge popular appeal and a person with close ties to a number of prominent businessmen – was uniquely qualified to tackle systemic reform. In a demonstration of the consensus style he wanted to pursue, he immediately called trade union organisations, employer groups and political parties to a national summit to formulate economic policy. A Prices and Incomes Accord, negotiated with the ACTU and its member unions during the election, brought the trade union movement into the economic management circle. The Accord traded wage restraint for industrial and social gains such as health care and insurance, occupational safety and superannuation. (In 1989 when the Pilots' Federation went on strike for pay increases outside the Accord it was given no ACTU support, and was dealt with so ruthlessly by the government that it ceased to exist.)

At the time that Julia Gillard joined the Socialist Forum, Labor's return to federal government and the breadth of the Hawke–Keating economic agenda, which would lead to profound changes such as financial deregulation and the lowering of tariffs, preoccupied thinking and debate in the left wing of Australian politics. Gillard organised a seminar on the Accord for the Forum. She understood the need for the changes, but sections of the Left within the Labor Party and trade unions saw the Accord as a sell-out to the Right.

After the 1955 Split, Victoria had become the stronghold of the ALP Left. Gradually the faction known as the Socialist Left came to dominate the Victorian party. But the Socialist Left – like Left factions and parties everywhere – was anything but monolithic. By the mid-1980s it had two main strands, the doctrinaire hard Left, whose members prided themselves on their adherence to traditional socialist objectives and were vehemently opposed to the Accord, and the group that supported a social democratic model.

The hard Left was led by Bill Hartley, a former state secretary of the Victorian ALP. He had gained national notoriety in 1975 when he, Prime Minister Gough Whitlam and the ALP's national secretary, David Combe, agreed to approach the Iraqi Ba'ath regime of Saddam Hussein for a loan of US$500 000 to help fund Labor's 1975 election campaign. At the time Iraq had close ties with the Soviet Union and its ideology. Fortunately this deal, which had the potential to make Australia's political system hostage to a foreign regime – and a radical, despotic one at that – did not go ahead. Bob Hawke, who as president of the ALP had the job of dealing with the fallout within the party, recalled in his memoirs: 'Hartley, in his fanaticism, obviously saw the enmeshment of the ALP with Iraq through this proposed transaction as highly desirable.' Hartley was threatened with expulsion from the party (and was finally expelled in 1986).

Hartley continued in the 1980s to be a strong supporter of pro-Soviet Arab governments, including the Palestinians and Gaddafi's Libya as well as Iraq, and an outspoken critic of Israel (another reason, if any were needed, why he and Bob Hawke detested each other). From 1978 to 1995 he had a platform for his hard Left causes with *Par Avion*, a radio program on community station 3CR.

Gillard viewed Bill Hartley as 'a strident demagogue from Central Casting'. For his part Hartley regarded the Socialist Forum as an attempt by ex-CPA members to infiltrate the ALP by stealth, and attacked it bitterly and relentlessly in his radio program and elsewhere. He also – unsuccessfully – put on notice for a state conference a resolution prohibiting Socialist Forum members from joining the ALP on the grounds that the Forum was de facto a competing political party.

In fact the Socialist Forum had developed into an organisation with several facets. For the former members of the CPA it was indeed a kind of think tank, a way of re-evaluating their approach to left-wing politics when it was clear that Soviet-style communism was a lost cause. For Forum members who had been in the political wilderness for years it offered a bridge to the ALP and mainstream politics. It gave some ALP members a neutral space in which to debate Labor issues, such as Hawke's consensus politics, that might have been contentious within party ranks. And for Gillard and her colleagues the Forum was their link to the ALP's so-called 'new guard', an informal grouping in the Socialist Left of mostly young people who were ready to take on the 'old guard' of Hartley and his forces.

The more progressive section of the Socialist Left was led by Kim Carr. A large, bearlike man even then, the thirtyish Carr had been a teacher before becoming a political adviser. According to one source, Carr ran the Socialist Left like a fiefdom, being much more interested in maintaining the numbers than in promoting talent. 'Stalinist methods of organisation is one lesson Kim learned early in life,' says an ALP colleague of Gillard. 'He was never particularly fond of people who were independent of him, and he didn't like critical supporters either.'

On the face of it, Kim Carr's sub-faction within the Socialist Left would have seemed the logical one for Gillard and fellow ALP members in the Forum to join. Both groups broadly supported the Hawke–Keating government's approach to industrial relations and economic reform, and any differences in ideology were minor. But Carr and his group basically considered the Socialist Forum ALP members a bunch of overeducated, know-it-all upstarts. Perhaps more significantly, they did not belong to Carr's world. In the words of former student activist Geoff Robinson: 'With Kim, there was this blokey in-group of unions, an old blue-collar Left milieu. Carr's people had moved with the times more than the old-school Left – but

Gillard's supporters still saw them as very blokey, and very ethnic, drawing on the Greek community. The Gillard group was very Anglo-Saxon, whereas the non-Anglo people in the Socialist Left were associated with Kim Carr.'

Julia Gillard applied to join the Socialist Left but was kept out of it for a year. Frans Timmerman, an influential Left factional organiser, succeeded in delaying her entry, objecting to her previous role in AUS. He now says: 'In hindsight I think that was a mistake, the organisation should have been as broad as possible, but I was feeling pretty shitty about her role in the national student union. Just as she now sits in the ALP, in AUS she was sitting in the middle against both the Left and the extreme Right, but she made some concessions to the Liberals and Zionists and the whole thing fell apart. The Left couldn't get solidarity with her to fight off the Right, so the whole organisation folded up. She was blamed for that by our group.'

The Socialist Left majority were not in ideological sympathy with the Hartley hard Left forces, but to Gillard and her Socialist Forum mates Hartley and his group were the outright enemy, and their instinct was to tackle them head on. Gillard's ally Paul Slape remembers one particular meeting: 'We had been used to being in a minority to the Bill Hartley forces. I remember Bill came onto the stage and this group of people started to heckle him. I thought, Jesus, you're brave. They gave him a rough time and I can still remember the look on Bill's face. He was used to his crew giving it to others, including us. It was the first time I'd seen open hostility to Hartley, and from a group of young people I hadn't expected it to come from.'

After Gillard's experiences in AUS, this must have seemed like exhilarating déjà vu – like facing the Trots all over again. And, as several observers have noted, Gillard never backed away from a fight and knew how to express her views forcefully. Naturally this confrontation and others did not endear her to the far Left. But nor did they alter Carr's view that the Socialist Forum people were uppity smart alecs who needed to be taken down a peg or two.

Relations between the hard Left and the Forum group soured further when history reasserted itself. The effects of the 1955 Split had been felt worst in Victoria, and the state ALP still harboured great bitterness towards the Democratic Labor Party. In 1985 the federal ALP told Victoria that if four DLP-affiliated unions (the so-called Grouper unions) were not allowed back into the fold federal intervention would result, and the Left might lose control of the Victorian party. (The federal party threat was probably made because Bob Hawke wanted to shore up his support base in Victoria.)

Grouper union readmission was put to the vote at a state ALP meeting at Coburg Town Hall. The new guard, including Gillard, Paul Slape, Michael O'Connor and other ALP members of the Socialist Forum, felt that it would be better to back off and readmit the unions. Paul Slape sums up the general view of both the Carr sub-faction and the Forum group of the Socialist Left: 'We weren't opposed to them coming back in. Our view was that Right versus Left factions was a tribal thing with no real ideological split. It wasn't like we were supporting Beijing and Moscow against capitalism. There were some differences with the DLP unions, but on social policy.'

The hard Left, on the other hand, was implacably opposed to any suggestion that the Grouper unions should rejoin the ALP. But it lost the vote and the DLP-affiliated unions were admitted. Some members of the hard Left considered the Socialist Forum lot to be partly responsible. A poster outside the Coburg Town Hall said it all: 'Stiletto Specialists'.

By the time she finished working part-time with the Socialist Forum, early in 1987, Julia Gillard was well on the way to learning how necessary successful factional warfare was for advancement in the ALP. Her initial exclusion from the Socialist Left had tightened her connections with an emerging Melbourne network of allies in the party, who were to become important in her future career. But she had not yet learned that youthful pushiness and self-confidence might make her some formidable long-term opponents. Inexperience prevented her from seeing that in politics one might win the battle but lose the war.

6

Mixing it with the blokes: 1

As a result of her plunge into ALP politics, Julia Gillard was mastering how unions operated within the party. By the mid-1980s many thought the union movement in Australia – as everywhere – had become a shadow of its former self. Its leaders even looked different. Almost gone was the older group of union officials: workers who had learned their trade as apprentices and worked their way up in the union from the shop floor. Trade union leaders were more likely to be well-educated graduates recruited from universities and student politics. Your standard union heavyweight was now much less likely to be a middle-aged man in a singlet than an ambitious young man in a suit.

At state and federal conferences Gillard and her group allied themselves with certain union members. In the words of Paul Slape, later national secretary of the Australian Services Union: 'We tended to sit close by them, the group of unions who were against the hard Left, which included my union (the Municipal Employees Union, now ASU), the Liquor and Hospitality Union, the Miscellaneous Workers, the Metal Workers, the Meatworkers – which were all fairly big. There was also the Painters Union, which was Michael O'Connor's and is now part of the CFMEU [Construction, Forestry, Mining and Energy Union]. Then he went to the Timber Workers. There was also the Clothing and Allied Trades Union. We were the group of unions opposed to those on the hard Left. They were more numerous, but mostly not as big. We used to call Gillard and O'Connor and co. the Youngies.'

Gillard might sit with the Youngies at ALP meetings, extending the range of her political network, but the union movement still had little time for ambitious young women. One of the traditional paths to advancement within the ALP was closed to her, and she knew it. If she wanted to make a career in politics – and she was considering the possibility with increasing seriousness – she would have to find another way.

When Julia Gillard graduated with a combined Arts-Law degree from the University of Melbourne, she was twenty-five years old. Feeling she had to make up time, she decided against doing the traditional year of articles in a law firm, opting instead for a six-month course run by the Leo Cussen Institute in Melbourne, which trained law graduates for admission to legal practice. The course was very practical, and an important component was work experience. 'They took notice of your preference, and I marked my form "commercial law, city",' she says. 'I felt I had spent so long kicking around student politics that I wanted to see how the other half lived.'

By what Gillard describes as 'some cosmic karma', she found

herself doing three weeks' training at the firm of Slater and Gordon. This Melbourne-based law firm has provoked strong reactions in its seventy-five-year history. When he was premier of Victoria Jeff Kennett loathed it, calling it 'that disreputable firm', a description adopted as a badge of honour and used as the title of Slater and Gordon's company history. Michael Cannon, author of the history, wrote in his preface: 'If I could live my life over again, I rather think I would like to be a Slater & Gordon lawyer of the rampaging kind. Can any author say more than that for his subject?'

Slater and Gordon started its life in 1935 in Melbourne, when young solicitors William Slater and Hugh Gordon decided to set up a law firm specifically to serve unions and their members, especially in the area of workers' compensation. By the 1970s it was doing well enough to open branch offices, both within Melbourne and in industrial areas such as Morwell in the Latrobe Valley. The firm also extended its practice and by 1980 was taking on not only workers' compensation cases but other areas of the law, including probate, local government, common law matters and commercial law. The firm's history has always been a struggle to balance keeping faith with its ideals and its need to turn a profit. Making money has never been its primary aim. As senior partner Peter Gordon says, 'Slaters perceives its raison d'être to be beyond profit.' At various times this has made life at Slater and Gordon interesting, in the Chinese sense of the word. One partner has said that working there is sometimes like flying an out-of-control plane: only so much can be done to defy gravity.

Slater and Gordon started really earning its spurs as a 'rampaging' law firm in 1984, gaining a reputation outside Melbourne legal circles in the process, when it conducted the first Australian asbestos-related cancer claim against CSR, the owners of the Wittenoom asbestos mine in Western Australia. This became the first of the mass tort actions – cases to rectify the harm done to many separate individuals by faulty mining or manufacturing – that the firm undertook. By the following year it was fighting hundreds of cases: so many that it opened an office in Perth.

Yet, despite Slater and Gordon's prominence, by the mid-1980s it was facing challenging times, partly because it had expanded too fast and was undercapitalised, but also because the Cain state Labor government had shifted the goalposts in terms of workers' compensation law. All Victorian law firms were worried that the 1985 WorkCare Authority would devastate their compensation practices, and Slater and Gordon estimated that it would reduce its income by about 30 per cent. Instead of pulling back, the firm increased its union client base, taking on a more diverse range of problems, from internal disputation through to fights for better pay and conditions.

When Julia Gillard walked through the front door of Slater and Gordon as a work experience temp in mid-1987, one of the first people she met was Bernard Murphy. Murphy, about five years older than Gillard, had recently been made a salaried partner. From a working-class background not unlike Gillard's own, he had bachelor and master's degrees in law from Monash and was active in left-wing politics. Indeed Clarrie O'Shea of the Tramways Union had recommended him for the Slater and Gordon job. Gillard and Murphy took to each other almost immediately. Murphy recognised Gillard's intelligence and drive from the first, and Gillard appreciated Murphy's humour and knew that she could learn from him. Learning could also be a two-way process, as Murphy discovered when he took his new recruit to a women's meeting. He had unsuccessfully acted for Susan Cooper, a keyboard operator who had claimed damages for work-related repetitive strain injury (tenosynovitis). Gillard says: 'On the way to the meeting, which was mostly leftie women, I said, "I think when you speak to this group, you should realise that they are not the kinds of women who take kindly to having women referred to as 'ladies'." He said, "OK", and then gave the speech. There were questions, and answering one of them Bernard described Sue Cooper as "a middle-class lass". It went down like a lead balloon, and I could hear a gasp from the audience. One woman said very coldly, "Mr Murphy, I don't think you realise that we don't like being called lasses or ladies." And Bernard, honest as the day is long, said, "Yeah, someone told me that only this morning . . ."

'As we walked back to the office he said, "I think we should offer you a job".'

Gillard began as a solicitor at Slater and Gordon in October 1987. Her job initially involved about 70 per cent commercial law and 30 per cent industrial law. She started work at a difficult time for the industrial law practice because the partner who had been running it had left after a dispute with the other partners. His colleague Ana Kokkinos took over briefly but she, too, decided to leave and went on to be a film director. (She is probably best known for *Head On*, the 1998 feature-length adaptation of Christos Tsiolkas's novel *Loaded*, starring Alex Dimitriades.) 'After that,' says Gillard, 'there was no industrial lawyer and no partner in industrial law and I got moved in to mind the practice until Bernard, who had a sizeable injury practice but wanted to be in industrial law, was able to finish his cases and move across. He became the partner specialising in industrial law and I worked with him.' The way she describes it is matter of fact but, for a newly fledged solicitor, being 'moved in to mind the practice' must have had its alarming moments.

Eventually the industrial law department numbered five solicitors, acting for about twenty-five unions at its peak. Industrial law was not an area that made much money for Slater and Gordon, as most of the unions could not afford to pay top fees for lawyers. However, representing unions had been a core part of Slater and Gordon's business since the firm was founded and – just as importantly – union contacts led to valuable work in workers' compensation and other litigation. Shortly after Gillard started, she became involved with women employed in the clothing trade. Historically women workers had been appallingly treated in this industry. In 1882 the recently formed Tailoresses' Union staged a successful strike of women workers, preventing clothing manufacturers from further reducing the wages of women who were already poorly paid. The union exposed the dreadful working conditions in Victoria's clothing factories, leading to a parliamentary inquiry into sweated labour. As a result of the inquiry, the Victorian government established boards to ensure regulation of wages, hours and conditions for all workers.

But by the 1980s a great deal of the work in the clothing trade was done not in factories – although these still existed, staffed mainly by migrant women – but by hundreds of women who worked at home. These women often worked fifteen-hour days and were paid on a per garment basis at a very low rate. Many of them were paid only one or two dollars an hour, excluding costs of materials, to make clothes that sold in the shops for forty to fifty times that price.

In November 1987 the Clothing and Allied Trades Union won an historic variation of the clothing trades award to create arrangements for outworkers. Under the new award it was illegal to pay contractors less money than they would have earned as regular employees. The variation carried stringent disclosure requirements, so records had to be kept by factories giving work to middlemen, who would pass it on to the women supervising the workers and thence to the outworkers themselves. Consequently the union had a large job to do making sure people complied with the new award and kept records.

Unfortunately the Clothing and Allied Trades Union had comparatively little industrial muscle. Almost every employer pleaded that their competitors had moved to the Philippines or India, and they could not afford to pay wages or workers' compensation and remain in business. It was often difficult to discover the employment arrangements made with outworkers: employers took enormous care to disguise them. Outworkers were often afraid of complaining because they might lose the work their family depended on, however badly it paid; most were migrant women who spoke little English and did not understand what they were entitled to. The union had multilingual organisers on staff and Slater and Gordon employed interpreters, but communication with the women worst affected was never easy.

Making sure factory owners complied with regulations caused many headaches. Companies would regularly go into administration or receivership on Christmas Eve to avoid paying holiday entitlements, and then would open up under another name in the same factory in January. Kate Hawkins, who worked with Gillard and is now a Melbourne magistrate, remembers once going to court on Christmas Eve to stop that happening, successfully arguing that assets should be frozen to prevent dispersal. Another time an owner set a savage dog on a union official attempting to inspect the company's books.

There were also problems with workers' compensation. Many women in factories suffered such severe repetitive strain injury that they would never work again. However, their wages were so low that they might win a settlement of less than $10 000.

'It's quite hard,' says Kate Hawkins. 'It's a systemic problem. These women are not heard and not paid properly.'

Gillard and her colleagues at Slater and Gordon did make some headway in protecting and enforcing the rights of this marginal group of women. Writs were issued against a number of employers, alleging breaches of the award. Some of these cases were resolved by negotiation, so disclosure of the names of the employers and the details of the settlement were prohibited. There were also cases in the Federal Court against manufacturers who seriously underpaid their factory workers: again, these were often settled out of court with disclosure prohibitions.

'It was a terrible job,' says Peter Gordon. 'A heartbreaking sort of job. We had a lot of people do that job and act for those people and it's pretty depressing. But nothing really upset [Julia]. Adversity didn't upset her, bad results didn't seem to distract her the way they do most lawyers.'

Brendan Soraghan, formerly an industrial officer with the clothing union, worked closely with Gillard over this period. 'When I started at the union, she said something I've never forgotten,' he says. 'It's why I still dress like this [in a smart suit]. She said, "When migrant women who work in the factories come to the union to see you, you'll find they dress up. It's like coming to their doctor or their lawyer. They want professional help and they want to be treated with dignity and respect, so make sure you look professional for them."

'I remember one time we met with a migrant woman in preparation for a case, and the woman said in broken English: "Oh, the case is on the tenth of April, that is my daughter ten birthday. I won't forget the day, Miss Julia." So we went to the case, and we got an outcome and as we were going and the worker was saying thank you, Julia pulled out of her bag a little present for her daughter. She gave it to her and said, "This will be good for your daughter to read, I liked this book as a child."

'Well, the woman burst into tears – and I just thought, Bloody hell, I wish I'd done that. I mean, here's someone who's working twelve hours a day at Slaters and then spending a good proportion of her evenings and weekends on what I always used to call ALP hack work, and she still had the time and foresight to do that.'

Trying to get results for a union has always been hard, sometimes thankless work if you are an industrial lawyer. In the words of Josh Bornstein, who had been a junior colleague at Slater and Gordon: 'In the union movement you need to have a tough hide. You have to be very tough with unions. Union officials work in a brutal environment where their members will abuse them if they think they're doing the wrong thing, let alone if they are, where the employers are trying to get them, where they have rivals in the union trying to knock them off. As a result they can be very abrasive and are often not big fans of the legal system. And often they have an underlying distrust of lawyers – in the eyes of some union secretaries, the best that can be said for labour lawyers is that they are a necessary evil.'

Gillard occasionally had problems with certain unions, mostly as a result of her time working for the Socialist Forum. Slater and Gordon's clientele included some hard Left unions, which were reluctant to use her. As time passed and she became more experienced and her talents became more obvious, this became a sticking point. One of the railway unions said that she was not to look at any of its files, which did upset her. However, she had forged very strong relationships with other unions, notably the Municipal Employees' Association – with whom she had made alliances during her student days – and the Clothing and Allied Trades Union, which preferred to deal only with her. 'She had the respect of a lot of male union officials,' says Kate Hawkins. 'Your blue-collar hard-drinking and swearing bloke, he respected her as well. She's just a very good communicator, she can work across many levels.'

Slater and Gordon was a very male-oriented environment – one source compared it to the locker room of a football team. In the words of Peter Gordon: 'People used language pretty freely, people expressed their views forthrightly and I suppose from her perspective that meant it was a boys' club. I never considered it that way, but it was rough and direct and people were confronted with their shortcomings. If someone felt something was wrong, if people felt they had been misled about something, there was no gentlemanly demurring to the better angels of one's nature, it was on.' Yet it was obvious that this was an environment in which Julia Gillard felt comfortable.

Those who worked with her and Bernard Murphy in the industrial law division remember that they complemented each other well, probably because their styles were so different. In the words of Josh Bornstein, 'Murphy was flamboyant, dynamic and energetic;

Gillard was quieter, well organised and more relaxed. They had different dimensions but it seemed to work.' As time went on, Murphy ran his union cases and Gillard ran hers.

They kept a happy team, and the industrial law division 'had a social element to it' as well as stimulating cases. Bornstein says: 'We enjoyed the odd long lunch or a drink at the pub. There were lunches with union officials, union functions, drinks on a Friday. It was fascinating, interesting work, getting good experience.'

In 1990 Slater and Gordon decided to introduce some of the younger lawyers into the partnership. One was Julia Gillard, the first woman to be offered a salaried partnership by the firm. She was twenty-nine and had been there three years.

She became a salaried partner at a prosperous time for Slater and Gordon. As well as the litigation against CSR in Wittenoom, which had gained it immense prestige, it had successfully mounted a class action for people suffering from medically acquired HIV. These were two very big wins, but perhaps more important for the firm's profile – Melbourne being Melbourne – was the fact that senior partner Peter Gordon became president of the Footscray (Western Bulldogs) football team. He now says that it raised his profile and that of the firm way beyond expectations. One of Gillard's new duties was to put on the red, white and blue scarf and barrack for the team, a job she took on with enthusiasm.

The political ambitions that Gillard was beginning to nurture were furthered by her new status in a leading industrial law firm that dealt with important trade unions. (At least one work colleague thought her such a political animal that, in accepting the salaried partnership, she might have been primarily interested in furthering those ambitions.) She continued to be very active within the Socialist Left faction at branch level in the seat of Melbourne.

Due to her drive to succeed as Slater and Gordon's first woman partner, plus her passionate interest in politics, Gillard worked very hard indeed, both in the office and out of it. She was equally able to be a union lawyer and to put together a political network, and her work ethic became legendary. It was not uncommon for her to be in the office at six on a Saturday morning.

Julia Gillard was never the kind of person who cared overmuch about her appearance: several former colleagues have commented about her relative lack of vanity. She dressed neatly, but the hems of her skirts were unfashionably long, the shoulders of her jackets disproportionately wide, and she favoured medium-high, thick-heeled shoes, which did not flatter her legs. With her hair in a long bob or pulled back and wearing very little make-up, she often looked, as one younger woman colleague observed, 'a bit of a dag'. The job was the important thing.

Although her factional alignment meant that she acted in very few internal union battles, which were generally handled by Slater and Gordon staff members without ALP affiliation, sometimes her two consuming interests collided. A former Slater and Gordon solicitor who worked with Gillard recalls: 'I vividly remember one meeting in the Socialist Left when Julia was accused of being a scab . . . because she was a partner in Slater's industrial department, which was running a case on behalf of the Painters and Decorators. Suffice to say the construction division [of the CFMEU] regarded her as a scab. She got up and said she had clients to represent and the client happened to be a union. She said that when she went to work for a union law firm, she never thought she would see the day when she would have to defend representing a union. Anyone would have agreed: here was a young woman standing up in a very strong and robust meeting, a hot environment where it got a bit out of hand. She was more than capable of getting up and giving it back, explaining why she and Slaters had taken this particular case.'

When Gillard's former colleagues are asked about her, the same comments are apt to come up again and again. Several male lawyers have described themselves in those years as emotional, perhaps even highly strung, and apt to become angry when things did not go their way. Gillard, their most senior female colleague, was quite the opposite. She never showed anxiety, rarely expressed anger, and above all was measured and unflustered.

Josh Bornstein, recalling his time as a junior lawyer, says: 'Just watching someone dealing with things slowly, methodically and calmly was a bit of an education. I don't recall her ever cracking. She didn't do what I did in those days. I'd say, "Oh God, I've stuffed something up." I was the anxious young lawyer. She'd say, "No, every stuff-up can be resolved."' Gillard wasn't detached – she was far too involved in her work for that – but she knew how to use humour to defuse potentially emotional situations and, perhaps, to get a bit of distance on a particular problem.

Kate Hawkins found her an excellent mentor: 'She was great to work with, she was highly intelligent, an extremely hard worker, but also very caring and a good teacher. She had high ethical standards and a high work ethic, she set exacting standards but helped a younger solicitor to reach them.'

Clarity and correctness of English expression were important to

Gillard as a legal practitioner, and she tried to make sure her staff kept to the traditional rules. Sometimes this meant unleashing her inner grammar obsessive. As she told a journalist many years later: 'I am a complete apostrophe nut. The misplacement of commas. The modern need to put a comma before the word 'and' in every sentence. What is going on with that? Dashes. Why does one need dashes in a properly constructed sentence? Sentences that start with "and". An inability to work out how to use its and it's.' Working for Slater and Gordon she instituted a grammar chant: 'I used to have them all chanting "one cat's hat, two cats' hats, where do the apostrophes go?" If I got a letter with it done wrong I would draw a cat with a hat at the bottom in the hope it would come back right the next time. They all thought I was kind of strange.'

Gillard's staff was a tightly knit group who worked hard and played hard. The age of the long lunch not yet having passed, there were times when Slater and Gordon continued to take full advantage of it. 'I don't think the National Health Council guidelines on alcohol were strictly adhered to,' notes Kate Hawkins dryly, 'but it was part of our good camaraderie.'

Josh Bornstein comments: 'When Kate and I were junior lawyers, watching Bernard and Julia, getting interesting work, there was a sense that the industrial department was going places, it was growing all the time. You had a good feel about it, you were enthusiastic about your job because the people around you were.'

Bornstein, now a principal at Maurice Blackburn in Melbourne, recalls that Gillard wasn't very enthusiastic about him when he first applied to join Slater and Gordon. 'Bernard kept pursuing me, saying he was keen, but he said, "Julia's not sure whether you'll be tough enough to litigate." Thankfully I think I've proved her wrong, which is good. So she didn't start off as a great fan of mine, but once we worked together, we got on very well, became friends and her loyalty continues to this day.'

In 1998, after he had left Slater and Gordon and was working for Maurice Blackburn, Josh Bornstein acted for the Maritime Union of Australia in the lengthy waterfront dispute that saw 1400 workers locked out of their jobs and replaced by non-union workers secretly trained in Dubai. The case grew dramatically bigger, reaching a climax around Easter, and he needed help in dealing with the media.

'I picked up the phone and said, "Julia, I need help." She said, "What's going on?" and in she came. I might not have talked to her for a year or two, but her loyalty is quite superb.' Gillard helped Bornstein fulltime to manage the media attention. Her involvement in the dispute was highlighted in Liberal Party advertisements as part of its anti-union blitz just before the 2007 election, and she was asked about it on the ABC-TV program *Insiders*.

She told *Insiders* that her only regret about having helped Bornstein was being photographed wearing a pair of 'bloody awful' sunglasses. (How well this played in the wider community could be gauged from a comment on a blog during the strike: 'Have you noticed the way that Gillard is getting portrayed as some femme fatale in dark shades lately? Jeez, it's laughable. I mean she supports the Bulldogs, how sinister is that!?')

'Once you become a friend, it's very hard to lose her as a friend,' says Bornstein. 'I don't know anyone else with that degree of loyalty.'

Some years earlier he had accompanied Gillard to a fundraiser for an ALP politician: 'She had asked me to go specifically because she feared an unwelcome approach from the politician, so I went along as her protection. The politician looked me up and down, and the heat generating from him, the anger . . . He was married but it didn't seem to matter. A number of people at that dinner asked me what I was doing there. I said, "I'm making sure that politician does not misbehave." One of the people took umbrage at that and criticised me over dinner for not understanding the sexuality of the Mediterranean male. That has stuck in my mind as one of the most ridiculous things I have ever heard.'

Although she was excellent at using legal process and knew how to marshal and deploy facts and how to negotiate, Gillard never pretended to be a black-letter lawyer; that is, one whose approach to the law is primarily intellectual, whose decisions are made as a result of the deep study of precedents and case law. She regarded the law primarily as a means of solving problems.

Nobody doubted her drive or intelligence, but her pragmatic approach led some colleagues to consider her efficient but not intellectually brilliant. Kate Hawkins sees her differently: 'She could get across a highly complex area of law and turn it into a simple concept that she could communicate to anyone, from a lawyer to a person from a non-English-speaking background. It's a rare skill to translate the intricacies of corporation law to someone with a primary school education. You watch her on telly now and the same skill is evident.'

Considering Gillard's initial reluctance to finish university and to embrace a law career, it is interesting that she achieved so much at Slater and Gordon so quickly. But in her area of abiding interest – politics – success would take much longer.

7

Welcome to first grade

There's a well-known football story about an eager young player who came down from the country to play first grade with a city club. During the match he brought the ball up to an opposing player, who tackled him and drove him into the mud. As the young player staggered up, his face bloody and his nose broken, his opponent grinned at him and said, 'Welcome to first grade, son.'

Julia Gillard's entry into the first grade of politics – going for preselection in a safe Labor seat – wasn't an affair of mud or blood, except metaphorically. But difficult it certainly was, with no shortage of people lining up to tackle her.

In early 1992 Gerry Hand, who had been minister for Aboriginal affairs and was presently minister for immigration and ethnic affairs, announced his intention to resign from Parliament at the next federal election. Hand had been a controversial minister. He had clashed memorably with Charles Perkins, the outspoken Indigenous secretary of the Department of Aboriginal Affairs, and as immigration minister he had introduced the policy of mandatory detention for illegal arrivals and asylum seekers (a policy that Gillard would be forced to confront some years later). Hand's electorate was Melbourne, a safe Socialist Left seat, which was now open for preselection.

It was a prize that, as Gillard realised, wasn't something that came up every day. 'I lived in a share house in the seat of Melbourne,' she says, 'I'd been president of a branch there for years and years. I thought I'd have a go.' It was a decision born of optimism and self-confidence.

Brendan Soraghan says: 'She rang me and said, "I have to buy a house and it has to be within the Melbourne FEA area." It didn't matter what kind of house, she wanted to live in the electorate – she had her eye on the prize. I remember her saying how crucial it was – and I thought, Shit, you're going to buy a house solely for that reason. Most people buy a house because they want to live in a certain area or close to amenities or near work or school or uni. She thought living in the electorate she represented was an important democratic issue.' There was no formal requirement that a would-be candidate, or even a candidate, had to live – let alone own a house – in the electorate.

There was also the question of Lindsay Tanner. These days Lindsay Tanner is the rather dour minister for finance in the Rudd government; then he was a clever young solicitor with an easy manner, a lot of street cred and great ambitions. He was also a skilled political operator, with an impeccable union background. He had started his career as a solicitor at Holding Redlich in Melbourne, and then become electorate assistant to Labor senator Barney Cooney, after which he was assistant state secretary and later state secretary of the Federated Clerks' Union.

The FCU had been one of the four DLP-affiliated Grouper unions that Gillard and other members of the Socialist Forum had voted to allow back into the ALP in 1984. Lindsay Tanner had gained immense kudos when he and fellow Socialist Left member Alan Griffin won control of the FCU at the union's first election after readmission. The FCU was the most important of the Grouper unions, and so a common view was that Tanner was owed by the Socialist Left.

Gillard was well aware of all this. She also knew that Tanner was a good networker, with steady support in many of the local branches, and an effective speaker. He had been active in the Melbourne electorate for at least fifteen years, and a leading figure in economic and environmental debates within the Victorian ALP. 'I knew Lindsay was the preferred candidate,' she says. '[But] I thought it was possible I could win Melbourne. Not likely, but possible. And if I hadn't put my hand up it would have been seen that I wasn't interested in a political career, so it was worthwhile doing from that point of view, too.' Her decision to run for Melbourne was, then, partly a strategic one.

The foundation of her support was the Municipal Employees' Association (which in 1993 would merge with several others to form the Australian Municipal, Administrative, Clerical and Services Union). She had met Darrell Cochrane, the union's state secretary, at Slater and Gordon when she gave legal advice for a campaign to cover home and community care workers, and she continued to be MEA's main contact at the law firm. With her help and advice the union recruited carer members in Tasmania, giving them the interstate representation they needed to get federal award coverage and therefore higher salaries.

Her other key supporter was a section of the Construction, Forestry, Mining and Energy Union under Michael O'Connor. There were also the members of the Socialist Left who had been her associates since her days in the Socialist Forum. As one source has pointed out, Gillard was already good at translating a network of people who shared her intellectual position into a network of political supporters. The question was, of course, whether Gillard's various networks, built up over time and immersion in the ALP system, would be powerful and extensive enough to have her preselected. According to the rules, preselection was 50 per cent controlled by the votes of ALP members in the electorate's branches, and 50 per cent by the ALP's 100-member Public Office Selection Committee chosen by state conference. That meant, as one source observed, one hell of a lot of networking.

There was no great animosity between Gillard and Tanner, who was five years older than she, but by all accounts they never really clicked. Both were ambitious, both were focused, both wanted the same thing for themselves: hardly a recipe for eternal friendship. Tanner subscribed to a view within sections of the Socialist Left that Gillard was a careerist – too pragmatic, too ready to make deals with whoever suited. Gillard says that the relationship between them was 'civilised'. Tanner's reservations about Gillard had been there since they first came across each other in the Australian Union of Students in the early 1980s. 'I think in part this was because he saw her as a rival,' says Andrew Scott, who has known them both from student days.

At the 1991 state ALP conference, a year or so before Joan Kirner's time as premier ended and with it the dominance of her Socialist Left faction in Victorian politics, Lindsay Tanner had spelled out what he saw as the fundamental divide in the Left of the Victorian ALP. He said it was beginning to split between 'rationalists' and 'traditionalists'. The rationalists included supporters of the Hawke government's brand of economic rationalism. These groups supported the Accord process and the restructuring of industry and the unions. He did not say so but clearly Joan Kirner belonged to this group, as did Gillard. The traditionalists, said Tanner, gained support from the sections of the old Left and Right in the party that were against privatisation, favoured greater government intervention in the economy and were suspicious of the Accord or opposed to it. Tanner said he would place himself between those poles, although he was probably closer to the traditionalists on questions of privatisation and the Accord. He also described himself as 'anti-corporatist'.

The traditionalists had already made their position clear. After the state conference the previous year the leaders of a group of Left unions, which became known as the Pledge unions, had come together and pledged to oppose privatisation. The Pledge Left demonstrated that the spirit of Bill Hartley still lived, and that it was carrying on his fight against the rest of the Socialist Left. Gillard and her supporters in the Socialist Left were all for expelling the Pledge Left members from the faction, on the grounds that their kind of ideological purity had no place in it. 'There was real bitterness between the Socialist Forum and the Pledge people,' says ALP colleague Andrew McKenzie.

Kim Carr, who still ran the dominant faction of the Socialist Left, continued to look on Gillard with a cold eye. Gillard's group was aggressively presented as reformers willing to be critical, says Andrew McKenzie, whereas 'Carr wanted to maintain control.

When the Socialist Left split, those pushing a very hard line on expelling the hard Left were the Gillard group. The Carr group felt they should not necessarily be driven out because they might want to deal with them in the future.' Carr prevailed.

The relationship between Carr and Gillard deteriorated further during Carr's 1992 battle for Senate preselection: he was up against Pete Steedman, a long-time supporter of Gillard, whom she backed in the contest. Carr duly got his Senate spot, but was not pleased that Gillard had been part of the alliance against him.

Gillard's irresistible force soon came up against the immovable object named Kim Carr in her own preselection contest. 'He didn't want her up there, he didn't want her at all,' says Darrell Cochrane. Carr's primary objective, according to Cochrane, was to have a factional supporter in the federal Parliament; he was always going to back Lindsay Tanner against Julia Gillard.

However, it was a three-way battle, played out within the Socialist Left, because Frans Timmerman had also put himself in the running. Not surprisingly Timmerman, who had been responsible for Gillard's delayed entry into the Socialist Left and was representing the Pledge Left, was no friend of Gillard either. Timmerman knew he would not be chosen, so his preferences would be crucial.

Even though the Pledge sub-faction had an affirmative action policy, its supporters did not want to vote for Gillard because they felt she was too conservative. Timmerman says: 'My supporters were lukewarm about Tanner, but most were certainly against Gillard. Even the women were against her, and many of those had never voted for men, but in this case they put Gillard last because they disliked her so much, they felt she wasn't a feminist. She never ran on her feminist issues at all. She was clearly ambitious.'

Gillard approached Timmerman for his preferences, but he directed them to Tanner. Tanner got ninety votes, Gillard sixty-six and Timmerman fifty-six. Had Timmerman delivered his preferences to Gillard she would have defeated Tanner easily.

But it was not to be. Hindsight is a wonderful thing, and in this case one conclusion is obvious: Gillard would have done better to be less implacably opposed to the Pledge Left. Who knows, perhaps she should even not have joined the Socialist Forum back in 1984. These days Gillard is philosophical. If she had won Melbourne, her political career would not have gone down the path it did a few years later and she would have missed out on some invaluable experience. All the same it was a setback – at the very least a blow to Gillard's pride – and at the time she would certainly have welcomed a blessing that wasn't in disguise.

8

Mixing it with the blokes: 2

In October 1992 Joan Kirner, Victoria's first woman premier and a warm friend, factional ally and supporter of Gillard, faced an election she had no chance of winning. Kirner had become premier in 1990 after the resignation of John Cain. Her two years in office had been turbulent, marked by inherited financial deficits and crises and by a divided party. She had been mercilessly lampooned in the press, referred to as Mother Russia or Auntie Joan, and portrayed in mumsy polka-dot dresses.

By early 1992 the government was in such a parlous state that ALP polling showed it would retain the seat of Sunshine and nothing more, according to John Lenders, then a head office organiser. The Hawke–Keating federal agenda, with its emphasis on privatisation and rejection of subsidies to unprofitable industries, was making inroads into the party's industrial base, and unemployment in Geelong and Melbourne was growing. Kirner was more popular than Jeff Kennett, her Liberal opponent, but voters agreed with him that Labor bore sole responsibility for Victoria's financial problems.

The Liberal Party won a landslide victory, with a thirty-four-seat majority. Kirner stayed on for a few months, then resigned her seat of Williamstown – to be succeeded by Steve Bracks – and left Parliament. Her place as leader of the Opposition was taken briefly by Jim Kennan and, after his retirement, by John Brumby.

Once in office Kennett lost no time in cutting costs, especially in various areas of the state public service. Between 1992 and 1995 about 50 000 public servants lost their jobs, and government funding for the public school system was slashed, with 350 government schools closed and 7000 teaching jobs removed. Thousands of public transport workers were sacked. At the same time Kennett oversaw a huge scheme for the privatisation of state-owned services, including the State Electricity Commission, the ambulance service, and prisons. On 10 November 1992 Melbourne's biggest public protest since the days of the Vietnam War took place, with an estimated 100 000 people marching through the city to demonstrate their opposition to the retrenchment of workers and Budget cutbacks. Peter Gordon believes that people don't remember how high the social costs of Kennett's first year actually were.

One Kennett action that directly affected Slater and Gordon, and other law firms that handled workers' compensation cases, was the introduction of the Accident Compensation Act, establishing WorkCover from 1 December 1992. The aim was to prevent law firms from winning what the government considered excessive damages for injured employees, and to force workers to accept much lower government offers (made in hearings from which lawyers were generally excluded).

All claims for compensation now had to be referred to a medical panel selected by WorkCover, claimants were not permitted to have their own lawyers or other representatives present, and there was no appeal against the panel's findings. Entitlements to weekly workers' compensation payments were slashed to ensure that only the most seriously injured employees were given compensation for longer than two years. And the right to pursue a common law claim for damages was restricted to those whose injuries met a 30 per cent impairment test. (A worker who lost a leg below the knee was considered to be only 27 per cent impaired.)

The process was so intimidating that in the following years many workers with claims preferred to drop out of the compensation system. Slater and Gordon, and other firms in a similar position, became alarmed that WorkCover would create an underclass of injured workers condemned to poverty for the rest of their lives.

The legislation also meant that if anyone's claim was stopped, the lawyer could take no steps to recover legal fees or any of the money the firm had spent. None of the clothing-trade workers represented by Julia Gillard at Slater and Gordon could afford to run their own cases; nor could many others. To make matters worse, the firm ran many cases on a 'no win, no fee' basis, so it could not charge clients who lost their cases either.

According to Peter Gordon, during that time Slater and Gordon was out of pocket by between $3000 and $5000 per case, for such things as medical reports, barristers' fees and court costs. And there were thousands of cases. At the same time Slater and Gordon was running several very big and high-profile class actions: representing local landowners in the Fly River district of New Guinea against BHP Billiton and Ok Tedi Mining Ltd; taking on Dow Corning over defective breast implants; and appearing against the Christian Brothers in Western Australia in cases of sexual assault. Kennett's

The Gillard family at their new home in Adelaide. Moira stands behind Julia, John behind Alison, c. 1967.

Schoolkid: Julia Gillard at Mitcham Primary, Adelaide.

A teenager at Unley High School, about the time she takes up debating.

President of the Australian Union of Students, 1983 – the second woman to hold the job in the organisation's history.

Members of the Socialist Forum at the Forum's office in Fitzroy, Melbourne, 1985. From left: Rob Read, Julia Gillard and Mark Taft.

A partner at Slater and Gordon, Melbourne, 1994.

Protesting against the Liberal government's handling of the 1998 waterfront dispute. Front row: Julia Gillard (sixth from left), Joan Kirner, former premier of Victoria (in purple top), ACTU secretary Bill Kelty (seventh from right), ALP senator Kim Carr (wearing grey gloves).

The newly elected Labor member for Lalor at her office in Werribee, October 1998.

Photographed at her Melbourne home soon after becoming shadow minister for immigration, November 2001.

new legislation had effectively removed the predictability of the firm's income on which the running of these cases depended.

'We had commitments in these areas,' says Peter Gordon. 'Our traditional union clientele were shitting themselves, the state was broke, the Labor movement was pretty much blamed, the tide turned fairly seriously against us. Slater and Gordon had invested more than $10 million paying for our clients' disbursements for their claims. Here was Kennett proposing, with the stroke of a pen, to abolish the clients' claims and to remove our right even to recover the money we had lent them. Kennett knew this. I believe he was deliberately setting out to destroy Slater and Gordon.'

Senior staff believed that Kennett's general antipathy hardened into implacable hostility towards Slater and Gordon in 1995 because of the Smith–Harris defamation case. Ian Smith, Kennett's finance minister, was forced to resign after it was revealed that he was having an affair with Cheryl Harris, his chief of staff. Bernard Murphy, acting on her behalf, lodged a writ alleging that Smith had assaulted her. Smith began defamation proceedings two months later in the Supreme Court against Cheryl Harris and Slater and Gordon. Before the full case was heard, a confidential settlement was reached. The question was asked whether taxpayers' money had been used, in order to stop the proceedings and avoid embarrassing the government. Certainly the episode did nothing to calm relations between Kennett and Slater and Gordon.

Peter Gordon says that for quite a while Slater and Gordon was the de facto Opposition: 'I think Brumby would concede that in the first couple of years the Opposition was fairly fragmented. Slater and Gordon was not fragmented and we were fighting for our lives . . . Kennett hated us.'

As a result of the Kennett workplace legislation and its consequences, Slater and Gordon were forced to sack about forty employees. Peter Gordon: 'Sometimes when you are running a business you have to behave like a prick. It's not pleasant.'

As a salaried partner, Julia Gillard had to do some of the firing. Now, for the first time in her life, she had to take responsibility for doing something she hated but that her position made necessary. Peter Gordon: 'Some people would probably have said, No, I am not prepared to do that, it's not what I do. Some would know it had to be done, but not by them. Some would say, No, let's continue as we are, and if we go broke we go broke. I had to sack senior people because I was more interested in Slaters being around in ten years than being on the right side ideologically. Julia innately understood that.'

This was not the first time Gillard had been responsible for other people's fates with Slater and Gordon. One of her jobs was to interview all prospective articled clerks for the firm. 'It was very regimented and compressed, and very fraught,' she says. 'Slater and Gordon would get 1200 applications for four or six slots, in a big round maybe eight slots. I'd read all the applications, [the general manager] Geoff Shaw would, [we would] compare notes, get them down to the final twenty-five, and I would interview them in twenty-minute cycles to get down to the final ten. The partners would then interview the finalists.'

Selecting staff like this was an exercise in honing one's skills of assessing people. 'It was very difficult,' she says. 'I had to make unbelievably fine judgements. And you're never sure how much your own reaction to another human being depends on your own prejudices.' She could have had worse training for a political career.

When Gillard debated Joe Hockey during the 2007 election

campaign, her opponent asked her to name one member of the Labor frontbench who had had to run a business or who had been responsible for making difficult management decisions. She replied, 'Yeah, OK, me.'

In this climate there was continuing and occasionally tense dialogue within Slater and Gordon about the direction the firm should take. The dispute crystallised around Peter Gordon, who generally favoured the large and potentially profitable class actions, and Bernard Murphy, who felt that trade union representation, compensation and personal injury work were essential to the firm's business. Julia Gillard was inclined towards her friend and associate Bernard Murphy, although naturally she understood that winning the big class actions brought in a great deal more money than industrial work.

Among the clients that Bernard Murphy had represented for a number of years was the Australian Workers' Union. In 1995 he acted for Bruce Wilson, the AWU secretary, in an intra-union dispute. Gillard worked with him, met Wilson and they began an affair. Their relationship caused raised eyebrows around the office. Wilson was regarded by some as a 'good bloke', but by others as somewhat slick, even 'quite an operator'. He was a smart and charismatic union leader who had worked in the resource-rich Pilbara region and risen through the ranks. While not well educated, he was intelligent and personable, and he had a sense of humour. He and Gillard had a good relationship, although her colleagues thought he was not in her league. But, as one observed, 'Julia always went for the rough diamonds.'

After several months Bernard Murphy discovered that Wilson was defrauding the union. As reported later, Wilson would go to construction sites and tell bosses that to ensure industrial peace they needed an agreement, which he would negotiate – but in return they must buy hundreds of AWU membership tickets. Wilson diverted the new membership funds to special accounts, using the money to maintain his power and to finance his re-election. As soon as Murphy discovered Wilson's dishonesty, he refused to act for him any further. Gillard did the same. As soon as the fraud became known, she ended her relationship with Wilson: cut it cold and never saw him again. Gillard was typically unsentimental in her attitude to the episode. She was never one to brood over losses, saying she preferred to go home, have a few glasses of red and maybe a good cry, and get over it.

Concerning her relationships with men, Julia Gillard has been considered very much in control. But just because you are controlled doesn't mean your heart is not engaged. Close friends knew how upset she was about what had happened with Wilson, and how bruised she felt. As one union ally said: 'I know it hurt her. It hurt her a lot. She put a lot of trust in the guy. She's never been the sort of person who had a lot of male friends personally – she has long-term partners, and then long periods of time without partners. It shows you have to be careful.'

Gillard said nothing about the episode in the office except to make a few mordant jokes about her taste in men. And there the matter might have rested, with Gillard chalking the whole thing up to experience. Except that shortly afterwards Kennett minister Phil Gude alleged under parliamentary privilege that Wilson was being investigated by the National Crime Authority and Victoria Police for the misappropriation of the funds, and that they had been used to renovate Gillard's house and to buy some personal items. However, nothing more was said until the 2007 election campaign, when the whole episode resurfaced in the pro-Coalition Murdoch press. There were headlines such as 'How Gillard's Ex Scammed' and 'Con Man Broke My Heart' and a repetition of the allegation that some of the money had been used to renovate Gillard's house.

'The story broke the Sunday before election day, and we knew it was coming,' says Gillard now. 'It was run by News Limited. I just put up with it. I was obviously concerned about my parents. Over the next two or three days I received phone calls from many of the biggest names in the Canberra press gallery expressing absolute disbelief that such things were said. Nobody followed up the story. It just died.' The *Sunday Telegraph* later apologised for its allegation that Gillard had used funds scammed by Wilson.

Slater and Gordon clearly did not believe in sexually transmitted misbehaviour, and it was agreed at the time that Gillard had simply made an error of judgement. But the whole Bruce Wilson episode exacerbated the tensions between Peter Gordon and Bernard Murphy, and Gillard was a Murphy ally.

Julia Gillard was now in her mid-thirties, single, with few financial responsibilities. She was a salaried senior partner at Slater and Gordon – affirmation that she was a very good and widely admired industrial lawyer. She had enjoyed her years with the firm and learned a great deal. But the acrimony between Peter Gordon and Bernard Murphy had badly affected the camaraderie that had once been such a feature of the industrial division. And then Murphy had suddenly resigned.

The atmosphere in the office was less pleasant than it had been. 'Working there wasn't as much fun, to be honest,' says Gillard. However, she could certainly take over the industrial practice, and things would settle down. But she was not sure that this was what she really wanted.

And so it was that many in Slater and Gordon heard with surprise that Julia Gillard was quitting the firm to try for a parliamentary seat she had little hope of winning.

9

'Sometimes you can say things happen for a reason'

Nobody has ever accused Julia Gillard of lacking persistence. Her unsuccessful campaign to win preselection for the federal seat of Melbourne in the 1993 election, and the knowledge that she had factional enemies, had not deterred her. According to several sources, she had never taken her eye off a political career despite her success as a lawyer. 'Politics was always what she wanted to do and law was always an offshoot of politics, rather than politics as an offshoot of law,' says Gillard's former colleague Andrew McKenzie. Initially when she told a few trusted people that she was likely to leave the firm – and the law – she had discussed her future in terms of getting a safe federal seat somewhere. But this began to look increasingly unlikely.

The logical alternative was to go for a Senate spot in the next federal election, which had to be held sometime in 1996. Half the Senate would be up for election, with the ALP defending two places in Victoria. There was a strong feeling within sections of the Socialist Left that Gillard, who had impressed many with the quality of her campaign in the seat of Melbourne, should be given the second spot on the ticket, which would probably ensure her selection. (The top spot was Robert Ray's.) At the time this was marked out for Barney Cooney, who had been in the Senate since 1984 and was in his early sixties. But there was very little chance of Gillard usurping his position, not least because Kim Carr, now a senator, was implacably opposed to any such move, as was Lindsay Tanner MP. Gillard had strong support within a sub-faction of the Socialist Left, but her union network was not enough to get her the second spot.

There was also some talk that she would be offered the third position on the Senate ticket: not unwinnable, but hardly a sure thing. Carr and Tanner were not having that either, and they offered the spot to Jennie George, an ebullient, no-nonsense former teacher and union activist who was assistant secretary of the Australian Council of Trade Unions at the time. George accepted. However, before the election she found out that the presidency of the ACTU was hers – she was the first woman ever to be offered and to take the job – and she withdrew from the ticket.

At this point Carr and Tanner said Gillard could have the spot. Gratitude was probably not her foremost emotion. She knew this was not much of a prize. Gillard was well aware by this time that the Carr and Tanner forces would never offer her a chance of winning – she felt she would never get a seat in federal Parliament if they had anything to do with it – but she accepted with good grace.

It is a tribute to Gillard's single-minded ambition that she was prepared to give up a lucrative and interesting career in the law in favour of a political future that might never materialise. Certainly her decision caused raised eyebrows among her legal colleagues. But she did not hesitate: 'I thought I had a chance,' she says. And, as with her campaign for the seat of Melbourne three years earlier, she felt she had to show that she was a serious political player.

Julia Gillard's departure from Slater and Gordon created a large hole in the industrial division, not least because Kate Hawkins and Josh Bornstein had left at about the same time as Bernard Murphy. By all accounts there were no hard feelings attached to Gillard's departure. She still sees some of her old colleagues occasionally, and she and Bernard Murphy remain good friends.

The federal election took place on 2 March 1996. The result was anything but good for the ALP: in the House of Representatives the Coalition, led by John Howard, resoundingly defeated Paul Keating and the ALP, which had been in power since 1983. The Coalition won ninety-four seats, Labor forty-nine, and the ALP recorded its lowest primary vote since 1934. Labor people were very depressed.

Gillard had to take into account that, if she succeeded in her bid for the Senate, she would be a member of a much-weakened Opposition party. She had about six weeks to wait for the final result of the Senate count, as well as no job and time on her hands. Victorian premier Jeff Kennett, of all people, came partly to the rescue. The day after the House of Representatives result, he announced a state election to be held on Saturday 30 March.

Gillard decided to get involved. 'I was on hold,' she says. 'I could have sat at home until I found what the count was, which would have been a bit mind-numbing, or I could help with the state election. They had short four-week campaigns then. Robyn McLeod, a friend of mine, was running in Mordialloc, a marginal seat, so I went to be her campaign director, as a volunteer.'

In the last week of the state campaign Gillard was visited by Andrew McKenzie, who was then assistant secretary of the Victorian ALP. He knew she was no longer working at Slater and Gordon and asked what she was planning to do. 'I said I hadn't spent much time making plans for the future, I just wanted to survive and suspend everything until after the Senate count,' says Gillard. 'I'd see whether I became a senator or not.'

McKenzie told her that John Brumby, leader of the Victorian state Opposition, was looking for a new chief of staff and that she should go after the job. It was a suggestion right out of the blue, and she said she would think about it.

On Saturday 30 March the expected happened: Kennett's government was re-elected. 'It was even worse than [what happened with] Howard,' says Gillard. 'We absolutely got thumped, we only held our absolute bedrock seats. Robyn was defeated, too. Every lower house seat we had was in the north or east of Melbourne, we won nothing south of the Yarra. It was terrible.' Despite Kennett's cuts to the public service and sales of state assets, he had gained a thirty-two-seat majority.

The week after another depressing defeat for Labor, John Brumby called Gillard to formally offer her the job as his chief of staff. By then she knew she would not be sitting on a red-covered bench in federal Parliament. 'I knew I had to make a decision,' she says. 'Either to say I shouldn't even think about getting into federal politics, and do something else, or to pursue possibilities, put more time into them. To be in a political job fulltime at the centre, instead of doing ALP stuff on evenings or at weekends, would be interesting. But I hadn't thought necessarily of a state job.'

And such a state job: as one source has pointed out rather brutally, Brumby's chief of staff in Opposition was not exactly a job for which people were stabbing each other in the streets. More than ever Jeff Kennett and his government absolutely dominated the political arena, and the general view was that the Opposition was likely to remain in the doldrums for the foreseeable future.

The question for Gillard was whether she was prepared to take a short-term step backwards in pursuit of her long-term goals. These days she talks about her decision as a logical one. But at the time many people saw it as a big gamble, and some questioned her political judgement. However, the more she thought about the opportunities a job with Brumby might present, the surer she became that this was something worth investigating. She would be learning new skills, making new contacts. Brumby was a member of the Victorian Right Unity faction, and it would certainly be sensible to widen her own contact and network base. For all these reasons Gillard agreed to take the job.

Her own factional allegiance was not a problem. 'John made a good call with her,' says Andrew McKenzie. 'She got the job in the way most people from the Left faction got jobs: she was good. Brumby decided that her factional allegiance didn't matter if it got him someone with her skills.'

Although Gillard and Brumby liked each other, to some of Gillard's colleagues they did not seem a logical pairing. The neat-featured Brumby was regarded as rather dour and uncharismatic: there couldn't have been a greater contrast between him and the exuberant bully Kennett. But he was very clear about what he wanted from his new chief of staff.

'I was coming in as a novice in a sense,' says Gillard. 'But I had obviously had a pretty responsible job before, and [my immediate predecessor] Mark Madden had had media experience. Brumby wasn't looking for that, he had confidence in his press secretaries. The office was small, there were seventeen of us in total, some part-time. Shadow ministers didn't have their own staff, that was it for the Opposition.

'We needed to churn out a lot of work, he thought it needed better organisation, better support to him, management logistics, plus better connection between him and party machinery. He knew I'd been knocking round for ages and had good connections.'

Gillard's responsibilities were wide and varied. As McKenzie puts it: 'The chief of staff is a vital job in terms of the influence you have on the leader and the mindset you inspire in the staff you employ.' Gillard's job was not only to run the office and manage the staff, but to keep Brumby's diary, get him on the road and help in developing campaign themes and slogans, managing policy output and dealing with the media, as well as maintaining the strategic connection between Brumby's office and the federal ALP. 'In the Victorian system that was one job,' says Gillard wryly. 'In the feds it would be four or five different jobs.'

Gillard learned from Brumby, and he learned from her. 'It wasn't factional, it's just that I knew more about party machinery than he did,' says Gillard. 'He had been a federal member for Bendigo, a country electorate, and had done marginal seat campaigning. But he had this grand naivety about the party in a way.

'He tells the story that when he was first Opposition leader he got an invitation to speak at a meeting of the Kingsville branch of the ALP, which he was told had 600 members. He thought, Yes, I should do this, and his wife Rosemary went with him. The

Kingsville branch then was a branch-stacked outfit, so there were a few blokes ticking off names as people came in and then left. Brumby had put all that effort into writing a speech and he had an audience of about seven people.

'I remember him telling this story and just from knocking around Melbourne I could have told him: John, I wouldn't even bother turning up to the Kingsville branch meeting. They don't even want a speaker. They send these invitations out and nobody ever replies. Brumby was the only bloke who had ever written back!'

Working in the state Opposition was often a dispiriting business because Kennett was so dominant. 'I thought Brumby was doing a difficult job at a dreadful time,' says Gillard. 'Kennett had been regarded as a lightweight buffoon, a clown – but [when he became premier he was] the only game in town. The state media were entranced with him, all state politics became concerned with what wild and wacky thing our Jeff was going to do today. We were trying to fight against that.'

Not only was the Opposition office underresourced, but in the state Parliament it literally had trouble getting a word in edgeways. 'Kennett had so altered the rules that Victorian Question Time was forty-five minutes on Tuesday, thirty on Wednesday, thirty on Thursday. On Tuesday we might get four questions in, the rest of the week two or three. And if a government minister spoke to each one for six or seven minutes, which isn't difficult to do, that's half of Question Time gone.

'With some of the stuff you get in federal Parliament, where one minister gets ten questions in a row that can be really forensic and searching . . . you have a minister under pressure. In Victoria that would be a fortnight's worth of questions. You could never get any purchase, there was no way the Opposition could hold the government to account in Parliament. It was really very difficult.'

There had been a tendency in the Brumby office – as in that of most political oppositions – to react very quickly to everything that members of the government said and did: to respond to Kennett's agenda rather than to push a program of its own. Gillard encouraged the staff to look beyond the twenty-four-hour news cycle, to not always seek to score points, to plan for the longer term. According to Andrew McKenzie, this was a break from the way Brumby's office had been run by Gillard's predecessors, especially Rob Hulls (who had left to enter state Parliament). 'Brumby and his parliamentary colleagues had the view that the most important thing in Opposition is what happens in Question Time. It is important in shaping morale and press gallery views about electability, but nine times out of ten it means nothing [to the voting public] the next day. She managed to get Brumby et al. to concentrate more on long-term planning.'

Brumby's staff was gloomily convinced it would be a long haul back to government. Gillard says: 'In our dark hours Brumby and I used to sit in state Parliament, between ten and eleven at night, having a glass of red wine together. Tim Holding, who is now a state minister, was the emerging bright young thing in the ALP then, and Brumby and I had this joke about the Tim Holding Labor government in about 2030. Brumby has a sardonic sense of humour, he can be very funny.

'And sometimes he'd say, "Look, the regions and country are reacting to Kennett differently from the city, they're being left behind, and you never know . . . we can pick up a swag of regional seats, we might just get there next time." And I'd sit there sipping my red wine and thinking, Should I tell him he's dreaming now, or just let him enjoy his fantasy?'

As it happened, Brumby would turn out to be right, not least about the regional seats.

The 1996 state election, although disastrous for Labor, had offered a few glimmers of hope. The ALP had won three seats – hardly a magnificent result, but enough to make the optimists in the state party believe that the tide might be turning, in large part because of the Premier's autocratic and bullying style. At first Kennett's capital works program had been popular, especially in Melbourne, but much of this had been made possible thanks to early cutbacks and Budget restructuring, and Kennett's scandals over allegedly corrupt preselections, his disputes with colleagues and especially his concentrated blitz against the public service, his sacking of hundreds of teachers and the closing of many small schools, imperceptibly eroded government support.

Early in 1999 Brumby, who had never really succeeded in changing his rather dull image, resigned as Opposition leader, to be replaced by the jovial Steve Bracks. To the astonishment of many, including his supporters, in the election on 18 September Bracks led Labor to a narrow victory against Kennett, which was dependent on the parliamentary vote of three country independents. Brumby remained an influential party figure as state treasurer. 'He'd been leader of the Opposition for so long in a divided party against a combative opponent,' says Gillard, 'he'd taken so much damage from that, which I don't think was his fault at all . . . The Brumby strategy could only come true with a different person.

'I remember watching the TV the night we won . . . Robyn [McLeod] and I saw the seats coming in, declared for Labor, and we thought, Nah, can't be. For a while I didn't actually believe we'd got there. A sort of perverse denial.'

By the time of the state election Gillard had moved on. In her time as Brumby's chief of staff, she had kept his office on an even keel and helped it use what resources it had efficiently and well. She was also partly responsible for a decision that ensured Sharon McCrohan became the head of media in March 1999. McCrohan was crucial in ensuring Bracks's election victory six months later.

In the lead-up to the 2007 federal election, when asked about Gillard as his chief of staff, John Brumby said, 'I think some of the time I was her boss and I think some of the time she was mine. She was a great chief of staff – very focused, very capable, very disciplined, great listener, enormous capacity for hard work, and a very safe pair of hands.'

Gillard says about the job: 'I'm not any kind of religious person, but sometimes you can say things happen for a reason. I don't believe I could have had the same career in federal Parliament if I hadn't had that period with Brumby . . . I would have gone in a lot greener, whereas having the opportunity to work with John and learn from him was vital. I learned a lot about campaigns, about polling, about messages . . . all the things I needed to learn. The personal attributes, the psychological toughness, the fortitude you need.'

10

Getting there

It is said that every picture tells a story – and those group photographs of newly sworn-in Cabinet ministers on the steps of Yarralumla are more eloquent than most. Especially when the governments concerned are Labor. Beneath those immaculate jackets and white shirts and blouses beat hearts toughened by years of factional disputes. Standing shoulder to shoulder are likely to be colleagues who have good reason to loathe each other, their bright smiles concealing the horrid realisation that they will have to work together for the next few years. The military theorist Carl von Clausewitz wrote that war is a continuation of politics by other means. Sometimes the converse also applies.

Julia Gillard echoes the words of others when she says that the ALP is a very tough school. If you succeed in getting its endorsement, you have probably already had the hardest battle of your entire political career. The corollary of that is, of course, that once you have come through you are much more resilient than you would otherwise have been. You have had the kind of training that cannot be bought: you know a great deal about how to make alliances, how to count, and how to think strategically. And if you are lucky enough to be a certain kind of person you will not succumb to the bitterness that combat, successful or unsuccessful, often brings.

That is, provided you get the chance to enter the fray in the first place.

After two unsuccessful tilts at federal preselection, one in the House of Representatives and one in the Senate, Julia Gillard needed to work out what her next move should be. This cannot have been easy for her, although she makes light of it these days. 'I think there might have been a time when she was wavering about whether she would go on, even,' says Andrew Scott. 'My sense was that after losing to Lindsay [in 1993] and then to Jennie George [in 1996] she was feeling quite wounded. But she kept coming to meetings, she kept showing her face, she didn't go away and sulk. She showed great strength and character, I think.

'She took it a lot better than others around her. She knew she had a good support base. She kept saying, We have to keep trying, even when she ran into brick walls.'

Caroline Hogg, a former minister in the Victorian ALP government, says: 'I can't see why they were so against her, other than seeing her as a potential rival. I really can't, it was so inexplicable. Either that or she was seen as an uppity female, but that again is irrational.'

Jeff Kennett and his government could never have predicted one of the consequences of their election victory over Joan Kirner back in 1992: that Labor women would have a better chance of getting into state and federal parliaments.

'When Joan Kirner was defeated as premier I think a number of women, including myself, were brought up pretty short,' Julia Gillard said some years later during an ABC radio interview. 'We thought we'd kind of succeeded and women were equal partners in politics, we'd had a female premier and female minister for health. But when in the early 1990s in Victoria we were forced back to our bedrock after that stunning defeat, we woke up to find hardly any women left in the Victorian Parliament, and that was of course because the women had the marginal seats, not the safe ones.'

Joan Kirner's friendship with Julia Gillard dated from the days when Gillard had shared a student house with David Kirner. (Indeed Kirner had secretly hoped that Gillard and her son might eventually marry.) Kirner had always encouraged Gillard in her political ambitions, but obviously the position for women in politics was fairly dire – and not just in Victoria.

'When I left Parliament I literally looked behind me and saw four Labor women where there had previously been fourteen,' says Joan Kirner. 'I was devastated. Carmen was in a similar position.' Carmen Lawrence had been premier of Western Australia from 1990 to 1993, and was the first woman premier in Australian history. 'And there were women in other states, too: Jan Burnswoods in New South Wales, Fran Bladel in Tasmania, for instance.'

Most of the women who had been defeated in various state elections at this time had strong connections to the women's movement of the 1970s and 1980s in different ways. 'Some were more into the Women's Electoral Lobby. I was more into the women's movement through community action,' says Kirner. 'I wouldn't have gone into or survived politics without the support of women's networks. Labor women's parliamentary caucuses, state and federal, operated in government on feminist principles and in partnership with women's organisations.'

Clearly the ALP's affirmative action principles needed work. These, written into the party's platform in 1981, had aimed to increase the representation of women in the Labor Party and in state and federal parliaments, but there were no mandatory targets or sanctions. They remained on the books, but by the end of the decade little had been done to make it easier for women to succeed in Australian politics by being preselected for winnable seats. In 1989, for example, there were only 100 women in state and federal parliaments, and that was from all political parties. 'It was time for our party to do something more innovative,' says Kirner. 'When push came to shove, many of the boys were unwilling to extend the power base for preselection. [Current federal treasurer] Wayne Swan's argument was that women weren't coming forward or, if they did, they needed training first. I've never forgotten that. I hope he's not still a dinosaur.

'So when we left Parliament we thought, OK, we have to change the rules. So we developed a nationwide campaign in Labor branches, involving three generations of Labor women.'

In January 1994 a national Labor women's conference passed a motion for affirmative action, proposing new rules to be adopted by the party's national conference in August. Kirner and Lawrence knew it was essential to get Prime Minister Paul Keating to take the lead, especially with any recalcitrant premiers or faction leaders. 'Keating was no feminist, but he did see the point,' says Kirner.

The new rules, formalised at the 1994 national conference, required that women had to be preselected in 35 per cent of winnable state and federal seats; at least one-third of all those selected for positions within the party had to be women, as did one-third of all delegations to state and federal party conferences (including union delegates, unless fewer than one-third of the union members were women, in which case the proportion of delegates should be representative). The requirement that 35 per cent of preselected candidates had to be women was the first step in a drive to have fifty-fifty representation by 2000. If the target failed to be met, the national executive would call preselections in the relevant electorates and do them again.

'Then we sat back and waited for it to happen,' says Kirner, 'but it didn't, because we handed it over to the male-dominated state and federal executives. The 1996 preselections were no better than the 93s.' Not only that, but the 1996 federal election saw the entry of sixteen new conservative women into Parliament. 'So we thought, bloody hell, this isn't good enough, we need to rethink this.'

Several Labor women had visited the USA and seen the work done by EMILY's List there. This was a national network of women that since 1984 had worked with the Democratic Party to help elect – to Congress, the Senate and governships around the country – Democratic women who were pro-choice on the issue of abortion. The name is nothing to do with a woman named Emily: it is an acronym for Early Money Is Like Yeast, a reference to the saying that 'Early money is like yeast because it makes the dough rise'. In other words, political donations early in a campaign can attract later, larger donors.

By 2000 EMILY's List had become the second biggest membership-based contributor to US elections (outdone only by the National Rifle Association, which supports the Republican Party). It has become so ingrained in the country's political culture that the character of C.J. Cregg, president Jed Bartlet's press secretary in the TV series *The West Wing*, once worked there.

The idea to develop the model for EMILY's List in Australia started with Leonie Morgan. A group of Labor women met to work through the idea. Leonie Morgan says, 'We met regularly for about a year, talking with people like Candy Broad, Julia Gillard, Joan Kirner and Kay Setches to work out how it could be done. And our conviction was that the women we supported would be pro-choice, and a section of the Right of the party didn't like that. There was also concern from some that we were setting up another faction, even though we wanted to extend membership to women within and outside the party. The third issue for us was that we were not prepared to accept any proposal that gave the ALP national executive the power to decide where EMILY's List money and support would go, and the amount each woman would receive. In the end we decided to set it up outside the ALP, where it still is today. And we only support ALP women.'

Because the organisation is independent of the ALP, it sees itself as a watchdog for the party's affirmative action rule. Leonie Morgan: 'The problem [before] then, of course, was that men chose the candidates because they had the numbers. Once affirmative action came into play we could say, Here's the target and if you don't meet it preselection will be thrown open. They were really scared of that.'

Gillard, who at that stage was working for John Brumby, gave practical as well as moral support. 'She was one of the first women who put up $1000 to establish EMILY's List,' says Morgan, 'and she wrote our constitution.'

A national committee was set up with members from every state, and there were teleconferences and meetings of Labor women around the country to discuss constitutional and organisational issues. Gillard helped to set these up and to run them. The organisation differs from its US parent in at least two important ways. It offers support to candidates only after they have been successfully preselected. And the kind of help EMILY's List Australia offers to candidates is not necessarily driven by or focused on funding, but can include a range of assistance, from mentoring by women MPs to arranging for child care.

Late in 1996 EMILY's List Australia was launched by Kim Beazley, leader of the federal Labor Opposition, and the following year it opened its own office. According to the organisation, it now has almost 3000 members nationally and at June 2009 had helped no fewer than 125 ALP women to be elected to parliaments around Australia, including assisting Carol Martin, the member for Kimberley in Western Australia, to become the first Indigenous woman elected to any Australian parliament (in 2001 and 2005). It has given a range of strategic and personal support to progressive Labor women and has commissioned research into the ways governments can meet the needs of women.

There have been mutterings among Julia Gillard's detractors that of course she did what she could for affirmative action and EMILY'S List – she wanted to get into Parliament so she stood to benefit, didn't she? But those involved with her all agree that she did an enormous amount of work because she believed in the cause. She is still a member of EMILY's List and continues to promote and support it.

In 1998 the Victorian federal seat of Lalor was safe, up for preselection and targeted for affirmative action.

Named after Peter Lalor, an Irish-born battler who became leader of the miners at the Eureka Stockade and later an Australian politician, the electorate sits on the western outskirts of Melbourne. About 990 square kilometres in area and including the city of Werribee, on the way to Geelong, it became a federal seat in 1949 and is now the fastest growing electorate in Victoria.

Lalor is not an affluent electorate and some of it is heavily industrial. Nor is it scenically beautiful. Although Werribee is near Port Phillip Bay and parts of the electorate are classified as semi-rural, a lot of it, such as Hoppers Crossing and Wyndham Vale, consists of commuter suburbs of roof-to-roof new houses sprawling across the flat coastal plain. In 1998 it contained the Altona petrochemical complex and Toyota manufacturing plant, as well as industrial estates, such as the one at Laverton, Melbourne's sewage farm at Werribee and the Point Cook and Laverton air bases.

Most of the people who live and work in Lalor are tradespeople, clerical staff, and labourers and workers in the production and transport industries. In 1998 48 per cent of its population were born outside Australia: the most heavily represented countries of origin were Italy, Macedonia, Greece, Vietnam and Lebanon, and Catholicism and Greek Orthodox were the most popular religions (followed by Islam, 'no religion', and then Anglican).

It is a place that can be roused to action when one of its amenities is under threat. In 1998 Lalor was fighting a bitter battle against CSR, which was preparing to fill its quarry at Werribee with toxic waste. The locals were tired of being treated as a dumping ground.

Lalor is a proudly Labor federal electorate: in its sixty-year history it has only been held by a Liberal member for three years. Among those who have represented the seat in federal Parliament are Dr

Jim Cairns, deputy prime minister in the Whitlam government, and Barry Jones.

Jones became a household name in the 1960s when, as a burly young schoolteacher with a photographic memory and an unerring grasp of facts, he became the star contestant of Bob Dyer's *Pick-A-Box* television and radio quiz show: a reign that lasted eight years. He also presented one of Australia's first talkback radio shows, considering talkback as 'an instrument for exposing people to new ideas and challenging them, rather than just reinforcing the ideas they already held' – which demonstrates how much talkback has changed since the 1960s. For five years in the 1970s he was a state politician, and then resigned to go into federal politics as the member for Lalor upon Cairns's retirement in 1977. Always an independent within the party but allied to the Centre Left faction, he was minister for science in the Hawke government from 1983 to 1990. In 1998 he announced his intention of retiring at the forthcoming election.

Lalor had been the subject of a cross-factional deal two years before, when Gareth Evans had left the Senate to seek a seat in the House of Representatives, hoping to further his ambition to lead the ALP. He had his eye on the safe seat of Holt, but it was controlled by the Socialist Left, which was not Evans's faction and had stymied his earlier attempt to move to the lower house. Barry Jones's seat, however, had no strong factional Left representation, and so Evans's Unity faction said to the Socialist Left: give us Holt and you can have Lalor.

The deal was done, and for the October 1998 election Lalor became a Socialist Left seat. Once again people suggested to Kim Carr and Lindsay Tanner that Gillard should be preselected. Her continued activities in the party, her work with John Brumby and everything she had done for Labor women – in short, her proven ability – meant that she should be given something. Once again the reply came back: nothing doing.

The greater animosity came from Lindsay Tanner. There was some evidence that Kim Carr was becoming resigned to the fact that Gillard probably had a future in federal politics, although he would not go so far as to help her. According to Gillard supporters, Carr was devoting his energies to dealing with his rivals Alan Griffin and Lindsay Tanner, especially the latter, having fallen out badly with him.

Tanner himself had not changed his view of Gillard. Observers felt he was determined to block her advance by all means possible, and he maintained his public position that she was a conservative and a careerist who could not be trusted.

So it was no surprise that Lindsay Tanner and the Socialist Left endorsed as their affirmative-action candidate Gaye Yuille, who was president of the Federated Clerks' Union and part of Tanner's reform group in the union. Tanner supported her, out of personal loyalty, and Kim Carr did too because, as someone said, she wasn't Gillard. The pro-Yuille forces were determined to have their way, according to Andrew Scott.

One of the Yuille supporters was Jenny Macklin, who had been elected to federal Parliament in 1996 as the MP for Jagajaga, an outer Melbourne seat. She was a member of the Socialist Left but had an uneasy relationship with Gillard. Although more strongly aligned to Kim Carr's group than Gillard's, Macklin had lobbied Gillard for support in the 1996 Jagajaga preselection contest, assuming that Gillard would show solidarity with another woman.

But Gillard declined, saying she was backing Pete Steedman, Macklin's opponent, whom she had supported in 1993 for Senate preselection. Macklin was considerably taken aback. In her eyes and those of her supporters this refusal betrayed the principles of affirmative action, which Gillard was continuing to support. She took Gillard's action very badly.

Gillard set to work to convince the preselectors that she was the better candidate. Victorian preselection rules remained unchanged since her Melbourne attempt: the local selectors' vote accounted for only 50 per cent of the total vote; the rest of the vote was controlled by the ALP's 100-member Public Office Selection Committee, elected by proportional representation from delegates to the annual state conference. Gillard says: 'When you're going for a seat in the House of Reps, you have to convince the central preselection panel that you are the right candidate. But if the locals don't like you, that's no help.'

She was well aware that, as a candidate who was not well known in the electorate, she had to work extra hard to win local preselectors over. She campaigned on local issues, including the upgrade of the Princes Freeway to Geelong, protection of the local wetlands and the defeat of the proposed toxic dump. 'There were about three hundred [local selectors],' she says, 'and I visited every single one.

'Working for preselection like this is extremely stressful. It's a lot harder than campaigning for the Senate, which means working with postal votes and visiting country places, including safe Liberal electorates.' She adds: 'It's like being interviewed for a job you really, really want – whether you get it or not will affect your whole life – but with an absolutely huge selection panel. And you may not know for weeks whether you've got the job either.'

The problem for Gillard was that Gaye Yuille had the numbers within the faction. Gillard, though, had a wider support base than in her previous two election attempts, one part of which was Martin Ferguson's Independent Left. Early in 1996 Gillard had found a new ally in Ferguson, the member for Batman, parachuted in from New South Wales on the retirement of former deputy prime minister Brian Howe. He was there more or less at the behest of Prime Minister Paul Keating, and had to undergo some messy preselection infighting before he prevailed. Ferguson had an impeccable Labor pedigree: most recently president of the ACTU, he was the younger son of Jack Ferguson, who had been deputy premier of New South Wales from 1976 to 1984. When Keating lost the 1996 election, Ferguson joined the Opposition shadow ministry. Not especially pleased with the way Kim Carr was running the Socialist Left faction, he formed a splinter group with his supporters, which called itself the Ferguson or Independent Left, and allied himself with Gillard. As a consequence she also gained the support of his union, the Miscellaneous Workers' Union.

In addition to the Ferguson Left, the MWU and the O'Connor group, Julia Gillard in 1998 could count on the Unity faction of the Right, which now dominated the Victorian ALP. The Unity faction was led by John Brumby and Stephen Conroy.

In the end Julia Gillard was widely regarded as the better candidate and won over both groups in the preselection process. She gained preselection over Yuille and, at long last, had defeated the Tanner and Carr forces.

On 3 October 1998, amid great rejoicing from her supporters, Julia Gillard, aged thirty-seven, became the new member for the federal seat of Lalor. At the election she got almost 70 per cent of the vote, with a 1.3 per cent swing towards her.

By most standards Julia Gillard had had to travel a long, hard road to become a federal MP. She didn't have a political machine behind her; nor could she count on family influence and contacts for preferment. And in the words of a former colleague: 'People were really really keen to make sure she never got there. I never understood it, but I don't understand much about the ALP. You can't say it's known for rewarding talent, and she came from the bottom up.' It took her five years of determined effort to gain preselection, but she never gave up, although she must have considered quitting more than once. As her friend Josh Bornstein says: 'If I ever meet anyone tougher than Julia Gillard I'll fall over. There isn't anyone.'

The ALP is a political party in which people have a strong tendency to brood over ancient wrongs. One of the interesting things about Gillard, attested to by several people interviewed for this book – opponents as well as friends – is that she does not bear grudges. She is very explicit about why this is.

'I have very clear recollections as a lawyer of seeing people come in with three lever-arch folders of stuff, and they plonk it on your desk and say, "It all started in 1962 when the boss said this to me." I'd say, "I'm a really quick listener but a really slow reader, so let's summarise . . ." I didn't want them to spend the first half-hour consultation, which was free, just going on about things.

'But their whole life has been on hold for twenty years as they obsess. And you want to say to them, "Well, you can spend the rest of your life brooding about this, or you can say, Well, shit happens, and go home and have a cry or a glass of red wine or kick the cat or whatever."

'If I don't bear grudges that's because of who I am and by dint of experience. I've seen [people ruin their lives by holding grudges] in life, in student politics, in the law and in Labor politics. And I decided I couldn't let myself live like that.'

This is both admirable and practical – and perhaps one does not have to be unduly cynical to point out that forgiving former enemies is much easier once you have prevailed against them.

11

New kid on the block

Julia Gillard came into Parliament at a time when the Australian Labor Party was feeling moderately optimistic. The 1998 federal election result had been encouraging. Not especially because of anything the ALP had done, it must be said.

In the previous two years or so, John Howard's Coalition government had, it seemed, ignored several rules about how to win elections. It had announced its intention of introducing a new tax that would affect everybody, had given oxygen to another right-wing party, which split its vote, had broken its own rules about accountability, had alienated a large section of the voting public because of its industrial relations changes – and it was going to the polls early. There had been fears within elements of the Coalition that the Howard government was a 'one-term wonder'. And yet, despite the proposed 10 per cent goods and services tax, the emergence of Pauline Hanson and One Nation and a raft of broken election promises, the Coalition had won.

But there was certainly cause for hope in Labor ranks. The

election had delivered an overall swing towards the ALP of 4.6 per cent, the party had won the highest proportion of the popular vote, and it had also won the two-party preferred vote, with almost 51 per cent. But as politicians tediously remind the electorate, there is only one poll that counts: the one on election day. It was cold comfort to the Labor Party that although the Coalition's majority had been cut from forty to twelve and the swing had been enough in all states to deliver government to the ALP, the uneven nature of that swing had denied Opposition Leader Kim Beazley the extra seats necessary to command a majority in the House of Representatives. Nevertheless on election night Beazley looked, if not exactly triumphant, buoyant in the belief that the ALP might well win the next election.

For Gillard, being in Parliament House at last was intensely satisfying – made all the more pleasurable because so many other Labor women had come into Parliament, too. The class of 1998 included Anna Burke, Jane Gerick, Jill Hall, Julia Irwin, Cheryl Kernot (this was the election when she left the leadership of the Australian Democrats to join the ALP), Kirsten Livermore, Jann McFarlane, Michelle O'Byrne, Tanya Plibersek and Nicola Roxon. A beamingly avuncular Kim Beazley was photographed with a group of the newly elected Labor women, his new 'stars': the intended message was that the ALP was the party of progressive change.

Julia Gillard made her maiden speech to Parliament about a month after the election, on 11 November 1998, the same day as Kevin Rudd and Nicola Roxon, two colleagues she later became close to. First speeches given by newly elected MPs generally follow certain conventions: they express a series of general statements of belief; tribute is paid to the seat's previous incumbents; and friends, relatives and supporters are thanked. Maiden speeches are listened to with respect and without interjection, and they are not widely reported. There are exceptions: in 1996 Pauline Hanson launched a strong and scathing attack on Australia's immigration and multicultural policies, making hers the most widely reported maiden speech in recent Australian parliamentary history.

While Gillard's first speech followed most of the conventions, it included some sharp observations and can scarcely be described as bland; in fact, for all its careful crafting, it was in part a youthful, fervent plea for a return to a politics of 'passion and conviction'. Her maiden speech is in some respects her manifesto, her statement of core values, and so it is worth looking at in some detail.

She began by positioning herself in the Parliament as the first woman ever to be chosen by the Victorian ALP for a historically safe seat. This was more than a personal honour, she said. It was 'a Labor landmark, as is the number of Labor women sitting in this House. It is a cause for celebration and will inspire us to ensure that many more women follow us into this parliament.'

Following tradition, she continued with a warm and graceful tribute to Lalor's previous member, Barry Jones, 'famed throughout Australia for his intellect and respected throughout Australia for his genuineness and compassion', and, she added, one of the few politicians of whom Australians were truly fond.

Gillard then spoke with feeling about her electorate. 'As part of Melbourne's industrial west, the people of Lalor have always had to try harder,' she said. Their fighting spirit was now being called upon in the major community campaign against CSR. 'There are only two reasons why Werribee has been selected,' she declared.

'CSR wants to make money by filling its disused quarry with toxic waste and the Kennett government thinks Werribee is no more than a dumping ground . . . When the Victorian Premier turns to the west, he holds his nose and closes his eyes.'

Significantly, perhaps, she did not describe her constituents as 'battlers' which, in traditional Labor terms, would have meant old-style working class, but rather as participants in a society transformed by bewildering global and technological change and prey to 'the prevailing mood of insecurity': 'As a community, in common with societies throughout the Western world, our response to insecurity has run from simple nostalgia to the spectacle of the frightened turning on the vulnerable' – a neat summation of what she saw as the two prevailing trends in the Howard government. 'So-called "wedge politics" sells the big lie that the answer to insecurity is to tread on the weakest amongst us . . . We [in the Labor Party] stand for the right of ordinary Australians – those who have neither wealth nor power – to a fair go, to be treated with dignity and respect in the workplace, to be recognised and valued as citizens and to have a say in their nation's future.'

She spoke with passion about the importance of equality of opportunity, framing it in the drama of the immigrant's story – that of her own family. 'Immigrants need courage and creativity; they need open minds and sturdy hearts. What the last red-headed woman who made a first speech in this place [Hanson] will never understand is that the vast majority of migrants come here determined to make a better life for themselves and their kids and they are prepared to work unbelievably hard to achieve that dream . . . [My parents] have contributed more to this country as workers, as citizens, than they ever cost it . . . Because they chose this country, they take nothing about it for granted: they celebrate and know its worth. And that is the truth of our history of migration, our history of multiculturalism.'

Australia had offered her opportunities denied to her parents: 'It would have been inconceivable to them that their child, and a daughter at that, could be offered the opportunity to obtain two degrees from a university and to serve in the nation's parliament.' This had only been made possible by South Australia's excellent state education system under Don Dunstan and the Whitlam government's abolition of up-front university fees.

'Around the world now there is a trend back to the Centre Left, to social democratic parties that stress the importance of raising the educational standards of all citizens,' she said. 'The students from my electorate are not any less intelligent than those from Higgins [Peter Costello's middle-class electorate] or Kooyong, but their educational opportunities are not the same . . . My predecessor, Barry Jones, used to say that unfortunately postcodes are probably the strongest factor in determining a person's expectations of success in life. It will be one of my priorities to ensure that in the Australia of the future the famous quiz master is, for once, wrong.'

The leitmotiv, here as elsewhere, was the importance of education. One of the things that makes Gillard's maiden speech so interesting is how consistently the ideas she expressed were reflected in her approach to government upon Labor's eventual return to power. The rhetoric running through it was that of the Centre Left she referred to, and similar to the so-called Third Way pronouncements of UK prime minister Tony Blair; that is, the expression of a centrist political position that seeks to transcend the old Left and Right by adopting policies from both. Gillard decried the free enterprise 'cult of individualism', while not denying the need for a strong modern economy. Instead she argued that a 'strong economy and a strong society' – a society based on 'community' and 'collective' values – 'are not contradictory goals', and that 'a nurturing and caring society is the best foundation' to 'ensure Australia competes in the global market'.

At the end of her speech she staked her claim to being a different kind of politician by drawing on her experience as a student activist. 'People today make a lot of the new generation from the other side of this House who emerged from the battles with left-wing students on our campuses in the 1970s. I come from the generation of students who followed . . . Ours was a radicalism fashioned by a desire to be practical.' That last sentence is not a bad summary of Gillard's approach to AUS politics in the past – and to some of the tougher policy questions that were shortly to come her way.

After she delivered her speech, Julia Gillard went back to her office. She was accepting congratulations from her mother and supporters when a tall, broad-shouldered man of her own age, with messy brown hair and small-rimmed glasses, tapped on the door and came in. He stood there, hunched and unsmiling.

'Good speech,' he said abruptly. 'You're obviously one of the few people in this place with a brain.' It was Mark Latham.

Like all new MPs, Julia Gillard spent some time finding her way around – not least working out how to get from point A to point B in Parliament House. With its long corridors studded on one side by anonymous doors and on the other by windows facing bushland blandly devoid of useful landmarks, the home of federal Parliament must be one of the most maddening buildings in Australia. 'I have a really bad sense of direction, and I kept ending up in the Senate wing,' says Gillard. 'Not very helpful when you've forgotten the vital bit of paper you need for a meeting and you have to find your way back to your office. And after ten years I still don't know where the Meditation Room is.'

Sitting in the House of Representatives chamber could be disconcerting, too. 'I had my views about John Howard and Peter Costello from watching TV, of course,' Gillard says. 'And when I saw them in Parliament, it was almost still as if they were on television, because I was a backbencher and they were in government, and they were sitting miles away.

'There was really nothing in a day-to-day sense that brought me into contact with Howard and Costello. Over the years I probably ran into Costello a bit more in flight lounges, the Melbourne scene, at football games. But to this day I would have had about three conversations with John Howard, all very superficial along the lines of, How are you Julia, isn't it nice to be at . . . wherever we happened to be.'

In some ways the new job presented less of a learning curve for her than some other newcomers. 'I knew some of it through working with Brumby,' she says. 'Stuff like the mechanics of Parliament, what an Opposition does, how the media cycle goes, how the place works. But there were all the other things, like choosing staff, linking into networks, balancing responsibilities as a backbencher and as a local member. And of course committees.'

New MPs are asked by the parliamentary whips, responsible for party discipline, to pick two committees they would like to join. 'There are the really popular ones, like foreign affairs and trade, and backbenchers have no chance of joining those,' says Gillard. She put her hand up for two fairly heavy-hitting committees: the House of Representatives Standing Committee on Employment, Education and Workplace Relations – a fortunate choice considering her later portfolio responsibilities – and the Joint Statutory Public Accounts and Audit Committee. She was readily accepted for membership on both: a certain indication that she was already marked as someone to watch.

One of the highlights of Gillard's first year in federal Parliament was to be chosen as a member of the official Australian bipartisan observer mission to the Indonesian elections in mid-1999. This was the first free election to be held in Indonesia since 1955. With the fall of Suharto, political activity was no longer restricted, and forty-eight parties contested 462 seats, with a further thirty-eight reserved for the army. Polling stations were independently monitored by Indonesians as well as 100 observers and support staff from twenty-three countries, led by former US president Jimmy Carter. John Howard asked Kim Beazley to nominate people from the Labor side: the Australian contingent advised to take their malaria tablets also included Kevin Rudd.

The atmosphere in Jakarta was tense and sporadically violent. There were very few if any tourists, and the hotels were empty, so the Australians stayed in plush suites in the Grand Hyatt for next to nothing. Then they split up and went to polling booths in various parts of the country. 'They confused me with someone young and fit, so I got sent to West Timor,' says Gillard. 'And a long way from Kupang, too. Close to the Indonesian border, we were.'

It was a hazardous trip along rudimentary jungle roads. There was no backup: if the vehicle broke down, finding help would be a problem. But Gillard and her small party eventually arrived at a village of about 400 people, many, Gillard observed, with vitamin and mineral deficiency diseases, including goitre. 'They were all sitting or standing outside the polling station, waiting for it to open,' she says.

When their names were called in alphabetical order, people went inside and cast their vote by driving a hole through their chosen party symbol on the ballot paper. They then dipped a finger in indelible ink to prevent them voting again. After the polls closed, people waited around while the votes were counted. Results were announced by an official giving the name of the party and holding each ballot paper up for everybody to see. 'They were waiting around for sixteen, seventeen hours,' says Gillard. 'I've never seen such enthusiasm. It was amazing.'

The process across the nation was peaceful, but the total count was slow, taking several weeks. The largest share of the vote went to the Indonesian Democratic Party – Struggle led by Megawati Sukarnoputri, with Golkar in second place. A total of twenty-one parties won seats.

After this extraordinary demonstration of republican democracy in action, Gillard returned in time for the discussion about Australia's future as a republic, one of the major political issues of 1999. The question, to be posed at a referendum on 6 November, was whether Australia should have a president appointed by a bipartisan parliament, the republican model decided at the constitutional convention the previous year.

Gillard, who had not attended the convention, took very little direct part in the debate, except for putting the pro-republican case to her constituents in Lalor (almost 49 per cent of them voted yes).

She did not think it was one of the most pressing issues facing Australia – she still doesn't – and like many of her colleagues she knew how much the whole discussion had been manipulated to favour the Howard government's position. Opinion polls suggested that the majority of the electorate favoured republicanism, yet when it came to the point the proposal was defeated, with roughly 55 per cent of the nation, and all states, voting no. The reasons for this have been widely agreed on in the ensuing years. Only eight out of forty-four proposals put to referendum in Australia have been approved by a majority of voters in a majority of states, as required by the constitution.

The campaign provided some interesting lessons. The proposal for a republic was defeated partly because of the perception that it was undemocratic: that the head of state would be chosen by a bunch of politicians – almost by Australian definition a shifty, untrustworthy lot – instead of by the people. (How John Howard managed to finesse distrust for himself and his colleagues into getting the result he wanted provided a fascinating demonstration of political tactics.) That those in favour of a republic were not united about the kind they wanted was another important factor. And the whole referendum experience reinforced the Coalition government's view that the Australian public was generally cautious and held the view that if it ain't broke, don't fix it.

The other emotive issue of Gillard's first year in Parliament was the question of reconciliation with Australia's Indigenous people. Like most on her side of politics, she thought this was imperative. But John Howard steadfastly refused to countenance making a formal national apology on the grounds that he did not believe the current generation needed to accept responsibility for the actions of previous generations. He would only go so far as to introduce a 'motion of reconciliation' into Parliament in August 1999, expressing 'deep and sincere regret'. No member of the Howard Cabinet went on the Reconciliation Walk because Howard said no, although several, including Treasurer Peter Costello, wanted to. The whole episode heightened tensions between Prime Minister and Treasurer, which did not pass unnoticed by the commentariat.

The undercurrent of public dissatisfaction with the Howard government's performance continued throughout 2000 and was exacerbated when, thanks solely to a last-minute deal with the Australian Democrats in the Senate, the Goods and Services Tax was introduced on 1 July. There was some public concern, resentment and confusion. Kim Beazley and the Opposition took advantage of this by announcing that they would roll back the GST, at least partially, should they win office at the next election.

Labor's cautious optimism continued into 2001, increased by the Coalition government's problems with rising petrol prices, ongoing public confusion and dissatisfaction with the GST and increasing inflation. The ALP's success in the Western Australian and Queensland state elections in February, the Howard government's bad opinion polls and its defeat in an important by-election were taken as further signs of a possible change of government. The government quickly went into rescue mode, decreasing the fuel excise, bringing petrol prices down and increasing benefits and tax cuts for older Australians in the May Budget. The economy just avoided recession that year, giving the government the opportunity to boast about its economic credentials, which it did as part of its new media expenditure of $20 million a month. In July it narrowly avoided defeat in the by-election for the seat of Aston, prompting Howard to comment that the Coalition was 'back in the game'.

But Labor could, and did, point to the opinion polls, which showed the ALP had been consistently ahead of the Coalition ever since the election of 1998. Things were still looking good for Labor to regain power in 2001 – but the old political hands knew more than to start taking victory for granted quite yet. It was a wise decision.

12

'We will decide who comes to this country'

In August 2001 Julia Gillard, like the rest of Australia, switched on the TV news and saw that a rickety fishing boat with 438 mostly Afghan refugees on board, which had been stranded in international waters north of Christmas Island, had just been rescued by a Norwegian container vessel, the MV *Tampa*. She could scarcely have known what an impact this event would have on the fortunes of the ALP in the forthcoming election, or on her own career.

The boat that the *Tampa* went to help was the most recent of a number of refugee vessels attempting to make their way across the Indian Ocean towards Australia, full of desperate asylum seekers. Once refugees stepped onto Australian soil they were legally permitted to apply for asylum, but according to Minister for Immigration Philip Ruddock the country's detention centres were full to bursting with asylum seekers and there was no room for any more. The government refused the request of the *Tampa*'s master, Arne Rinnan, to proceed into Australian territorial waters and land at Christmas Island, four hours away.

Rinnan, whose vessel was not designed to carry such a large number of people, many of whom were ill, pleaded vainly to be allowed to bring the asylum seekers to Australia. After several days he lost patience and entered Australian waters without permission. The Australian government dispatched Special Air Service troops to board the ship and prevent it getting any closer to Christmas Island. When Rinnan refused to move the *Tampa* back into international waters a standoff ensued. The incident had escalated to the point where Australia was reported to the United Nations for failure to obey its duties under international law.

At this stage John Howard introduced into Parliament an emergency border protection Bill, giving the government power to contravene international law by removing any ship inside Australian territorial waters, using force if necessary. The government needed the assent of the ALP for the Bill to pass in the Senate, but Kim Beazley refused to support it, basically on the grounds that it contravened the rule of law because the courts had been entirely cut out of the process.

It was a position that many outraged voters did not really understand or accept, enabling Howard to place Labor as the party that dithered on questions of national security – the party that was deliberately blocking all attempts to safeguard Australia's sovereignty. As Kim Beazley said later, 'There was a profound conviction that John Howard was taking a stand on principle and that the Labor Party was playing politics.'

Then on Wednesday 12 September Australia woke to appalling and unforgettable images on breakfast television: the flash of metal as two planes ploughed into the World Trade Center in New York, the billows of smoke from its smouldering twin towers, the cascade of glass and concrete as the south one collapsed. Next came the news of almost simultaneous attacks on the Pentagon and the crash of another aircraft in Pennsylvania. Nineteen Islamic hijackers in four planes were responsible for it all, causing their own deaths and those of 2974 others, mostly civilians.

Expressing the public's widely felt fear and outrage, John Howard immediately committed his government to work with President George W. Bush and the USA in combating international terrorism, a commitment that by October would see Australian troops joining the fight against the Taliban in Afghanistan. Within days of the World Trade Center attack Australian talkback radio callers were declaring it a well-known fact that the terrorists of New York were linked to Muslim asylum seekers forcing their way into Australia. The Coalition government responded quickly: Australia's engagement in the war against terrorism meant possible threats at home, and tough action needed to be taken.

This soon included the introduction of the so-called Pacific solution. To prevent boat people having to be assessed for refugee status on Australian land, thousands of territorial islands were excised from Australia's migration zone, opening the way for asylum seekers to be transported to detention camps on small island nations in the Pacific Ocean. Under this scheme some of the *Tampa* refugees were sent to detention camps on the island of Nauru. New Zealand agreed to take the others.

Eligibility for protection visas was also tightened. Refugees accepted into Australia on a three-year temporary protection visa who applied for an extension were ruled ineligible if, while their cases were being processed, they had stayed for seven days or more in another country where they could have received protection.

For many Labor supporters opposed to John Howard's harsh measures the last straw came when the ALP accepted the government's revised border protection Bill. It was useless for Kim Beazley to insist, as he did, that the revision was a totally different Bill, which met all of Labor's objections. Many voters perceived that Labor was heartless, unprincipled and too weak to stand up to the government.

At the beginning of the *Tampa* crisis Labor had assumed that the issue would soon be resolved and that, in the lead-up to the election that must soon be called, the debate could be turned back onto ground that favoured the ALP. Since the 1998 election the ALP had kept ahead in the polls largely by proposing greater public investment in health and education and a more regulated approach to the labour market – issues Julia Gillard, for one, considered the core of ALP and modern government policy. But now she and other Labor MPs watched with dismay as the government surged into the lead, chiefly because the public approved of its attitude to national security and border protection. Kim Beazley tried to make up ground by declaring that Labor would fight the election 'on the security issues at home and the security issues abroad, a secure future for all Australians'. But it was no use.

Julia Gillard says: 'I always thought we were going to struggle in 2001. Sure we were ahead in the polls for a while, but our vote was too soft. And 9/11 and the *Tampa* just showed we were underprepared to deal with the immigration issue.'

John Howard called the election for 10 November 2001. A few days into the campaign Philip Ruddock claimed that asylum seekers on a fishing boat approaching Australia – later known to the press as SIEV 4 (Suspected Illegal Entry Vessel 4) – had thrown children overboard in order to force the Royal Australian Navy to rescue them and take all on board to Australia. The government released alleged photos of children in the water being rescued by RAN personnel. This fuelled Australian xenophobic and anti-refugee sentiment, as the government had known it would.

In the last week before the election there were strong assertions that the photographs showed not children thrown into the water, but people being rescued while the boat was sinking. But two days before the election Defence Minister Peter Reith released a video that, although it simply showed a man standing at the railing of a boat holding a child, he claimed was proof that children had been thrown overboard. Right up to polling day the Coalition ran ads repeating the key line in John Howard's election launch speech: 'We will decide who comes to this country and the circumstances under which they come.'

Gillard's majority was reduced in Lalor, largely she says because of the *Tampa* crisis, and the election result as a whole was very bad for Labor, which received its lowest primary vote for sixty years. Labor's small-target strategy of concentrating on domestic issues, especially health, education and the workplace, was simply no match for the government's electoral focus on immigration, defence and foreign affairs, and its adroit use of xenophobia.

And Labor had been damned if it supported the government's stand on asylum seekers, and damned if it didn't. The party's conservative blue-collar voters turned to the Coalition because they thought Labor was weak on the issue of asylum seekers, and the socially progressive elements supported the Greens and the Australian Democrats, perceiving that Labor had abandoned its humanitarian obligations to refugees. Kim Beazley maintained that if Labor had not adopted the government's approach to immigration the electoral damage would have been even worse, a view that is still contested among Labor supporters.

After the election the Senate, which remained dominated by the ALP, the Greens and the Democrats, set up a Senate select committee of inquiry into the children overboard affair. Military officers and other witnesses were exhaustively cross-examined, and the claims that children were thrown overboard were shown to be false.

In view of the divisiveness of the election campaign, the government played down the role of immigration and terrorism issues in its victory. There was evidence that the polls had begun to turn the Coalition's way even before the *Tampa* incident, and the government said it had campaigned and won mainly on issues of economic and financial management.

Julia Gillard may have suspected that the party was always going to struggle in 2001, but it was a view that Labor comprehensively rejected. In the words of Tim Gartrell, the ALP's assistant national secretary: 'We [had] turned the corner on domestic issues. We were pretty much getting to a situation of neck and neck and I think the Liberal Party decided to hit that refugee button, which is what they did.'

Whatever the reasons for the loss, the situation was clear for the ALP and especially for Kim Beazley. He stood down as leader shortly after the announcement of the election result. The new leader of the Opposition, elected unopposed, was Simon Crean.

It was not the most surprising choice: Crean had been Beazley's deputy and shadow treasurer, and he was from the same faction, the Right. As president of the ACTU in the mid-1980s, he had played an important part in negotiating wage agreements with the Hawke government until he went into politics in 1990. After he won the Melbourne seat of Hotham, he took the ministerial portfolios of science and technology; primary industries and energy; and employment, education and training. In almost twenty years of federal politics he has never been a backbencher.

When Crean took over the leadership he promised a fresh start and promotion of new talent. It was a declaration that many greeted with scepticism: Lynton Crosby, director of the Liberal Party, observed that 'Labor's idea of generational change is to replace as their leader the fifty-three-year-old son of a former Whitlam minister with the fifty-two-year-old son of a former Whitlam minister.' It was a sneer that the Coalition directed against Labor for years.

Like most political one-liners, its accuracy was in inverse proportion to its quotability, for Simon Crean, an impatient man who links determination with a disarming friendliness, was intent on remodelling the ALP's frontbench as a prelude to reforming the party. 'Crean is proposing Party reform but it's not clear how far he is willing to go,' wrote Mark Latham in his diary. 'The fact that he has even placed it on the agenda is remarkable enough. Who would have thought? The son of a Whitlam minister, a former ACTU President, a Beazley loyalist talking as if he wants to shake out the machine and democratise the Party. He's got my support simply because he's having a go.'

Crean was determined to do whatever was necessary to get new people on the frontbench. He demoted a number of former ministers from the Keating government and long-term Beazley frontbench supporters. 'Crean is certainly not afraid of making enemies,' observed Mark Latham. 'First he took on the factions to get new blood onto the frontbench, and now he's threatening the power of the State-based machines. Already as Leader he's made enemies of Con Sciacca and Arch Bevis, two Queensland duds he kicked off the frontbench; [Leo] McLeay and [Steve] Hutchins, the Sussex Street gang [the New South Wales Right]; plus Ray and Conroy from the Victorian Right.'

Crean had made it his business, with Senator Peter Cook, to take an interest in and to look after new MPs, including fellow Victorian Julia Gillard. Despite factional differences, she and Crean got on well from the first. They shared a sharp, legal-based intelligence – Crean had also studied law and economics – a clear understanding of the union movement and a strongly pragmatic streak. 'Simon also got on well with women and wanted to promote them,' says Gillard. He agreed to have Jenny Macklin, a woman from the Socialist Left, as his deputy and shadow minister for education.

As well as Macklin, his new shadow ministry included some political names that have become increasingly familiar: Lindsay Tanner (communications), Kevin Rudd (foreign affairs), Kate Lundy (information technology), Craig Emerson (trade), Nicola Roxon (child care, family support and youth) and Kim Carr (science and research). There was also the contentious Mark Latham, the brilliant, fiery idealist disguised as a boofy bloke, who had been shadow minister for education but had quarrelled bitterly with Kim Beazley over Labor's policy directions and taken himself to the backbench: he now became shadow minister for housing and urban development.

And Julia Gillard?

'I volunteered for immigration,' she said. 'I knew it was bloody hard but I put up my hand.'

It was probably one of the most difficult shadow portfolios offering. In the wake of an election where the public had voted overwhelmingly in support of the Coalition's approach to border protection, and where suspicion and distrust of foreigners, especially Islamic foreigners, had come to the fore, her job was to hold the government to account. She was also charged with looking at and possibly reformulating Labor's own shaky and somewhat muddled immigration and refugee policy.

Gillard had no illusions. 'We were always going to struggle to make ground on immigration,' she says. 'But I knew if I handled it successfully it would be good for my career.'

13

'A desire to be practical'

In March 2002 Alan Moir of the *Sydney Morning Herald* published a cartoon showing an ALP politician about to enter the shadow Cabinet room to discuss refugee policy when he sees a security guard with the sign 'Please leave your spine here'. It summarised at least half of the problem Gillard needed to confront in her new job as shadow minister for immigration: the perception among many Labor supporters that the ALP had simply rolled over in the face of government thuggery on immigration issues and forfeited any claim to be the party of compassion.

The other half of the problem was that if Labor came out in favour of less draconian treatment for asylum seekers the government could position it as soft on national security and willing to harbour potential terrorists. When the issue had hit the headlines after the *Tampa* and during the election campaign this had been thrown into alarming focus. The party had been caught unprepared and had never recovered. Gillard was well aware, as were the ALP strategists, that immigration, and particularly its refugee policy and border protection aspects, was the most important issue Labor needed to address if it was to have any hope of recovering its electoral losses. It continued to be a highly emotive issue among voters of all political colours, and had real potential to split the ALP for a long, long time.

In strategic terms the party desperately needed to be united around a refugee policy as swiftly as possible, since the issue was not likely to disappear. Its policy had to be firm enough to mollify those who thought Labor was soft on border protection, yet include enough humanitarian elements to satisfy supporters who had been disgusted by Labor's acquiescence in government policy. Howard clearly had no compunction in being tough on refugees, but Labor saw itself as better than that. The policy, then, had to be acceptable to the electorate and to disarm Howard: it had to combine tough border protection with a respect for human rights – and it was Gillard's job to draft it.

Immigration has always been a difficult issue for the ALP, as indeed it has been for political parties in most western countries. The party has a lengthy history of compassionate language sitting alongside labour-market protectionism, with a bit of racism and xenophobia thrown in – reflecting white Australia's own history really. Immigration to Australia had been legally restricted since the Australian colonies enacted anti-Chinese legislation during the gold rushes of the nineteenth century. In 1901 the new Federation had passed the Immigration Restriction Act, generally taken to be the beginning of the so-called White Australia Policy, which was supported by the labour movement.

The suspicion of 'aliens' meant that German Jewish refugees were kept in detention by the Curtin Labor government during World War II. However, Australian attitudes in general to European refugees changed after the war, not least because they were white and their labour was needed for the large postwar infrastructure projects. In the 1950s both Robert Menzies, the Liberal prime minister, and Arthur Calwell, the ALP Opposition leader, continued to be committed to the country remaining white, and still largely British.

When Gough Whitlam succeeded Calwell as leader of the Opposition in 1967 and declared his antipathy to the White Australia Policy, he met resistance and criticism from older members of the ALP (as late as 1972 Calwell was still railing against a 'chocolate-coloured Australia'). In office Whitlam abolished the policy, but his government was somewhat inconsistent in its application of the more relaxed immigration requirements. It let in very few Ugandan Asians fleeing Idi Amin's government, for example, yet accepted about 3000 Vietnamese refugees, and a number of Chileans escaping the 1973 coup against Salvador Allende.

In 1992 Gerry Hand, minister for immigration in the Hawke Labor government, overturned the existing discretionary detention policy for boat people and introduced mandatory detention. It was argued that this would make refugee claims easier to process, prevent de facto immigration and eliminate the cost of locating boat people in the community while their cases were assessed. Under Hand's successor, Nick Bolkus, detention became mandatory for all immigrants without valid visas. Liberal immigration minister Philip Ruddock actually softened the policy in 2001 by introducing community detention and providing residential housing for women and children.

Mandatory detention had strong support in the ALP, but equally strong opposition. Those in favour of it believed it was necessary for maintaining efficient visa and border controls, pointing to the problems caused in Europe by asylum seekers who entered countries without going through the official processes; they also said that if detainees did not like the Australian arrangement they were free to leave at any time. Opponents argued that mandatory detention was unnecessarily punitive and had proved useless as a deterrent (about 9500 boat people had arrived between July 1999 and August 2001), that it shamed Australia internationally, and that it was psychologically damaging to refugees and unnecessarily cruel.

The question of temporary protection visas was also contentious. These had been introduced by the Hawke Labor government in 1989 to protect Chinese students studying in Australia after the Tiananmen Square massacre. Labor subsequently abolished them, but then supported their reintroduction in 1999 by the Howard government as an instrument of control and a way of avoiding giving boat people permanent residence if their claims for refugee status were successful.

Labor might have considered itself the defender of human rights, but in the past decade or so its actions and attitudes over questions of immigration and refugee policy had hardly conformed to the highest humanitarian standards.

Gillard was aware of all this when she set out at the beginning of 2002 to develop ALP immigration policy. Because this was her first shadow portfolio, and a difficult one, she was determined to do well in it, and issues of immigration and refugee policy consumed her energies and thinking for months. Raising the stakes even higher was the fact that Gillard would have to get final endorsement from Caucus. This decision had been made by Crean in the interests of showing parliamentary party unity during the policy debate that would surely follow within the ALP organisation.

There was already an ALP immigration policy framework in existence, in a paper prepared pre-*Tampa* and during the 2001 election campaign by Con Sciacca, then shadow minister for immigration, and Duncan Kerr, shadow minister for justice. Beazley had asked the two to put together a preliminary paper clarifying some of the main problems in the refugee debate. Their work had not been made public for two main reasons: there was a great deal of disagreement within the party at the factional level, and – just as importantly – Beazley was keen for the pre-election agenda to be Labor's preferred small-target domestic policy, not immigration. As it happened, of course, Howard gave him no choice.

The differences of opinion within the party cut right across the factional divides. Labor's support of the government's position during the election had been condemned by members of both the Left and the Right in the parliamentary party, and by prominent figures in the labour movement. At the same time these sections also had their Beazley supporters. By January 2002 an internal ALP group named Labor for Refugees, outside factional control and with no input from Gillard, had formed to urge support for a softer policy than the one Beazley had taken to the election. Most of its members were from the Left; notable among them was Carmen Lawrence, shadow minister for reconciliation, Aboriginal and Torres Strait Islander affairs and for the status of women. Others on the Left, influenced by electoral pressures in working-class electorates and by traditional labour-market protectionist beliefs (which could be summarised rather crudely as 'foreigners will come here and take our jobs') found themselves in agreement with a large proportion of the Right. Conversely there were members from the Right – often those influenced by Catholic social teachings – who sided with the Left. One influential member, for instance, was John Robertson, the Catholic secretary of the unions' peak body in New South Wales.

On 11 February 2002, during the first parliamentary sitting since Labor's election loss, Gillard presented a submission to Caucus, based in large part on the Kerr–Sciacca paper, outlining what needed to be considered in the formulation of ALP policy. The submission discussed issues related to the detention of refugees, set out alternatives, and proposed a re-evaluation of Labor's support for the Pacific solution, on the grounds that it was costly and unsustainable over the longer term.

In the minds of some Caucus members the terms of reference were wrong. Gillard's submission called for a review of the Pacific solution; Duncan Kerr called for its total abolition. The submission laid out the ways in which the existing treatment of refugees might be modified; Carmen Lawrence argued for the complete abolition of mandatory detention and temporary protection visas. Lawrence won support across the factions, from hard Left to Right. But Gillard's general terms of reference were endorsed by a majority of Caucus, and so became the framework for the policy Gillard was charged with fashioning.

Carmen Lawrence promptly and publicly called for mandatory detention and temporary protection visas to be abandoned, and led a public campaign in favour of a softer refugee policy. Others who supported her stand kept the dispute within the party.

Following the Caucus meeting, Gillard embarked on what she describes as 'a huge learning curve'. 'I went all over Australia, to detention camps, to Manus Island with Philip Ruddock, learning how the whole process worked, and it was very fraught indeed.' By all accounts, she and Philip Ruddock managed to deal together amiably.

In an interview Julia Gillard gave in March 2002, she outlined what her approach to her new job would be. She drew a picture of an admirably comprehensive and inclusive consultative process: 'I see my role initially as informing people, because this is a complex area and people can really only engage in the debate if they are across the facts, secondly [as] listening to the views that people form, having heard those facts, and then thirdly, [as] putting together a proposal which I believe is good public policy for Australia.'

To accomplish the first two steps, Gillard needed to consult both the parliamentary and the organisational wings of the ALP. Accordingly she ran seminars on refugee policy in different parts of the country, and invited submissions from ALP and union members. 'I went all over the country seeking electoral support,' she said some years later. 'It was hard. We had schisms in the union movement, there were union organisers who were pro-refugee while their members were anti. I understood the reason for the anger, the fear that a small population on a large isolated island would lose control if a lot of migrants came in and took jobs, the resentment of newcomers who might have come in and jumped queues. I didn't want to neutralise the issue. I wanted to craft good policy, one that was right for this country and one that could be lived with.'

Although Gillard insisted that consultation with all stakeholders was an important part of her work, according to some of her colleagues the process was patchy at best. Sections of the ALP saw it as an exercise in persuasion, rather than consultation – maintenance of control from the most senior party level down. For some the anger has lasted to this day.

There were parliamentary ALP members who said Julia Gillard spoke to them at length, while others claimed they were excluded from the process because they did not agree with the policy they felt convinced she was pursuing or with the framework for that policy. One of these was Duncan Kerr, who had spoken out so strongly against mandatory detention.

Another was Carmen Lawrence, who had worked with Gillard in the early days of EMILY's List but parted company with her over the kind of immigration policy she was putting together. Lawrence said that Caucus had not been given enough time for discussion initially, and that Gillard had told Labor for Refugees from the outset that she was not about to recommend the abolition of mandatory detention. Gillard had never been interested in discussing the fundamentals with the party, simply in gathering support, and without the work of Labor for Refugees ALP party members would not have been involved in the refugee issue at all, Lawrence claimed.

Throughout the period Labor for Refugees did provide a national forum for challengers of mandatory detention, temporary protection visas and the excision of Christmas Island from Australia's migration zone. The group also campaigned to influence the election of each state's delegates to the annual national conference, and the resolutions put forward there; as a result the dominant Right allowed a conscience vote at regional and state levels on the Labor for Refugees proposals.

There is some evidence to support the claims that Gillard's persuasive powers controlled the consultative process. Asked whether, in the light of party division, she saw her role as coming up with a hard policy, one way or another, or as forging a compromise, Gillard said: 'I actually don't think that the polarisation in the ALP is anywhere near as bad as some of the media reporting would have you believe. When you actually sit down with people and talk issues through at a level of detail you find that people aren't as far apart as the sloganising would have you believe . . . I've had party members say to me that they support ending mandatory detention and when I ask them what they actually mean, they say, "Oh no, I understand that it would be necessary for identity checking and security checking and for health issues and there might be people who are at risk of absconding and they would still have to be detained." '

And some of the public statements Gillard made over the next months as shadow minister for immigration sounded too uncompromising to have resulted from wide consultation, and angered sections of the ALP. In an interview with Laurie Oakes on Channel Nine's *Sunday* program in mid-April she acknowledged that border protection had been electorally 'a very good issue' for the Liberal Party, and added, 'I agree with John Howard's statement . . . that we and only we should decide who comes to this nation.' She also supported Philip Ruddock on the new Baxter detention facility, making it clear that it fitted Labor's idea of a detention centre and saying that for some people 'because they have exhibited behavioural problems, security problems . . . you might need electric fences or even razor wire'.

At the same time, Gillard made the point that '[T]here is a level of [discussion] about this which is rational and then a level used for political advantage. I agree with protecting our borders . . . But then there's an area where it's just used to make people feel more insecure, an area that's just spin or, at worst, lies.

'We know for example that the claim that asylum seekers threw children overboard was just a lie, but it was about exacerbating fear, fear of difference, fear of the sort of people who were seeking asylum in Australia. And when it's used for those purposes then I think it's an unacceptable electoral strategy, and I think it generates long-term community division and problems. We don't want, in this country generally, to have issues of race dominating our politics.'

Occasionally during this period there were public and parliamentary exchanges between Julia Gillard and Philip Ruddock. Her spirited responses laid the foundation for her current reputation as a good performer in Parliament and the media. The press and the public loved the idea that a young 'feisty redhead' was taking on the ever-courteous but chilly and measured Ruddock, one of the least popular ministers in the Howard government, and apparently giving him a run for his money. They might not have been able to spell out significant differences between the immigration policies followed by Labor and the Coalition government, but the public perceived that the Opposition was on the case and would hold the government to account, especially in urging more humane treatment of women and children in detention centres.

Gillard's tactic in confronting Ruddock was to avoid disagreement – and in fact at times to agree with positions he took on asylum seekers – when she could see the political advantage and perhaps even the merit in doing so. She attacked when Labor could argue that an issue such as the incarceration of families under duress called for a more ethical and caring approach.

In terms of political advantage – not quite the same thing as public perception – Gillard did not really lay a glove on Ruddock until the 'cash for visas' scandal in the latter half of 2003, when she no longer held the shadow immigration portfolio. This issue essentially allowed her to demonstrate her relentless parliamentary style.

The Howard government had restored the immigration minister's discretionary powers, meaning he could grant residence and temporary residence status in cases that the department might refuse. (These powers had been removed from the legislation by Robert Ray when minister for immigration in the Hawke government.) Ruddock had obtained significant campaign donations from a number of organisations and individuals, which Gillard linked to a subsequent granting of visas; one of these involved a shady Filipino businessman named Dante Tan. Ruddock, although not considered corrupt, had nobody but himself to blame for the scandal because of his extensive use of ministerial discretion.

Gillard moved a censure motion in Parliament, and her attack on Ruddock was devastating. It was delivered with considerable relish, not least because she was able to kick him over an issue on which he and Howard had previously bested Labor.

She told Parliament: 'He would sashay into Liberal Party functions to standing ovations and cheering . . . we thought it might be because of his attitude about *Tampa*, about having created the Pacific nightmare, about having started the children overboard conspiracy . . . But now we know the truth . . . half the crowd were shouting "show me the money" and the other half "show me the visa" . . . Minister Ruddock was always an unlikely man for the status of conservative superhero . . . He was always more super shadow than Superman.'

This speech, perhaps more than any she had made previously, marked Gillard as a parliamentary heavyweight. Not everybody admired her for it. Some journalists believed that she had gone over the top in attacking Ruddock personally, especially as she had previously supported many of the things he had said. But by then she had learned the value of publicly winning political battles.

Julia Gillard presented the ALP's immigration policy to its parliamentary wing in December 2002 in a document entitled 'Protecting Australia and Protecting the Australian Way: Labor's Policy on Asylum Seekers and Refugees'. As one source pointed out, take away the word 'Labor' and the title could have been written by any conservative politician since Federation, except perhaps Malcolm Fraser. Its opening paragraphs carry the assurance that a coastguard will put 'a cop on the beat', and it promised to put the protection of Australia first and to 'crack down on illegal workers', 'smash onshore and offshore people smuggling' and 'impose harsher penalties' on people traffickers. It is tough language that could have been used by John Howard.

But the wording of the policy document softened somewhat after that, and there was a nod towards the plight of refugees: 'Labor understands that unauthorised boat arrivals are the worst possible outcome both from Australia's point of view . . . and from the point of view of the asylum seekers who risk and sometimes lose their lives.'

In essence 'Protecting Australia' sought to steer a middle course between hardline demands for border protection and the equally strong demands for humane treatment of refugees. It recognised the plight of people forced to move because of poverty, natural disasters, conflict and environmental degradation. But, while it rejected Howard's excision of thousands of islands from the migration zone, it retained the excision of Christmas Island, Ashmore Reef and the Cocos Islands: all those farthest away from Australia, it might be noted. Christmas Island was recommended as the prime asylum-seeker processing and detention facility. Mandatory detention was upheld, although not for unaccompanied minors.

Gillard's policy document also reflected Labor's traditional support for international institutions and solutions, promising increased financial contributions to the United Nations High Commission for Refugees and more aid to countries of first asylum.

If the question is asked whether Crean and Gillard succeeded in moving the issue of boat people away from fear and xenophobia, the answer is no. Given entrenched Australian attitudes to refugees, however, such a task would probably have been almost impossible for the party. But some ALP members did think – and still do – that they should have done better. Carmen Lawrence resigned from the frontbench of the parliamentary party in December 2002 over the asylum seekers issue, and a number of MPs supported her stance, including Duncan Kerr. Gillard had also alienated a swathe of other people from the Labor Left, including state and federal MPs and human rights advocates, for her acquiescence in aspects of the policy pursued by Philip Ruddock.

By the time the document was presented to the ALP national conference in 2004 for acceptance, when Gillard was no longer shadow minister, a softer line had been taken. This included concessions on temporary protection visas, which were now to be issued for only two years instead of three, with resident status then granted if there was no other option for those found to be genuine refugees. However, the excision of Christmas Island was retained. The 2004 policy, with modified language and some non-crucial concessions, was voted in along broadly factional lines. It was essentially Julia Gillard's.

When Gillard was asked a few years later whether she considered the policy she had fashioned was ideal, she said: 'Look, I was very proud of it when we finished it . . . It was a bit like writing a PhD thesis . . . dealing with policy input from all over the place . . . I think it did balance what we need to balance in our refugee and asylum seeker policy, which is a humanitarian view and a view of our role in a world system that deals with people movement and refugees, but also properly deal[s] with security issues.'

There is no doubt that Gillard's time in her first shadow portfolio brought her prominence inside the party and beyond. Her hard-won ability to focus on essentials, to reduce an enormous amount of material to manageable proportions without sacrificing accuracy, was displayed nationally in a policy review critical to the party.

Her crafting of the policy also demonstrated her political skills. She had done what was asked of her: she had managed to steer the ALP away from the shoals and reefs that Howard had prepared for it. As a successful lawyer she knew how to follow a brief. The service she saw herself as being able to render the party was summed up in her words: 'I wanted to put together a policy that would cover all the problems that might be faced, from the arrival of a small boat on Ashmore Reef to the death of a child in a detention centre. We couldn't afford to be tough one day, soft the next.'

At the same time she attracted a lot of criticism. Sections of the party believed she had allowed expediency to get in the way of proper policy formation. There were echoes of the old charge against Gillard, extending right back to her AUS days, that she was a pragmatist first and foremost, for whom principled policy making would always come second to politics. One opponent expresses the feeling succinctly: 'I wouldn't trust her as far as I could throw her.' Any perception that Julia Gillard is a divisive force in the ALP stems from her stewardship of its immigration policy.

14

The life of the party

Julia Gillard was Labor shadow minister for immigration for just over eighteen months. She was a member of a shadow frontbench that the press and commentators widely considered successful, saying that it balanced the need to bring new faces to the Opposition with the experience required to be effective in Parliament. This was a media-generated point in the ALP's favour, but no corresponding response showed up in the polls. Behind the scenes a lot of soul searching was going on about the state of the ALP.

The party was now in its sixth year in federal Opposition, with no apparent prospect of regaining government, and there was no shortage of insiders ready to explain what was wrong. In June 2002 a trade union seminar in Melbourne sponsored by the Socialist Alliance put forward the view that much of 'the present conservatism in the ALP' was due to the dwindling influence of the union movement within it. The rot had started with the Accord in the 1980s, speakers said, as the union movement ceased to have a separate voice – by implication, as the ALP ceased to be the party of the workers – and the party moved further to the Right. They believed that perhaps the union movement should disaffiliate from the ALP altogether, which would shock the party to such an extent that it would be forced to smarten up.

There were other, sometimes contradictory, views about the reasons for Labor's less than stellar electoral performance. Under the heading 'The ALP, A Renovator's Nightmare' Lindsay Tanner, Gillard's old foe within the Socialist Left, who was now shadow minister for communications, argued in the *Age* that the party needed to reject knee-jerk views that 'We lost because of the *Tampa*, it's all the unions' fault, we've got to cuddle up to small business'. He argued that the labour movement had taken insufficient account of changes in Australian society, including the shrinking of trade union membership, the increasing complexity of political issues, the decreasing willingness of people to be involved in politics because of other calls on their time, and the dwindling base of committed voters. The ALP, he said, was still being hampered by an outdated structure, culture and organisational approach, and Labor's future as a political force depended on its ability to reform and revitalise the party.

Simon Crean held similar views. Once he had become leader of the Opposition, he had announced his intention of reforming the party's organisation and commissioned a national committee of review to recommend changes to ALP rules, headed by Bob Hawke and former New South Wales premier Neville Wran. The most contentious recommendation – strongly supported by Crean and subsequently adopted by the party in 2004 – was that only half the number of delegates represented at state ALP conferences should be from the union movement. Previously unions had comprised 60 per cent. The new '50/50 rule' was potentially troublesome for Crean, and his authority was certainly not increased when the New South Wales seat of Cunningham, a former Labor stronghold, was won by the Greens in a by-election in October 2002, with a 6 per cent swing against Labor.

Faced with mounting speculation about his leadership, Crean had earlier given a rather telling self-assessment in a radio interview. Asked to reply to the description of himself as a snarling 'junk-yard dog', he had said he would like the theme song to be changed from 'Bad, Bad Leroy Brown' to 'Don't Let Me Be Misunderstood' with its plaintive 'I'm just a boy [sic] whose intentions are good'. It was only a throwaway remark in a jocular interview, but they were words unlikely to have been chosen by someone who saw himself as a strong and forceful leader.

Like her colleagues, Julia Gillard was watching Crean's performance with apprehension. And like many of them, she spoke up in defence of her leader. What differentiated Gillard from a number of her colleagues was that she was genuinely a Crean loyalist, who knew how much he had done for the ALP, as well as a friend who had gone on holiday with him and his family. But she must have had misgivings about his approach to strategy. During one shadow Cabinet meeting after the Cunningham by-election Crean had listened closely to Lindsay Tanner's contention that he should go in harder in attacking interest groups associated with the Coalition, but had then, as Mark Latham recorded, 'continued down his well-worn path, talking about the importance of consensus and electoral inclusion. It's not in him to pick a fight to prove his point. He likes long meetings – a process-driven approach to politics.' To Gillard, always focused on results and invariably a devotee of outcomes, this must have been as disquieting as it was for Latham.

Crean's problems worsened with the early months of 2003. This was the time of public and parliamentary uproar over Iraq. On 18 March Australia joined President George W. Bush's so-called Coalition of the Willing, which included Britain, in sending troops and naval units to support the US's invasion of Iraq and the removal of Saddam Hussein from power. Howard had earlier told Parliament that only 'Full disclosure by Iraq of its chemical, biological and nuclear weapons programs and immediate and total co-operation by Iraq with the provisions of resolution 1441 of the Security Council will remove the need for military action', but that 'Of at least one thing we can all be absolutely certain – if the world turns its back on the threat posed by Iraq . . . other rogue states . . . will be encouraged to flout the international conventions on arms control and develop their own chemical, biological and even nuclear weapons.'

There was already scepticism about Iraq's possession of weapons of mass destruction, and public opinion was decisively against war (although not, as it turned out, against Howard protecting the alliance with the US). Crean had said that Labor would not approve military action that did not have the backing of the UN, but he became muddled in expressing what he meant, leaving Labor's position ambiguous. Latham wrote bluntly: 'Crean is bleeding to death on Iraq. He's incapable of coming up with a clean, straightforward position . . . I've never seen policy making by caveats before – it's the political equivalent of water torture . . . [Greens leader] Bob Brown is killing us on this issue through the power of a simple, commonsense message: Bush is an imbecile and Australia should not be part of his war.'

In April the *Bulletin* published an interview with Kim Beazley entitled 'If I Were PM: Kim Beazley Finally Takes a Stand and Ignites the ALP Leadership Debate'. He did not tell Crean of his intention, and Crean was stunned and appalled, as were his supporters, including Julia Gillard. It was bad enough for Crean to have been white-anted for the past twelve months by his enemies and ambitious colleagues – all, of course, reported faithfully in the press. But to be deliberately undermined by the man whose loyal deputy Crean had been for three years: that was something else.

'There's a lot about being involved in politics that does have the capacity to turn your stomach. There's just no doubt about it,' Gillard reflected in 2006. 'When the destabilisation of Simon Crean's leadership was at its awful height, you [did] see some of the worst aspects of human behaviour on display. I knew him well, I cared about him, I knew the family, you know – Carole, the girls – and to just see someone who I thought was such a lovely human being caught up in this awful sort of animalistic environment, there is a sense of repugnance about it.'

Crean decided to stick it out. As Gillard observed at the time: 'If it is part of anyone's strategy to wait for Simon to fold his cards, they will be waiting forever . . . No part of his demeanour suggests he has in any way dropped his head – and you'd have to say that is remarkable given what he has endured.' It is fair to say that the relationship between Julia Gillard and Kim Beazley was not improved by the *Bulletin* article.

Naturally any suggestion of a possible ALP leadership challenge sent the commentariat running in all directions. Beazley told the press that he was not considering running against Crean, even though his supporters in Caucus were busily gauging his support. These included Stephen Smith, Wayne Swan and Stephen Conroy (the group Mark Latham had dubbed the Roosters), Leo McLeay, Con Sciacca, Anthony Albanese and Kevin Rudd. Crean had his own support team, chief among whom were Mark Latham and Julia Gillard, who worked the phones with equal diligence. Gillard told the ABC, 'I believe Simon Crean will lead Labor to the next election and he is undoubtedly the best person to do that.'

When the vote was taken during a Caucus meeting on 16 June 2003, Crean won by 58 votes to 34. (Most of the women in Caucus had voted for him.) One of the reasons for his victory was the widespread perception that Crean should not be the first Labor leader to be denied the chance to fight an election. Crean followed the script given to Labor leaders on these occasions: he was gracious in victory, and spoke of the need for healing. But in the minds of some who knew their Labor history was the axiom that it usually takes two goes to finish off a Labor leader.

Crean's victory on this occasion could be described as pyrrhic. But for his supporters his win was real. Mark Latham replaced Bob McMullan as shadow treasurer and manager of Opposition business, with Julia Gillard his deputy manager and shadow minister for health. The shadow health portfolio, left vacant by Beazley supporter Stephen Smith, was gratifying affirmation of her performance in the shadow immigration portfolio as well as a reward for her support of Crean. Health policy had been the centrepiece of Crean's Budget reply speech, and the portfolio was set to be one of the Opposition's highest profile jobs. ABC-TV's *Lateline* reporter Alexandra Kirk commented: 'The main interesting point [in the reshuffle] is Julia Gillard and Mark Latham. They have been strong supporters of Simon Crean, [and] I think their promotion is a sign that Simon Crean wants to go on the attack, rather than the defence, in Parliament . . . I think now he's going for the gloves-off approach.' It was recognition that Gillard, like Latham, was one of Labor's most effective parliamentary performers.

Public interest in Gillard was growing. From this point on longer stories about her started to appear in magazines and newspapers, with taglines such as 'She's Smart, Tough and Giving the Government a Run for Their Money'. (Many of these stories give the impression that she should take naming rights on the phrase 'feisty redhead'.) For the first time the Australian magazine-reading public also became aware of her working-class and student-activist background, as well as her firmly held views on the importance of education and belief in the crucial role of opportunity.

Less welcome to Gillard, however, was the publicity given to her relationship with Craig Emerson, the workplace relations shadow minister. They had been together for a year, but had kept their liaison under the public radar for a number of reasons, not the least of which was that Emerson was married with three children and left his wife during the relationship. (According to one tabloid newspaper story, Gillard and Emerson were 'dubbed Elizabeth Taylor and Richard Burton by colleagues aware of their affair' and 'one senior ALP colleague' – a character who always seems to crop up in stories like these – had advised them to marry.)

Julia Gillard has said very little about their relationship, which lasted for a couple of years, except that it was important to her. 'Being involved with a colleague has got its downside in the sense that drawing the line between what's work and what's not work becomes increasingly blurred,' she observed a couple of years later.

Of course she was well aware of these pitfalls, having already had relationships with associates, but for a woman whose work is so central to her life such liaisons also have their advantages: both parties understand workplace pressures, and in this case both had similar interests. Gillard had known Emerson from the day she entered Parliament – the same day that he had, as it happens – and they had worked together in support of Simon Crean, even though they were not factional allies. Gillard's experience of working with unions was probably helpful to Emerson, who came from an academic and bureaucratic background. Their personal styles are very different, however. Gillard's straightforward, no-nonsense manner stands in sharp contrast to Emerson's milder, more intellectual focus. To put it bluntly, Gillard has a greater ability to cut through quickly, a certain killer instinct.

The break-up, when it came, was painful. 'Craig and I lived in different states [and had] very demanding positions,' she has said. 'And in the hurly-burly of the Labor world, ultimately it was just too difficult.' Although the relationship remained private while it was continuing, Gillard did discuss it briefly, when asked, a couple of years later. She was even able to joke: 'Craig and I were staying together at a hotel and I'd managed to forget to pack my contact lens holder. So I was just storing the contact lenses at the bottom of a glass, which wasn't exactly the smartest thing in the world to do. Er, so . . . in the bathroom, this glass with the contact lenses and a bit of solution in them. So, you know, during the course of the night, Craig gets up and thinking it's water, grabs the glass and drinks it. So I was wandering around National Conference blind for the next morning. I did have to give the Health Policy Report at the podium not basically able to see my notes or see the audience.'

Simon Crean had bought himself time with his clear majority vote in Caucus, but his fortunes, and those of the ALP, did not improve. Mark Latham: 'We are in a terrible position. Simon is unpopular, but it goes beyond the personal standing of one individual . . . we are yet to create an identity that the electorate can relate to and support . . . If we talk about the success of our economic model, people associate that success with Howard/Costello. If we talk about the Hawke/Keating legacy, people associate it with high interest rates.'

By mid-October Crean's popularity rating was way down and Robert Ray and John Faulkner, the Right and Left factional leaders respectively, decided that something had to be done. Crean, they felt, just was not grabbing the public's attention, and the chances that he would lead the ALP to victory at the next election were growing slimmer by the day. Despite the tradition that Crean should have the opportunity to fight the next election, it was felt that a new leader needed to be found.

But who? There was little enthusiasm for a return to Beazley, although he indicated that he would stand again if necessary. Back in June there had been a significant meeting between Mark Latham, Laurie Ferguson, Peter Cook and Kim Carr. According to Latham's diary: 'Excellent news: Cook and Carr have adopted me as the next Labor Leader, either after the next election or if Simon falls over beforehand. They don't want to be caught on the hop by the Beazley forces. A possible scenario: Martin Ferguson to tap Crean on the shoulder before Christmas.'

As it happened, the tap on the shoulder came on 26 November when John Faulkner and Bob McMullan visited Crean and he agreed to step down as leader. All this went on behind closed doors. They did not consult factional colleagues.

Julia Gillard, who was dismayed by this turn of events but perhaps not surprised, was asked to contest the deputy's position. She said she did not think about it seriously, telling journalist Annabel Crabb, 'Obviously there were people who thought I should consider the deputy leader issue, but it's one of those things that just get canvassed at the time of hurly-burly.' It is just as likely, indeed more likely, that she took a look at the numbers, thought the change was going to be a near-run thing and that she probably would not win.

And so the parliamentary Labor party embarked upon yet another round of number-crunching: Beazley versus Latham. There was an added sense of urgency this time. Everybody knew that whoever was chosen would lead the party to the next federal election. Latham was able to take advantage of Crean's numbers, and the counting began in earnest. His lieutenants, including Peter Cook, Laurie Ferguson, Julia Gillard, Kim Carr and Craig Emerson, set about trying to stop Beazley. The bedrock of Latham's support was the Centre, plus the Ferguson Left, and some members of the Right, including Joel Fitzgibbon and Penny Wong. Jenny Macklin had told Crean she would vote for Latham, but in the end supported Beazley.

The whole exercise demonstrated how easily the parliamentary factions could fracture, something that often happens during leadership contests. Right-wingers in every state except Western Australia defied their leaders' support of Beazley; some members of the hard Left supported him. Simon Crean and his allies worked tirelessly on Latham's behalf. Con Sciacca's opinion was that the Crean loyalty factor was worth twenty votes to Latham in the end.

Julia Gillard threw herself into persuading Caucus women. Despite her sadness about what had happened to Crean, she rather enjoyed having a role to play. She later commented: 'Beazley was fundamentally damaged by the "shock and awe" campaign in June, the nightly coverage trashing the name and brand of the Labor Party. There was a deep and lasting resentment about it, and I think it fed into support for Mark.' She was almost certainly describing her own feelings.

The leadership ballot took place on 2 December 2003. Latham defeated Beazley by 47 votes to 45. It was the narrowest of votes, a fact that caused problems later on. But supporters of Latham, and journalists too, could say that if the ALP had wanted generational change they now had it. Mark Latham was the first genuinely new leader on the Australian political scene for nearly a decade.

15

Taking care of business

Mark Latham's ascent to the leadership of the Opposition caused a surge of media and popular goodwill towards him and the party he led. Early indications were that the public was intrigued and interested. Much was made of the so-called generational change in the Labor Party, for Latham at forty-two – born in the same year as Julia Gillard – was twelve years younger than Simon Crean, thirteen years younger than Kim Beazley. Unlike them, he carried no baggage from previous Labor administrations.

Latham looked like the fresh start that the party needed, his youth providing a contrast to John Howard and other members of the Coalition, and ALP supporters felt they were now in with a chance for the next federal election. His policies and focus were also different from those of previous leaders.

He had already written and co-written several books setting out his views about society and politics, including what he saw as the challenges for the ALP. The thoughtful tenor of his writings, in books such as *Civilising Global Capital* (1998), surprised people who knew only Mark Latham the street fighter, the man who had told the ABC's Maxine McKew that he was a 'hater'. Here was something new for the ALP: a brawler intellectual.

In general favouring globalisation, Latham's work emphasised the concept of social capital, involving mutual trust, cooperation and the building of networks, which he believed would improve the efficiency of society by enabling people to work together more effectively, given their mutual interests. He was suspicious of what he called 'government handouts', believing that welfare, like other 'big government' initiatives, stifled the impulse towards trust and connectedness that was essential for a successful civic society. Globalisation meant that the old divisions of Left versus Right needed to change, in Australia as elsewhere. The new way forward for all governments was what he called the 'new radical centre', which was 'formed by moving to the centre of the old Left/Right spectrum and, most critically, lifting above this plane of politics through the expression of new and radical social values (conceptualised as the apex of a triangle, with the Left/Right divide forming its base).'

Some of Latham's ideas and attitudes unsettled traditional Labor people. Latham believed that unions served little purpose in the new 'knowledge economy' and that the information age had collapsed the traditional distinction between labour and capital. He saw the main distinction in society as being between the elites – in the media, the corporate sector, the bureaucracy and the parliaments – which controlled the political process, and the majority of Australians, who lived in the suburbs and had been denied a political voice. There was no place for the operation of social capital in Australia as currently constituted. Latham in his speeches and writing sought implicitly or explicitly to identify himself with the majority. John Howard, too, had sold himself as the defender of the suburban battler against the professional, intellectual and media elites. The difference between his suburban dweller and Latham's seems fairly minor from this distance, except that Latham made a very strong point of saying directly, 'I am one of you', not 'I understand what you want.'

At the beginning Latham was generally greeted with enough enthusiasm to drown out faint 'I hope the party knows what it's doing' mutterings from the sidelines and the union movement. Doubts were also eclipsed by his early poll results. When Latham took over the ALP in December 2003 the Coalition was the preferred party by 44 per cent against Labor's 35 per cent, and the two-party-preferred measure was 53–47 in favour of the government. In the week of 11 March 2004 Labor was ahead 44–41, and on the two-party-preferred indicator the ALP was 55 to the Coalition's 45. Latham's approval rating was 62 per cent. He was still five points behind Howard as preferred prime minister (39–44) but optimists, who included journalists, thought he would probably catch up fast.

Following the rhetoric of previous Labor leaders after internal upheavals, Latham made a point of emphasising healing within the party. His deputy, in a cross-factional deal, was Jenny Macklin and he appointed Simon Crean as his shadow treasurer. Stephen Smith came from the backbench to take over immigration, and Nicola Roxon was shadow attorney-general.

For Julia Gillard, Latham's ascendancy meant two things: more work and greater opportunity to do well. She kept the difficult, contentious shadow health portfolio, which she had held for less than six months, and took on a second job as manager of Opposition business in the House of Representatives, the first woman to be given that role.

This is one of those subterranean parliamentary jobs that surfaces mainly in House of Representatives information sheets. But it has a significant bearing on the effectiveness of the Opposition in Parliament, because the MOB's responsibility is to negotiate with the leader of the House of Representatives – that is, with whoever is in charge of managing government business in the House on matters such as the time allowed for debates and the priority of items of business. It is not a glamorous job, but an astute member of the Opposition can gain a real insight into a government's tactics and personalities. Gillard is nothing if not astute, and the job gave her a good opportunity to observe and judge the strengths and weaknesses of government members. It is fair to say that her stint as manager of Opposition business, a position she held for just over three years, has been a strong contributing factor to the effectiveness of her own parliamentary performance.

That, and her own verbal skills. In early October 2003 she had had a perfect opportunity to sharpen these when Tony Abbott, previously minister for employment and workplace relations, took on the health portfolio. Their parliamentary jousting tournament lasted for more than three years. Being manager of government business in the House, Abbott was doubly Gillard's opposite number once she became MOB, and he had already acquired a reputation as one of John Howard's most formidable supporters and debaters. Almost from the minute he became minister, Gillard was on the attack: 'The Minister at the table wants us to believe that the divisive, whirling dervish boxer is now gone and he's been replaced by cute and cuddly Tony, Tony with Toffee the dog on the front page of the newspaper, Tony listening to doctors.'

Abbott was an important target for Labor. Research had shown the ALP that Labor was the party most trusted on health issues. And in the minds of the majority of Australians, the centrepiece of the country's health policy was Medicare.

Like so many other areas, health policy in Australia has always had a chequered history. After World War II, under Liberal prime minister Robert Menzies and his successors, an increasingly complex system of private health insurance, subsidies, tax concessions and pensioner health benefits developed, frustrating both doctors and consumers. The whole ramshackle edifice crumbled under the weight of scientific and technological advancement: those who had insurance wanted more for their money, those without had to get by as best they could.

When, in 1974, Prime Minister Gough Whitlam introduced Medibank, Labor's universal health scheme, it was bitterly opposed by the Coalition and most of the medical profession, who described it as socialism and an attempt to dictate doctors' fees. They also said Medibank was prohibitively expensive, which in its first form it probably was (it was funded through taxation because Whitlam had failed to get Senate approval for a levy of 1.35 per cent). But the electorate loved it, and when Malcolm Fraser came to office he had no choice but to retain it – at least at first.

In Opposition Labor watched while the Fraser government, with John Howard as treasurer, weakened and then abolished Medibank, replacing it with a system of rebates on fees and tax and pensioner concessions. Fraser, sensing electoral danger, established Medibank Private, a government-owned private health insurer.

That did the trick. The number of people with private health insurance increased dramatically.

Back in office in 1983, under Bob Hawke, Labor retained Medibank Private, but in 1984 set up Medicare, a modified version of Whitlam's Medibank, on which taxpayers paid a levy. The private health insurance system dwindled.

As prime minister from 1996 John Howard knew that his dismantling of Whitlam's Medibank had done the Coalition little good with the electorate. He was committed to the privatisation of health insurance, but even more committed to staying in government. He had made it clear in Opposition that he regarded Medicare as simply insurance cover for pensioners and other low-income earners. He and Treasurer Peter Costello had added that bulk billing was aimed at assisting only the same group. For Howard the challenge was to move people into private health insurance cover without appearing to dismantle Medicare. The ALP and Gillard needed to defend Medicare by limiting Howard's ability to undermine it and drive people into private insurance.

Because health policy was Labor's strongest suit, the one area in which it was perceived to be strikingly different from the government, Gillard's approach needed to be the opposite of the one she had taken for immigration policy. This time her job was to emphasise as sharply as possible the contrast between Labor and the government – an entirely different brief. Throughout 2004 she followed Mark Latham's lead, emphasising Labor's credentials on delivering services and reminding the electorate that the ALP was the party of good schools and good health services – practical things that made a difference to people's lives.

She had set out the contrasts between the Coalition and the

ALP in a talk she had given to the Evatt Foundation the previous September: 'Throughout the 1980s as Medicare gained strength and became the foundation for an equitable health system, John Howard was Medicare's greatest enemy . . . But John Howard could never win an election while threatening to dismantle Medicare and kill off bulk billing. So something happened between 1987 and 1995. In 1995 John Howard told Australians, "We absolutely guarantee the retention of Medicare. We guarantee the retention of bulk billing" . . . John Howard is now the prime minister and now that the government has ordered the words "bulk billing" to be deleted from the government's vocabulary, his absolute guarantee to retain bulk billing is worth nothing.'

It was a foreshadowing of the 'mean and tricky' rhetoric Gillard would later relentlessly apply to John Howard's government. And she hammered the point that Australian families – not yet known as Australian working families – were having difficulty in meeting increased health costs under Howard, with higher co-payments to doctors who would not bulk bill, increased insurance premiums and gap charges, and rises in the cost of essential medicines. Her opponent in Parliament might have been Tony Abbott, but her target was John Howard: she knew he was driving the government's health policy, as he drove almost everything else.

Gillard's attack went beyond the pragmatic. She sought to refute Abbott's contention that 99 per cent of the time the health portfolio was an exercise in allocating resources. 'The minister could not be more wrong,' she said. 'Our health system is an expression of our values. You can choose to design a health scheme based on the foundation stone of universality, a system on which we can each rely and for which we pay. Or you can choose private provision as your foundation stone.' Although the rhetoric was different, the sentiment could have come straight from the Gillard family hero Aneurin Bevan, the Welsh-born firebrand who had driven Britain's national health policy more than half a century before. John and Moira Gillard must have been pleased to hear their daughter publicly espousing Bevan's principles.

In February 2004 Mark Latham wrote in his diary: 'A good meeting this morning with Gillard's health experts . . . If the Federal Government takes over the public and private health insurance costs of senior Australians (say, 70 years and above) it can make significant savings on the cost of the rebate – an electorally appealing policy that partially pays for itself. This would also be a significant move towards the integration of the public and private health systems in Australia . . . The health economists are going to crunch the numbers/costings and see how they look.'

That meeting probably marked the adoption of Medicare Gold, the controversial health policy that Gillard would take to the federal election later in the year, and that probably caused her more strife than any other of her portfolio responsibilities.

The idea of Medicare Gold in embryo form had come up during Crean's term as leader, although it was not developed until later. The argument was that the Howard government had underfunded nursing-home care, forcing the public hospital system to take aged people as inpatients. It had then squeezed the states' ability to support the hospital system, decreasing their proportion of federal funding. The result was that acute-care beds in public hospitals were being occupied by frail aged people.

The intention behind Medicare Gold – which did not significantly change in the eight months before the 2004 election – was that Labor would invest $2.9 billion in a plan to guarantee health care for all Australians aged seventy-five and over, with the federal government taking full responsibility for their hospital costs. These costs would be met by using the resources of both public and private sectors, by giving public hospitals extra money and by negotiating fee schedules with private providers for in-hospital services. It would enable older Australians, many on limited incomes, to save money on private health insurance hospital cover.

The idea for Medicare Gold was developed by the large and influential lobby group Catholic Health Australia, representing the interests of more than seventy public and private hospitals and 500 aged-care services across the country. It was originally offered to Tony Abbott as well as to the ALP by Francis Sullivan, then CEO of Catholic Health Australia. According to Sullivan, Abbott was very interested in the idea and thought it could well be looked at in more detail. In the light of Abbott's later denials that he had approved of the concept in any way, this is certainly interesting.

The two experts charged with evaluating Medicare Gold for Labor were Stephen Duckett and Hal Swerissen. Both were, and are, highly respected health policy analysts. Duckett, an economist specialising in health, was a former secretary of the Australian Department of Human Services and Health, and had held several senior professorial positions. Hal Swerissen was dean of health sciences at La Trobe University, with a strong background in health reform at state and federal levels.

The Medicare Gold issue would blow up dramatically during the 2004 election campaign. But at the beginning of the year it was a policy quietly in development: so quietly, in fact, that Gillard started to refer to it as 'the policy that dare not speak its name'.

It was a joke that Latham appreciated, as he did many of Gillard's jokes (she also referred to John Faulkner, the mandarin of the parliamentary Left, as the 'governor-general' because of the way 'he straddles the sub-factions of the Left', presiding over party affairs 'without going too far into the muck'). On paper Latham and Gillard had quite a lot in common: a quizzical, irreverent sense of humour, a working-class background and a similar set of priorities in support of the social good. The similarity of Gillard's beliefs to Latham's would become more evident in her policy making in the years that followed.

But at this stage Gillard was not in Latham's inner circle, which was basically reserved for Tim Gartrell, the party's secretary, John Faulkner and Laurie Brereton, Latham's chief backer and adviser. Each appreciated the other's capacity for hard work and the ability to summarise an issue. Latham wrote: 'I like Gillard because she has a go. She's the opposite of white bread: feisty, irreverent, good sense of humour, the closest thing we have to charisma in Caucus. Not afraid of policy innovation but also steady and sensible.'

All of which qualities were about to be severely tested.

16

Implosion

Depending on the ALP's fortunes, national conferences can be occasions for revelling in self-delusion, workmanlike forums for debating and refining policy, or, in the words of the ABC's Michael Brissenden, 'a cauldron of factional poison'. They can also be all of the above. What they invariably are, though, especially these days, is theatre.

The forty-third national conference, held from 29 to 31 January 2004 in the cavernous convention centre at Sydney's Darling Harbour, had followed the pattern. It was big – 400 delegates meant twice as many as usual – and those in the public gallery were enthusiastic. As writer Mark Hearn observed, these were a heterogeneous bunch, typical of Labor faithful across the board:

> [They comprised] the gay activists of the Rainbow Labor group, the predominantly young, black T-shirted squad of the Labor for Refugees supporters, old loyalists and dissidents in flannelette shirts, often armed with bags and folders of ideas and papers, small groups of

women of polite appearance given to sudden outbursts of sharp interjection, a formidable trio from the National Union of Workers, in shorn heads and black suits with the NUW logo and slogans stitched into the breast pockets of their jackets. All came in the expectation that Labor might speak for them.

All delegates were well aware that any serious squabbling with their new leader over policy could easily destroy Labor's election chances. And so the conference's theme was a nice blend of the celebratory and the reassuring: 'Enduring Labor Values'. The conference started with Allen Madden from the Sydney Metropolitan Local Aboriginal Land Council welcoming delegates to Gadigal country and reminding them that his grandfather had been unable to vote. This was the rather uneasy cue for Carmen Lawrence, the party's president, to welcome to the podium Warren Mundine, who the following year would take his place as the ALP's first Indigenous president. Labor, Mundine said, would put an end to the Howard years and restore equality in society and humane and progressive values.

The lights dimmed and overhead screens showed images of a young boy, a youth, a university graduate and a family man, to the strains of 'New Sensation' by INXS. Then Mark Latham descended to the podium through crowds of supporters – a touch of symbolism that might or might not have been intended, but probably was. He spoke on the theme of Labor's enduring values, reminding all present of what the party had already achieved: Medicare, the expanded education system, the move towards Indigenous reconciliation, a competitive economy. There were surprises: nobody could recall a federal political leader declaring that 'there is no more powerful force in our society than a good government school'. Latham also introduced his own theme of the 'Ladder of Opportunity', and his belief that strong economic growth was being 'matched by record rates of depression, loneliness and isolation'.

Julia Gillard opened the discussion on health, declaring that health issues would determine whether Labor won the next federal election. So rattled was the government by perceptions that the Coalition hated Medicare, she said, that cakes sent to Medicare offices all over Australia to celebrate its twentieth anniversary were not to be cut in public because they would seem to be taking a knife to the scheme. Clearly should such a knife be poised over such a cake, Gillard would be there to say exactly that. She and Mark Latham also announced that in office Labor would set up a new national dental scheme, which would reduce the waiting lists for half a million Australians who could not afford to have their teeth fixed. In addition there was a commitment to spend more on mental health services.

This was the national conference where the policy Gillard had drafted about the treatment of asylum seekers was accepted after considerable debate. Carmen Lawrence repeated her contention that mandatory detention was wrong, Christmas Island should be restored to the nation's migration zone and temporary protection visas should be abolished. The party's first directly elected president, Lawrence was seen as the party's conscience on the issue of asylum seekers, and her comments recalled the divisive policy that Gillard had put forward. Lawrence and her supporters maintained that the policy proposed by Gillard's replacement, Stephen Smith, was still far too close to that of the Howard government. Not surprisingly, Gillard rejected this, saying that the recommended policy was consistent with the United Nations's, and was not racist. She summed up her position with 'We have to draft a policy that can win public support', which had always been her approach.

There were resolutions calling for early childhood literacy and national reading programs: two policies very close to Mark Latham's heart. Extra university places were promised, as was needs-based funding for schools. The press gave these measures some attention in its reporting of the conference.

Latham's view of the vital importance of education as a social good – a means of upward mobility and wealth creation and hence important almost solely in utilitarian terms – had already made an impression on the electorate. His understanding of young families and their anxieties about education, encapsulated in a clever campaign to put a book in every child's hand, was clearly something people liked, according to the opinion polls. Maybe, just maybe, Latham could revitalise the party.

It was a view expressed by Dick Morris, ex-US-president Bill Clinton's former staff tactician. In a memorable interview on 4 December 2003 he had told John Shovelan of ABC Radio's *AM* that Latham had a 'wonderfully penetrating, inventive mind'. He saw Latham's approach as similar to Clinton's and Tony Blair's Third Way emphasis on upward mobility for the ordinary person, education and retraining, rather than social-welfare props for the unemployed. Latham was likely to be successful, Morris believed.

Morris also had some tactical on-air advice for Mark Latham about dealing with his chief opponent: 'Howard is like a fixed piece of artillery that's planted in the ground and has a field of fire in front of him, and if you walk into the field of fire you get hurt, and if you set up your office there, as Beazley did, you get annihilated. But if instead you play a mobile game . . . Howard isn't a tank. He doesn't know how to swivel his turret and attack other areas.' He added, 'I think Latham will confuse Howard in a way that Clinton confused the Republicans and Blair confused Major, and ultimately makes it possible for him to win because he's not the enemy they're prepared to face.'

This strategy appeared to be working when Latham announced his intention of modifying the Commonwealth contributory superannuation scheme, essentially chopping out a large chunk of federal politicians' superannuation. This was an audacious move, based on the electorate's perception that politicians were ludicrously overpaid. It was instantly attractive to voters, if not to their elected representatives. John Howard recognised a popular policy when he saw one and reluctantly agreed. Round one to Latham, said the media. But some of Latham's colleagues in the ALP had misgivings, mainly because the idea seemed to have come from nowhere very much, was not policy but populism.

Latham and Labor continued to dominate the polls and the newspaper columns. The first glitch came in March when Kevin Rudd, the shadow foreign affairs spokesman, told ABC-TV's *Lateline* that the ALP wanted Australian troops out of Iraq sooner rather than later, but was conscious of international obligations and would wait until the country attained interim self-government. Latham contradicted Rudd – the ALP would have troops out by Christmas, he said – and Rudd was forced to try to retrieve the position, which would scarcely have endeared his leader to him. Latham had badly miscalculated. Some polls said that support for immediate withdrawal was running at only 35 per cent and that 65 per cent of the population thought the troops should stay until the job was finished. For the first time Latham's own poll numbers dipped.

It was as though the electorate had taken its first long look at Latham and started to think, Hmm . . . maybe not. And as the months passed, business began to look askance at Latham, and Labor, too. Some of his colleagues became concerned at his reluctance to meet with business leaders, which seemed like a refusal to try to win them over. He was obviously trying to position himself as a new kind of leader, one whose strength came from his community-based roots and who was not beholden to the elites of capitalism, but the result was unsatisfactory. Some felt he had a working-class chip on his shoulder and was too inclined to demonise businesspeople as exploiters. This was a time when most Australians' investments in shares and property were doing well, so they were not enthusiastic about attacks on business. Latham made speeches attacking the influence of Australia's retail giants, and called for increased accountability to shareholders, none of it done in a conciliatory spirit. And because business interests did not feel Latham and his party were sympathetic to them, they were not about to discourage their constituency from voting Liberal. There was the danger, too, that Latham was beginning to alienate the 'soft' Labor voters, small businesspeople.

All in all Latham's tone deafness – his lack of understanding of the wider electorate and apparent inability to respond as a leader to the expectations of a range of people – was shaping up to be a big problem. This gave the members of the Coalition a great opportunity, and they took full advantage of it. The Coalition's strongest suit among voters had always been its management of the economy and national security, and Latham seemed fairly wobbly on both. The policy of bringing the troops home from Iraq the instant Labor got into power could easily be positioned as the populism of an inexperienced leader who had not given the issue of Australia's international commitments sufficient thought. Latham's plans for tax reform were thwarted because of resistance within the ALP itself, which could be seen as a lack of unity within the party. And the Coalition used the financial difficulties Latham had experienced as mayor of Liverpool to suggest that his economic credentials were not good.

In July, stories surfaced that Latham had punched a political rival during his time on Liverpool Council. There was also the story that an angry Latham had broken a taxi driver's arm. Latham said the Coalition had established a dirt file on him. But the voters were left wondering, Well, what else do we have to find out about this man?

The Coalition's attacks and the bad publicity began to have their effect. Voters started to question Latham's experience and temperamental suitability to be prime minister, and his approval rating went down from 54 to 47 per cent late in July. Julia Gillard, like her colleagues, watched with growing apprehension. She had really thought at the beginning of the year that the ALP had a chance of winning government, and her own work on health policy had been a mainstay of Latham's social equity agenda. But by the end of July she and the party sensed that, although the polls were basically still in Labor's favour, the party was not far enough ahead of the Coalition to translate the lead into a convincing victory. As Latham himself wrote, 'My numbers are still okay, but they need to be in the stratosphere if we are going to win.' Running an agenda that concentrated on social inequity and the ability of Latham's Ladder of Opportunity to redress it was problematic when the national mood was fairly optimistic and the economy – as far as anyone could see – remained strong.

The problems were succinctly stated in a polling and focus group analysis prepared for Labor by researcher John Utting of UMR Research:

> [The voters] don't directly link the Prime Minister with the blame [for their concern about problems in the health and education systems]. It's surprising when one reflects on this. Consider the facts: the Prime Minister has launched and orchestrated a ferocious personal attack on the Opposition Leader, presided over the wholesale destruction of Medicare and bulk billing and skewed higher education policies against average Australians. Despite all this, he remains popular and respected by voters . . . [Howard] has managed to triangulate himself out of the political equation, riding serenely above the tumult and combat of day-to-day politics.

Latham quoted this in his diary, and was honest enough to evaluate the critical comments: 'The electorate is pretty perceptive. According to Utting, "Concerns have emerged from the most recent focus groups that Mark Latham appears distracted, tired or disinterested" . . . I have been distracted and disinterested, and people have picked up on it.'

All the same the sustained attacks by the Coalition exacerbated a tendency on Latham's part to turn inwards, to behave as though the world were against him. His colleagues found him increasingly unapproachable and unwilling to discuss what he was doing and its possible consequences.

Besides his health was not good. On 17 August he had a bad attack of pancreatitis, a vicious and potentially life-threatening illness for which there is no cure, although rest and a controlled diet help. Latham believed his pancreas had been permanently damaged from the radiotherapy he had undergone for testicular cancer a decade before. Life-threatening experiences are likely to alter one's perceptions and priorities considerably (a fact that has not really been discussed by the media in relation to Mark Latham). 'Forget politics and the Labor movement, what about making sure I see my children go to school, play sport, graduate from university – my primary responsibility and priority in life?' he wrote in his diary.

But, he added, 'Let's do the election and see what happens. If I have another attack and the problem is chronic, I can give it away then . . . I've given up too much of my private life, but not this time. Howard won't commit to serving a full term and let people know about his plans for the future, so why do I need to blurt out everything? The media can get stuffed.'

The combination of detachment, self-pity and impetuousness expressed in his diary entries during July and August must have been seen by Gillard and her colleagues behind the scenes, and it was deeply worrying.

Howard finally called the election for Saturday 9 October. Latham was still determined to fight the election on Labor's turf, not the government's. He could point to the fact that Labor remained ahead in all polls and on 31 August, two days after the election had been called, Labor was still ahead 52–48 nationwide. This, however, came within the ambit of that favourite pollster's phase 'too close to call', and Howard, who had consistently outpolled Latham as preferred prime minister by an average of almost twelve percentage points, chose as his theme 'Who Would You Trust?'.

Even though Labor had been waiting all year for Howard's announcement, the party was seriously unprepared for an election.

Julia Gillard and federal Opposition leader Simon Crean at a shadow Cabinet meeting in Churchill, Victoria, 2002.

With Craig Emerson at the National Press Club, Canberra, 2000.

Mark Latham and Julia Gillard launch Labor's health policy at the Royal Brisbane and Women's Hospital, late September 2004.

Just back in January 2005 from a holiday in Vietnam, Julia Gillard speaks to the media at Melbourne airport about Labor's federal leadership crisis.

The infamous 'empty fruit bowl' photograph: Julia Gillard at home in Altona, early 2005.

Conflict and consultation: from 2003 to 2007 the relationship between Julia Gillard and Tony Abbott was marked by both parliamentary aggression and behind-the-scenes co-operation.

New leadership, 4 December 2006: Julia Gillard (with partner, Tim Mathieson) and Kevin Rudd (with his wife, Thérèse Rein) on the way to their first press conference after winning Caucus's vote to lead the ALP.

Sturt Krygsman's comment on the reaction to Liberal senator Bill Heffernan's remarks about Julia Gillard, May 2007.

Shortly before the 2007 election the conservative media depicted Julia Gillard as a dangerous radical.

The early days of the campaign were distinguished by confusion and a series of avoidable glitches, some caused by staffers, others by scrambled policy detail. To the increasing frustration of party members – not least former prime minister Paul Keating – Latham chose not to emphasise the economic policies of the previous Labor administration, allowing the Coalition government to claim all the credit for the benign economic climate. Latham quarrelled with his staffers and with campaign managers, was often unapproachable, and made a number of decisions that were widely regarded as quixotic, to say the least.

And events in the lead-up to the election did not help. On 9 September a car bomb exploded outside the Australian embassy in Jakarta, killing nine people and wounding more than 150 others. The government issued dire warnings about security and border protection, and Latham made the extraordinary decision to cease campaigning for a couple of days as a mark of respect to the dead. He lost momentum there, but regained it on the twelfth when he was judged to have won the sole TV debate with John Howard.

As part of his plan to direct education funding to poorer schools, an important plank in his education reform agenda, Latham announced on 15 September that he would slash government subsidies to sixty-seven private schools. 'Labor's Hit List', screamed the headlines. Latham's decision flew in the face not only of policy commonsense but of Labor history. Gough Whitlam and Bob Hawke had both learned that 'don't cut funding to private schools' was the education policy equivalent of 'don't march on Moscow'. The press and popular fury unleashed as a result of this decision was considerable. It was a lesson of which Julia Gillard, watching from the sidelines, would take advantage in the years to come.

Following the rather odd convention that campaigns are formally launched only a couple of weeks before an election, the government unveiled its policies on 26 September, basically throwing money in as many directions as possible. Despite this, Howard and his ministers sought to position the Coalition as the party of fiscal responsibility, cashing in on the myth that Labor governments equalled record interest rates. Howard and his ministers kept up their personal attacks on Latham, emphasising what their polls had been telling them: he was perceived to be unstable, erratic.

The ALP launched its campaign three days later and the centrepiece was the announcement of Medicare Gold, the policy that Gillard had been working on since February. In its final form the policy was a plan for the Australian government to take full responsibility, from 1 July 2006, for the hospital costs, public or private, of all Australians aged seventy-five and over. Public hospitals would receive additional funds to cover their costs for this group, and fee schedules would be negotiated with private providers. Because at present the presence of the over-seventy-fives drove premiums up, private health insurance would now be cheaper for those remaining on it. The policy would have the effect of placing both aged care and aged hospital services under the Australian government, allowing it to 'get the balance right' (a favourite phrase of Gillard's then and later) between beds in nursing homes and hospitals. Journalists picked up on its potential electoral effectiveness: it was intended to woo the Coalition's core constituency by promising to end waiting lists and take over all the private and public hospital costs of the over-seventy-fives.

Latham's diary states that it was a miracle that word about Medicare Gold never leaked until the actual election campaign. It seems strange that the ALP should release such an important policy so late in the campaign, but perhaps Latham and Gillard did so for fear the government would take it as its own – after all, Abbott had looked at it with interest when it was first presented to him. Judging by entries in his diary, Latham had always intended to spring the policy on the electorate late in the day, possibly wishing to use it as a circuit-breaker if the polls were not favouring Labor as strongly as they had previously.

And perhaps, too, Latham and Gillard did not want possible opponents to have too much time to savage Medicare Gold before the election. As it was, those opposed to it took full advantage of the time they had. The Australian Medical Association, which had commissioned Access Economics to analyse the policy, said that Medicare Gold could only be available at the cost of other patients' access to hospitals, an objection supported by the Doctors Reform Society. Medicare Gold, they said, was simply not sustainable over the longer term because of the increasing numbers of aged people, the effect of inflation on health costs, and the expense of removing price and queue constraints. They went so far as to say that this would cause money to be siphoned away from other public goods and services.

The Australian Health Insurance Association agreed that the policy would place an increasing burden on the Budget over time, and was dubious that the states would agree to give back some of the funding already allocated to hospital treatment. This objection particularly irritated Gillard, who had spent a great deal of time and effort persuading the states, all of which had Labor governments, to support the scheme.

There was also a certain amount of 'tis/'tisn't arguing. Minister for Health Tony Abbott naturally supported the negative criticism, and said the costings did not hold up. Gillard said they did, and questioned whether the economic critiques had really looked at the impact an ageing population would have on Australian society.

The policy was given for costing to the Department of Finance on 1 October, three days after it had been announced and eight days before the election. Gillard has said that this was enough time and as much as was normally given. Whether this is true or not, the Coalition managed to give the electorate the impression that the policy had been hurriedly put together and costed on the back of an envelope. Treasurer Peter Costello insisted that there was a 'black hole' in Labor's Medicare costing. This was shown to be wrong: savings of $800 million from other areas of health would have eliminated the $726 million shortfall identified by the Department of Finance. But the mud stuck – another problem with releasing the policy so close to the election. And for some reason, possibly because Labor was unwilling to be seen to be cutting other areas in the health budget, Gillard and her advisers omitted this savings item. This seems an odd mistake, which might have reflected inexperience on the part of Latham or Gillard. Or perhaps there simply wasn't time to make the point.

After an initial leap in support – Labor's vote among older people increased from the low to the high forties – Medicare Gold didn't get a great deal of bounce from the electorate. It was an example of policy overcome by politics, and a difficult experience, but one that Gillard learned from. She has since said: 'To the extent that Medicare Gold had demerits, it had them because of the political context. There is nothing in the research that ever showed an internal demerit in Medicare Gold.'

The wrangling about money made many voters' eyes glaze over, and the boldness of the policy made people cautious. Medicare Gold also fed into the growing perception that Mark Latham, although highly intelligent, was apt to take unacceptable risks: he was not a safe pair of hands. He also continued to be seen as aggressive, a view confirmed for many by footage that showed him looming over John Howard to shake hands with him, hard, when the two men met at the ABC. Latham dismissed the effect of this, but according to the Liberals that handshake attracted more criticism of the ALP leader than anything else.

The disappointment that Labor's major health policy had not given the ALP the boost it needed to win made Gillard less than optimistic about the election result. And then Latham released his forest policy.

Gillard greeted this with a sense of foreboding. She later said: 'In the few days before the policy – the policy was announced on the Monday [that is, 4 October] – the rumours were flying thick and fast that Mark was going to announce the policy and it was going to be very green. I actually was in Tasmania with Sid Sidebottom, who was the member for Braddon at that stage and who lost Braddon at the election solely, in my view, because of the timber policy. And Sid was hearing the rumours and was very disheartened . . . I knew he was fearing the worst.

'I started trying to call Mark [to] say, "What's going on with the timber policy?", and ended up having a conversation with him on the Sunday night. He'd been at the NRL Grand Final. It was obvious to me that he was going down the next day to announce this big bad policy, and . . . my political instincts were saying to me that this was going to be a fiasco. This would cost us seats in Tasmania, it might well cost us seats in the mainland, it's bad policy, stupid policy.

'I was saying to Mark, "Please don't do this, just please, pull out now" . . . And he was convinced that it was the right thing to do, and was committed to making the announcement the next day, and it was clear to me that there was nothing at that stage that I could do to change his mind.

'It was like watching a child tottering towards a fire. A sense of being completely immobilised, nothing I could do.'

In Hobart Mark Latham vowed to end logging in most of Tasmania's old-growth forests and to spend $800 million on a job-saving package for timber workers. The idea was to put a moratorium of ten months on new logging in old-growth forests outside existing plans while an expert panel looked at the scientific and conservation arguments for locking up 240 000 hectares of disputed forests of high conservation value, and examined the wilderness and heritage worth of eight different bioregions. Loggers of old-growth forests would find jobs in plantation-timber logging and the craft industry. There would be no net loss of jobs, but many workers would be retrained and reskilled.

'Politics is not a consideration,' declared Latham. 'We're doing this because it's the right thing to do.' In fact part of the reason Gillard thought this such a stupid policy was that Latham was wedged between, on the one hand, a state Labor government that heavily backed the loggers and, on the other, those who wanted to see the forests protected – swinging voters on the mainland and the Greens, whose preferences the ALP needed. Latham and his advisers believed that a few seats might be lost in Tasmania but they would be made up on the mainland by approving environmentalists.

Almost immediately 500 Tasmanian timber workers declared Latham unfit to lead the country and accused him of throwing workers on the scrapheap. Scott McLean, the state secretary of the Construction, Forestry, Mining and Energy Union, said his members felt betrayed and disappointed, and the chief executive of the Forest Industries Association of Tasmania accused Labor of ratting on workers and industry. 'It's quite clear to us that they are prepared to sell out Tasmanian jobs to get a few votes in CBD Melbourne and Sydney,' he said.

It was therefore a simple matter for John Howard to declare the policy a sell-out of Tasmanian workers – not a forestry policy but a grubby preference deal with the Greens. 'If Mark Latham can break his word to the workers of Tasmania, why should any Australians believe any promise he makes to them at any stage during this election campaign?' he asked.

Gillard comments, 'Howard was smart enough, having watched Mark go right out there, to pick a policy [in which] he was going to be seen to be doing something a little bit environmental but also having the timber workers cheer.'

That is exactly what Howard did. The following day he fronted a rally of 3000 timber workers in Launceston and promised to lock up 170 000 hectares of Tasmanian forests without costing any jobs. Dick Morris was proved wrong in this case: Howard was not just a fixed piece of artillery, he was a tank, too, and he had swivelled his turret in a sudden devastating attack on Latham.

Howard told the rally: 'I said when I commenced the current campaign that the goals of ending old-growth logging and preserving jobs had to be compatible and had to be preserved. That I am not willing to pursue a desirable environmental objective, as seen by the great majority of Australians, at the expense of the jobs of a limited number of Australians in isolated communities or indeed anywhere else in Australia.'

He was cheered to the echo and the CFMEU – including Michael O'Connor, who had remained a close friend of Julia Gillard – backed the Howard plan. O'Connor immediately came under fire from the media. How could an allegedly left-wing union support John Howard? But he remained firm, saying that Howard's policy offered a better deal and pointing out that the trees that would be locked up against logging, according to the Prime Minister, were probably inaccessible or not needed for the industry. He described the ALP's forest policy as a job destroyer, and added '[W]e hope the Labor Party has learned their lesson from that'. The issue, he said, was basically whether voters wanted to support the caffe latte set and the middle class or the ordinary working people. Yes, he said, he did have a left-wing point of view – that 'you do not sacrifice blue-collar jobs to appease the middle class of this country'.

Gillard, who might well have been incensed and disappointed that one of her staunchest former allies had chosen not to support the Labor Party, was both pragmatic and loyal to her old friend when she spoke about the election a couple of years later.

'Michael [knew] that every other policy the Liberals were coming out with – whether it be on industrial relations or health or education or whatever – weren't in his members' interests. But when it's your job, what you're going to vote on is your job, and that's what his members were going to do. So it was a dreadful position for him to be in.

'Michael's job is to represent his members . . . he's got one job and one place he gets his salary from and that's the amount of money the members put into the union pot. On the question of whether his people were employed or not employed, he had to take the position he took.'

Whether the forestry policy tipped the balance or not, the election result on Saturday 9 October 2004 was conclusive. The Liberals won seventy-four seats, the National Party twelve, and Labor sixty. The ALP's total vote was 37.6 per cent, making Latham the first Labor opposition leader for eighty years to fail to make a net gain in seats at his first election against the government. But the real net gain for the government was in the Senate, where the Coalition won thirty-nine out of seventy-six seats. It became the first government to have a majority in the Senate since 1981.

The result was not only discouraging for Labor, it was ominous. Gillard and her colleagues had to come to terms with a depressing fact: in only ten months their party had gone from the real possibility of victory to irrelevance.

17

'Much more than a job'

Coming back to Parliament after your political party has lost an election must be a profoundly depressing experience. The members of the parliamentary Labor Party found it particularly hard after the election of October 2004. It wasn't just that the Howard government had walloped them, it was that the Coalition had control of the Senate. Howard and his ministers now had three years to push through whatever agenda they liked, and the ALP would be powerless to stop them.

'Everybody was shattered,' says Julia Gillard. 'I mean, this is much more than a job. And while you're under a lot of scrutiny, you have to keep your emotions in check because people are tracking them. You know enough to say you don't feel badly about losing, but you've got a lot emotionally invested in it, and you take it personally. You do. Not in the sense you feel bad about yourself as a person, but it hits you hard.

'And election night hit me really hard, and in the days that followed it became increasingly clear that the Howard government were going to get the Senate, and I knew what that meant. So you're depressed about the future of the country, you're depressed about the future of your brand of politics because you've lost again. And you've lost some really good mates in the process.'

And, as always happens to the losing party after a federal election, leadership speculation started up once again. Very soon journalists began asking whether Mark Latham would last as Labor leader, or whether his erratic temperament and health problems would prevent him from going through to the next election.

But in the aftermath of the defeat Latham seemed calm. His immediate task was to work out who would be on his frontbench. '[I]n the old days, the Leader simply issued a statement, announcing the positions without consulting his colleagues,' he wrote in his diary. 'A much better system: it would have rescued my weekend at home from a thousand phone calls.'

It was a tricky exercise, with a lot of factional toing and froing. Latham had to exert all the authority he still had in order to guarantee Simon Crean a spot. He wanted Gillard as shadow treasurer, but it was not to be. 'Gillard is the best person for the job, our rising star, but her own people have vetoed her. The leaders of the Left have lined up, one by one, to blackball her: Faulkner, Evans [Chris Evans, ALP leader in the Senate] and Combet [Greg Combet, ACTU secretary], plus expected criticism from Macklin and Albanese . . . I told Julia I couldn't give it to her because I had run out of petrol after saving Crean. I didn't have the heart to tell her about the rats in her ranks. Anyway, my feeling is she will be better off as Health Shadow and Manager of Opposition Business; it gives her a chance to grease Caucus and line herself up as the next Leader. That was certainly my experience: MOB won me Caucus support, while ST cost me votes.'

It's an interesting entry for a couple of reasons. First of all it clearly shows how ambitious Julia Gillard was perceived to be – shadow treasurer is a highly influential portfolio – and it also demonstrates that she posed a threat to the ambitions of others on her own side. Asked about this now, she shrugs it off as the fortunes of politics. But clearly the 'Gillard must be stopped' faction was still operating, and the knowledge must have hurt. However, true to her credo of not allowing herself to be embittered, Gillard exercised her formidable self-discipline, bowed to the inevitable and concentrated on doing the best job possible as shadow health minister.

And there is also this entry in Latham's diaries for Tuesday 30 November: 'I sat down with Gillard at my dining room table in Parliament House for a frank discussion about my situation. I've still got the numbers in Caucus (on my count, 50–38) but then again, so did Crean until the leaks and treachery wore him down. That's my point to Julia: "We need to learn from Simon's experience and make sure there is some sort of succession plan in place, especially if there's a challenge to my leadership. If worst comes to worst and the enemies can do me in, I'll dive-bomb their candidate and try to set it up for you to win." It's not an admission of defeat, rather a recognition of reality, something Crean never did.

'Gillard was reluctant. She's never seen herself as a parliamentary Leader, but I convinced her to go through her numbers (in a notional contest against Beazley, the strongest of the possible machine candidates). Close, but not enough: she would lose 39–49.'

So Gillard knew the time was not right to make a leadership move.

Wayne Swan became shadow treasurer, with Stephen Smith in charge of industry infrastructure and industrial relations. (Already known as two of the Roosters, Smith and Swan were now dubbed the Glimmer Twins, after Mick Jagger and Keith Richards.) Latham wanted to promote progressive young women, observing that 'all the talented Labor women are in the Left, an area where we have a clear advantage over the Coalition', and so Tanya Plibersek took the shadow portfolios of work, family and community, while Senator Penny Wong became shadow minister for employment and workplace participation. Others in the shadow Cabinet were Jenny Macklin (deputy leader and education and science), Robert McClelland (defence and homeland security), Simon Crean (trade) and Kevin Rudd (foreign affairs).

Several prominent ALP parliamentarians, however, chose not to contest or recontest frontbench positions, and went public with criticism of Latham's personal style and policy priorities. These included Bob McMullan, Annette Ellis, John Faulkner and Kim Beazley (whose mid-year appointment from the backbench to the shadow defence portfolio had been interpreted as Latham's attempt to undo the damage of his 'home by Christmas' misjudgement). The media naturally jumped on yet another story that seemed to demonstrate problems with Latham's leadership, saying that he was not powerful enough to control the factions in his own party.

After Latham gave the senior economics portfolios to Swan and Smith, one anonymous colleague spoke up in support of Gillard, in a background briefing given to *Age* journalist Shaun Carney and quoted on 6 November. Latham recorded: 'The article said that my backers found it galling that Gillard had been overlooked and Swan/ Smith's bad behaviour [as Beazley supporters] had been rewarded. Then the quote: " 'Julia was a stand-out all the way through that last term. With no front bench experience, she managed to fashion an acceptable policy on refugees and then took on health and made that a winner too. She had earned a promotion,' one Labor MP said".' Latham's view was that this was Simon Crean – 'I saved Simon but now he's backgrounding against me' – and that Crean had praised Gillard as a way of making his own tenure of leadership look better.

The pressure and criticism were building, and Latham could not be immune from them. Gillard later observed: 'Mark at that stage was very, very tired, but saying he wasn't going to allow himself to die the death of a thousand cuts the way he thought Simon had. He was quite aggressive about confronting his critics, which led to more criticism that he was not dealing with defeat, so he was already on a bad cycle.'

But he had made some interesting choices for his frontbench, picking people who would show great potential in the years to come – surely one of the things a successful Labor leader should do. He might have taken some comfort from that. And, more pragmatically, from the fact that there was no obvious successor to him as Labor leader. Lindsay Tanner and Bob McMullan, two of his harshest critics, did not have enough cross-factional support to be seen as viable leadership candidates and there was little enthusiasm for a return to Kim Beazley. Whether or not Latham felt safe as leader at that point, he was.

This is how things stood when Parliament rose and everybody went away on holidays at the end of 2004, thankful for some time to recover. And then, on Boxing Day, an undersea earthquake triggered a devastating series of tsunamis in the Indian Ocean. Large areas were laid waste in countries in Australia's region: Indonesia, Sri Lanka, India, Thailand and the Maldives. Almost 230 000 people lost their lives. The Boxing Day tsunami has been ranked as the second deadliest ever recorded.

As Australia's prime minister, John Howard quickly expressed national sympathy over the disaster and promised aid. But nothing was heard from Mark Latham. Senator Chris Evans, who was acting leader of the Opposition in the absence of Latham and Jenny Macklin (also on holiday), made a statement on the Opposition's behalf. Predictably all the media speculation about, and criticism of, Mark Latham started up again. Where was he? Was he ill? Would he be able to continue as ALP leader?

Julia Gillard was on holiday in Vietnam with an old friend, Julie Ligeti. She was not expecting to hear from any of her colleagues, so although she had taken her mobile phone with her she was using it as an alarm clock. Before going to bed one evening in her Hanoi hotel room she set the alarm as usual, but forgot to turn her mobile off. A few hours later she was awakened by its ringing.

The caller was a desperate Chris Evans, who had been trying to contact Latham without success. Latham was not returning his calls. 'I've rung you to see whether or not he will return your call,' Evans said to Gillard, 'because I have to know what's going on.' He knew that Latham was ill – he had suffered a further bout of pancreatitis – and Evans was planning to make a statement about his leader's health.

Nobody would have been surprised that Evans called Gillard. He knew that she was one of the people Latham talked to, someone with whom he had never quarrelled, whose loyalty to him and the party he had never questioned. They were known to be friends – not bosom buddies, but two people who liked working together, had similar views about social policy, enjoyed each other's sense of humour and respected each other's sharpness of intellect.

Gillard called Latham on his mobile immediately, left a message and went back to bed. The next day she and Julie Ligeti visited the Ho Chi Minh mausoleum. They were outside in the garden, having just filed past the leader's body, when Gillard's mobile rang. It was Latham.

Julia Gillard says: 'Mark at that stage was holed up in his house in the west of Sydney, he was there by himself, and the media were camped out the front. He just sounded dreadful, sad, besieged, clearly unsure what to do next . . . concerned about his health for the future, concerned about [his two sons], trying to weigh all of this up, under incredible pressure . . .

'I said to him, "What can I do? What do you want me to do? Do you want me to come back?"

'He basically said, "Well, unless you have some magic that would clear the media off my doorstep there's not much point in racing back."

'By the time I got off the phone I was dreadfully worried about him on a personal basis. He just did sound so desperate and sad and obviously there by himself. I'd seen Mark in all sorts of circumstances, from absolutely elated as he was when the leadership stuff worked out the right way . . . I'd seen him from time to time angry and upset with the way people were conducting themselves, when people weren't being loyal enough to the Labor Party. But I'd never struck him sad like that.'

Senator Evans made a statement about Latham's illness, saying that his leader was thinking about what to do in terms of his own health. 'He meant that as a genuine effort to try and curb the media swell,' says Gillard, 'but of course the implied suggestion . . . that Mark was thinking about his future as Labor leader actually continued to provoke it. The media were after the story.'

As a result for the next five days Gillard was besieged by phone calls from colleagues: did she know what was happening, was Latham intending to resign, what would happen if he did, was she coming back to Canberra early? 'I took the view that Mark needed some space to make his own decisions and to announce them, and if I'd raced back to Australia that would have been interpreted by the media as me almost announcing his decision for him.'

She decided to continue her holiday in Vietnam. But by the time she and Julie Ligeti left Hanoi, Gillard was becoming the object of attention from journalists and press photographers. In Ho Chi Minh City, their next stop, Gillard learned that Mark Latham intended to resign.

Latham in fact had made up his mind as early as New Year's Day 2005. 'First, the good news,' he wrote in his diary for Saturday 1 January. 'I can retire from Labor politics, get out of that rotten, debilitating culture. And the bad news: another attack of pancreatitis . . . That will do me . . . My covenant with Janine and the boys will take me to a better life. My pancreas is struggling: a lifetime of uncertainty about these attacks. Work stress is a killer, so I need a private life, not a public one.

'There is no reason to stay. In fact, I've missed too many chances to get out: the first pancreatitis attack, then after the election. Third time lucky. And the timing is perfect: I'm on leave until 26 January, so I can choose the day that suits me.'

When she heard what Latham had decided, Gillard was not surprised. 'I knew after the election defeat it was going to be hard to hold Mark in the leadership. He would have arranged against him a lot of forces who would spend their time basically undermining him. But I'd mentally settled for supporting Mark for as long as he wanted to be there . . . I thought he deserved another go.'

Her own account of the late-night conversation with Latham on 30 November, during which they had discussed the possible leadership 'succession plan', corroborates Latham's diary account to some extent, although the emphasis is not the same. 'He wanted me to do a rough count with him about my numbers if he decided he didn't want to continue. I'd walked away thinking it was the tiredness talking. He was desperate to get some time with Janine and the boys and [I thought] after the summer break he'd be back and . . . back to business as usual, as much as business is ever as usual in the federal Labor party.' (It is worth noting that she said this after the publication of Latham's diaries.)

Mark Latham resigned as leader of the federal Labor Party, and as member for Gough Whitlam's old seat of Werriwa, on Tuesday 18 January 2005. He had been federal Labor leader for only thirteen months. He read a short prepared statement, thanking Labor, his supporters, his staff and his family, and saying he was proud of Labor's achievements in Opposition, including reforms to parliamentary superannuation.

It was a somewhat graceless exit, and a sad one, too, with a gaunt Latham standing in a local park alone. Journalist and political commentator Mungo MacCallum probably wrote Latham's best political epitaph: 'In other circumstances he could have developed into a formidable leader, even prime minister. As it is, he remains one of the great what-ifs.'

Who would follow as Labor leader? There was at least a small coterie who thought it should be Gillard. They argued that the ALP's blokey culture had allowed the party to become sclerotic: having a woman at the head of the party would represent a major culture shift and display an entirely fresh ALP to voters. Furthermore Gillard was one of Labor's most effective parliamentary performers. Although putting her forward as leader would be yet another experiment by the ALP – and the last one had demonstrably failed – Gillard was a far more stable character, a woman of steely determination and, just as importantly, self-discipline. Latham's larrikinism had proven attractive to the electorate at first, but it became alarming when people perceived his tendency to shoot from the lip. And in a Caucus largely made up of former staffers and union officials, Gillard had at least had a reasonably diverse life experience.

Gillard gave the prospect serious thought after Latham went. Very likely this was the point where she began for the first time to consider party leadership as a realistic goal for herself. But the numbers were against her, she felt: 'I thought, I will get no more than a third of the vote, I won't win,' she says. Although the circumstances were now entirely different, she was perhaps adopting the stance she had taken when she stood for the seat of Melbourne against Lindsay Tanner more than a decade before: by not firmly squashing all talk of her running for the leadership she was letting people know that she was a serious player.

In the same position, but from a different faction, was Kevin Rudd. However, there was only one person whom the party could see as a serious leadership aspirant. Kim Beazley announced that he would put his name forward at the special Caucus meeting to elect a new leader on 28 January. While Beazley led other Labor

MPs in the polls as preferred leader of the Opposition, the public still showed no enthusiasm for promoting him to prime minister. (Indeed there was a rather cruel joke that Beazley's job in the Howard government was leader of the Opposition.) But right then, to a shell-shocked party, Beazley at least represented continuity.

Gillard says now: 'As he rang around the Caucus colleagues, he would have been getting the same feedback as I was . . . people saw in him stability, people were hurt by the election defeats, stunned by what had happened to Latham. But they did want things to be different, and I think Kim carried that sense with him . . . And then we had to go up to Canberra to go through the ritualistic non-vote, as it turned out, for Kim to be leader . . . It was a pretty tough day for everybody really, but probably even more tough for Kevin and me. You wouldn't be human if you weren't [thinking]: What if?'

The newly elected Beazley wisely made no significant changes to Latham's frontbench, and the shadow Cabinet settled down to running their portfolios. And so life continued, more or less, through the rest of 2005 until another potentially damaging upheaval in September: the publication of *The Latham Diaries*.

Mark Latham's diaries are unique in Australian political history. Rarely do politicians burst into print so soon after retirement, and leaders of political parties never have. The usual form is to publish memoirs or diaries some time after the author is out of office, as Gough Whitlam, Bob Hawke, Graham Richardson, John Button, Jim McClelland and Tom Uren all did. (Admittedly Peter Costello's memoir appeared while he was still in Parliament, although he was a backbencher and no longer federal treasurer.) There is also something self-serving about political memoirs and diaries in general. While not exactly immune to this charge, Latham's diaries are extraordinary for their combination of candour, spite and penetrating analysis. They certainly show warts and all, and some are very large warts. And, not least, the diaries are well written and funny, which alone makes them standouts in the annals of Australian political memoir.

Predictably when they appeared, journalists lined up to condemn them and their author. 'Rancid' was one popular adjective applied to both. The press picked over every mean-spirited phrase, while the government chortled on the treasury benches. None of Latham's colleagues, it seemed, emerged unscathed. None of them, that is, except Julia Gillard, the woman whom Latham had anointed as a future leader.

A less level-headed and astute politician than Gillard might well have engaged in a panicky tirade of self-justification and condemnation of Latham. The way she managed to pick her way through the minefield of *The Latham Diaries* reveals some interesting things about her handling of potentially difficult political situations.

Just after the diaries were published Gillard spoke at a conference sponsored by the Equal Opportunity for Women in the Workplace Agency. She began with a declaration: 'I do not keep a diary. But as you may have noticed in the media, others do . . .

'Understandably the media is loving the feeding frenzy over Mark Latham's diaries . . . Each insult or nickname or piece of plotting or intrigue is great grist to the media's mill. But politics is – or should be – about so much more . . . Mark Latham, at his best, had insight about many of the big issues which confront us as a nation and a people. It saddens me greatly to see Mark's loss of faith in the power of politics to make change for the better. It saddens me even more to see Mark's loss of faith in the Labor Party. It saddens me and I do not share it . . .

'I have struggled overnight and from early this morning to put into words my reaction to Mark's diaries and what it means for Federal Labor. I suspect the truths in the book will be ignored because the focus will be on the spleen, not the substance. I think this is a great pity. I also think it is a great pity that the diaries have diverted us, even for a few days, from our true task of holding this extreme and arrogant government to account . . .'

This refusal to engage with the personal and comment on Latham's view of his colleagues was something Gillard steadfastly maintained. Far more useful, she thought, to look at the bigger picture. It was also, of course, not in her interest to be perceived as another opportunistic politician, going with the anti-Latham tide, even had she been inclined to do so. She had always been loyal to Mark Latham, and she continued to be.

Gillard had to justify her position more thoroughly in a long interview with Monica Attard on ABC Local Radio's *Sunday Profile*. Its tenor could be gauged by Attard's introduction: 'Mark Latham's pin-up girl Julia Gillard on that kiss of death [Latham's approval of her], the Latham diaries and what's wrong with the ALP.'

Asked why she was still loyal to Mark Latham, Gillard diverted the question neatly: 'I don't agree with what Mark has done with these diaries and I've said that publicly . . . I'll always be a member of the Labor Party and something that damages the Labor Party is not something I'm prepared to support. So Mark and I diverge very sharply on the question of these diaries.' Pointing out that Latham's loss of faith was sad, she added: 'Mark's topped out on the highs and had the most crushing lows. To end up Leader of the Labor party . . . to have taken Labor from that position of early 2004 where we'd have to concede magic just fell from his fingertips and of course the crushing lows and to end up with a disease . . .'

Attard asked, 'So you can forgive him the excesses?'

Gillard was far too sharp to fall for that. 'No,' she said, 'I don't believe he has done the right things with these diaries . . .'

When Attard asked whether Latham's endorsement of Gillard had made life more awkward within the party, Gillard said it was five minutes of discomfort and then it would pass.

'You don't think you're forever going to be seen as a Latham ally?'

'I'm going to forever have the history that I've had. You know I was one of Mark's key supporters. I supported him for election to the leadership, I went out of my way to discuss supporting him with my other colleagues . . . that's a matter of history. I don't walk away from it, I don't try and rewrite it. I don't try and respin it. I did that, I believed I was doing the right thing,' Gillard replied.

And the press gallery and the voters, she believed, would move on.

By refusing to indulge in any personal criticism of her former leader, Gillard did a great deal to defuse the problem of *The Latham Diaries*. Not everybody was impressed. *Bulletin* columnist Laurie Oakes criticised her for not supporting her colleagues whom Latham had attacked and quoted anti-Gillard party sources who regarded her continued defence of Latham's leadership as treachery.

Mark Latham probably didn't do Julia Gillard any favours by describing her as a future leader. Whether she will be is a question that has dogged her in the media ever since.

18

The national health

Julia Gillard and her colleagues in the federal parliamentary ALP faced the years to be got through in Howard's fourth term of office with less than total enthusiasm. Losing the election so comprehensively had been bad enough, with a huge amount of work to be done in order to claw back support across the country, but they had also to come to terms with the fact that, for the first time in almost twenty-five years, the same political party had control in both houses of Parliament. This, said some bitter Labor insiders, was Mark Latham's parting gift to his party.

Sure enough Howard was soon flexing his Senate muscle, and one of the first things he did was break a promise he had made law, in the area of health policy.

'The Howard Government ministers are the truest of true believers in a Medicare system,' Tony Abbott was still declaring several months after the election, to predictable mockery from Gillard. It is fair to say that the subject of Medicare and health insurance gave Gillard most of the ammunition she deployed during her three-year running battle with Abbott. One particularly fertile field for scorn was the so-called Medicare safety net, which the Coalition had put in place before the election and which refunded 80 per cent of all out-of-pocket expenses above $300 for low-income families, and above $700 for other Australians. Abbott had declared at the time that the government would maintain those thresholds if re-elected.

Gillard and Labor's policy was to abolish the safety net altogether, as a fundamentally flawed policy that advantaged the well-off at the expense of those who were poorer. There was evidence that people in the predominantly Indigenous electorate of Lingiari in the Northern Territory, for instance, had benefited least, while those in Bradfield on Sydney's affluent North Shore had done best. The safety net, said Gillard, was nothing but a political stunt. She declared that it had nothing to do with Medicare, would lead to the inflation of doctors' fees and would spell the end of Medicare as a universal system. While Abbott ignored this criticism in Parliament, he gave one of those rock-solid guarantees that both Medicare and the threshold levels would remain the same.

They didn't. Within six months of the Coalition's election victory, Abbott was forced to announce that the safety net had been too expensive, and that thresholds must rise. The new figures were $500 per annum for pensioners, health care cardholders and families, and $1000 for other Australians. Gillard and the ALP went on the attack on two fronts, somewhat confusingly: the government had broken another promise, and Abbott should resign for making worse a policy that it should not have adopted in the first place. The electorate regarded the whole issue with cynicism, Abbott stayed in his job, and no poll results rose or fell.

When it was hinted in April 2006 that Medibank Private might be sold off, Gillard hailed this as further proof that the government was really determined to demolish Medicare altogether. 'If Howard wins the next election Medibank Private will be sold,' she told ABC-TV's Tony Jones. 'A Labor government would not buy it back. Once an asset is sold it's sold, that's the depressing news. It will be bad news for premiums and for the structure of what is essentially a not-for-profit sector.' She might well have been hoping that the government would continue with its plans, especially as the electorate was dead against the sale, but the Coalition backed off after realising it would be an unwise move when the government was about to float its holding in Telstra.

At about the same time, Tony Abbott put up the idea that public hospitals could be managed by private organisations, including for-profit organisations. This, he said, was already happening with some hospitals in some states, notwithstanding that they were run by Labor governments. Gillard was having none of that: 'The free public hospital is a great Australian institution. What's public about a hospital that is managed for profit, and who is generating this profit? Patients? Insurers? We'll have a for sale sign on our public hospitals as well.' She added: 'I don't have any difficulty with not for profit managers. Where I come from, Werribee Mercy Hospital is a public hospital run by the Sisters of Mercy.'

Gillard watched while the government fudged, played with retaining Medicare, blamed the problems of the public hospitals on the states. She rarely lost an opportunity to draw a distinction between Abbott's summation of the health portfolio as the allocation of resources and her own and Labor's principled policies.

Occasionally Gillard was able to dart in, land a blow on Abbott and dart away again. (Cartoonists could have made more of this as an image – they tended to show Gillard and Abbott facing each other with scalpels poised over a supine body marked 'Health System' or something similar.) Abbott retaliated, usually accusing Labor of being opposed to private health insurance, but there was little evidence that this did Labor much damage. Gillard was well aware that Abbott was no more the primary driver of the government's health policies and positions than he had been in the previous term: that remained John Howard, who was far too cagey to get into a real fight over Medicare when the polls consistently showed that Labor was the party most trusted on health issues.

The controversy over mifepristone or RU 486, the so-called abortion pill, shows another facet of Gillard's handling of the shadow health portfolio. This drug had been restricted by the Coalition government in 1996 in an amendment to the Therapeutic Goods Act. It could only be imported with the specific approval of the federal health minister. This had come about as the result of a Coalition deal to secure the vote of Senator Brian Harradine, who opposed the view that a woman should have the choice to continue or to terminate a pregnancy, and who held the balance of power in the Senate at the time.

Liberal MP Sharman Stone urged the government to get rid of the virtual ban, saying that women in her country Victorian electorate found difficulty in arranging abortions. Her Liberal colleague Mal Washer, a general practitioner, supported her, pointing out that RU 486 was allowed in most European countries, as well as Britain, New Zealand and the USA, and that US research had shown that women preferred it to the surgical termination of pregnancy. The cause was taken up by women on all sides of the House:

if surgical termination was considered acceptable, why not medical termination?

Gillard supported overturning the amendment, but she still had to take account of the fact that in 1996 the ALP had voted in favour of it. She said that while Labor had supported a system requiring ministerial approval to import RU 486 nine years before, it had not realised that this would turn out to mean a ban on the drug. The situation had changed since 1996, she added, and the government should commission some independent medical experts to review the new information. Gillard felt she had to be cautious on such an emotive subject, but in this instance she was actually more conservative than her Coalition women colleagues. However, she could not resist having a go at Tony Abbott: 'A minister's personal opinions should not influence policy decisions on this matter. The current Minister for Health has decided views and we have always said his personal opinions should not be what guides policy here, and we maintain that.'

A Bill overturning the restriction on RU 486 was introduced to the House of Representatives on 16 February 2006 by Fiona Nash, a member of the National Party. Tony Abbott strongly opposed it, not just because he was against it on religious grounds, but because it very pointedly removed him as the minister responsible for making the decision to import the drug. John Howard also opposed the Bill, but was astute enough to see that a conscience vote would help defuse a difficult and emotional issue. In fact frontbenchers on both sides of politics, including Gillard, could see the advantage of letting an issue like this be driven by numbers and by the backbench. The Bill was passed overwhelmingly by MPs on all sides of politics. Julia Gillard, Kim Beazley and Kevin Rudd voted for it.

At the same time as RU 486 was being debated, another emotive health issue was coming to the fore, one with even wider ramifications. This was the question of stem cell research. In 2002 legislation had been passed allowing stem cells to be extracted for research from embryos left over from IVF programs – although the creation of human embryos for this purpose was banned – and had provided government funding to extend such research. The legislation allowed for a review to see how it was functioning, and in December 2005 a panel of experts in law, ethics and science, chaired by former Federal Court judge John Lockhart, presented its report to Parliament.

The Lockhart report was tabled in February 2006. It basically recommended the continued use of embryonic stem cells for research under the existing guidelines, without additional legislative restrictions. But it also recommended that the creation of embryos, using eggs and sperm or genetic material from more than two people, be permitted provided it was all under strictly controlled conditions and for medical research alone. This raised the moral issue that under the right conditions such embryos could develop into human beings. Accordingly the Lockhart report recommended that embryos should not be allowed to develop for more than fourteen days.

Any discussion about the ethics of human reproduction for any purpose always runs up against the definition of the word 'cloning'. In science this applies to the creation, from a single cell, of genetically identical cells that will never become complete humans or animals. But the word can also mean the genetic duplication of a complete living being from a single parent cell. The distinction is sometimes not made by people who, for religious or ethical reasons, are against any interference with 'normal' reproductive processes. One of those who opposed the adoption of the Lockhart report most strongly was Tony Abbott, who told the National Press Club that 'so-called therapeutic cloning is basically translating Dolly the sheep type situations to human beings'. (Dolly was the first mammal to be cloned from an adult cell, proving that a cell taken from a body part could recreate a whole individual. As the donor cell was from a mammary gland, Dolly was named after the lavishly endowed country-and-western singer Dolly Parton.)

Abbott's objections were echoed by many others on both sides of Parliament, and there were equally passionate supporters. John Howard, who was against the recommendations, floundered on the issue and clearly did not want to touch it, but his government was under pressure right across the parliamentary spectrum. At one point the government suggested commissioning a new report, which caused Gillard to ask why this was necessary when the Lockhart review had already released its findings. She added that the government was normally very good at making sure it was only given the advice it wanted.

Like discussion of the RU 486 issue, debate about stem cell research was driven largely by backbenchers from both sides of politics. At times it generated more heat than light, and threatened to combust. The potential for the treatment of genetic disease was seen as the most powerful argument in favour. Liberal senator Kay Patterson brought forward a private member's Bill and Howard surprised many when he agreed to a conscience vote. Late in November 2006 the Prohibition of Human Cloning for Reproduction and the Regulation of Human Embryo Research Amendment Act of 2006 passed narrowly in the Senate (34–32) and more convincingly in the House (82–62). John Howard, Tony Abbott and Kevin Rudd voted against it.

Julia Gillard, like other supporters of the legislation, endorsed the Act on the grounds that it was practical. As she observed to ABC Radio, 'We don't know whether, if we could fast forward the clock fifty years, that scientific progress will have come through embryonic stem cells or adult stem cells. We don't know that now, and we can't know that now, and the only way we will ever know is to allow both sorts of research to proceed.' She said she had considered the fundamental ethical issue – 'whether it was right to create an entity with a theoretical capacity to become human for research purposes' – and was satisfied that under the legislation it was prohibited, with the embryo not permitted to grow beyond fourteen days.

The RU 486 and stem cell issues demonstrated some intriguing differences and similarities between Tony Abbott and Julia Gillard. There was the obvious contrast in their religious orientation – conservative Catholic versus a woman who has declared she doesn't think she has a religious bone in her body – and what that meant in terms of the conscience votes. Yet their parliamentary styles were eerily similar. Each was vociferous and knew how to use Parliament as theatre. They were well-matched antagonists in many ways, both at ease with complex issues, each quick to score points off the other. Much was made of their political ambition. According to Michelle Grattan, the *Age*'s political editor, Abbott desperately wanted to be deputy when Peter Costello became leader and Gillard was being talked up as a future deputy in the ALP, with Jenny Macklin said to be feeling pressure from her colleague.

In the conscience debates, however, an interesting difference emerged. Abbott's arguments against RU 486 and stem cell research were often quite emotional and doctrinaire; Gillard's were measured and careful, always treating the issues as ethical questions for individuals to explore and never seeking emotional hegemony on the grounds of gender. As has been observed, the frontbench was not driving either debate, and Gillard seems to have been willing to let her women colleagues get on with it.

During the fourth term of the Howard government, the friction between Gillard and Abbott was one of the more entertaining political spectator sports. They were usually sharply critical of each other when asked about their personal relationship. On ABC-TV's *Australian Story*, for instance, Gillard said playfully: 'Hello. Abbott's out there for a doorstop where he'll be complaining that everyone's being mean to him because he's Catholic . . . I'm going to walk out and just say, "Tony, this isn't about you." Try and get him off talking about himself.' She added: '[I]n private, we've never had a cross word. At one level I think he's a, you know, a sort of likeable knockabout Australian character. But he's a deeply eccentric human being . . . I think I'm a much more normal person than Tony Abbott.'

Abbott's view was: 'On those rare occasions when she lets her hair down she can be a charming companion. I've certainly enjoyed her company a couple of times in a social context.' But the competitiveness between them was never far below the surface.

Their mutual antagonism, friendly or not, made for interesting TV viewing for most of 2007, from the beginning of the undeclared election campaign in January until a couple of weeks before the ballot. Abbott and Gillard were on Channel Nine's early morning *Today* program every Friday during that period and spent the time sparring and trading friendly insults, interspersed with the occasional foray into policy discussion, while the program's host,

Karl Stefanovic, and a series of female co-hosts chuckled and threw in easy questions. These sessions – some of which can still be seen on YouTube – are notable for the variations in Gillard's hairstyles over the months and the good humour of both participants. Most obvious, however, is Tony Abbott's smile, the panic-stricken rictus of a male who thinks he is being got at by a woman but doesn't quite know how to counter it. Gillard is totally at ease, giving an impressive display of flirting as a martial art.

Possibly their sharpest war of words came towards the end of the 2007 federal election campaign, when point-scoring had some real weight. In early October Abbott attacked Gillard for being obsessed with politics and said that voters wanted 'a bit more humanity' from their political leaders. 'The thing about Ms Gillard is that she is very bright, just uber-professional and a formidable debater,' he was quoted as saying. 'But it would be a lot easier for her to realise her ambition [presumably to rise to the top in politics] if there was evidence of a broader lifetime experience . . . She's somebody who has lived, breathed, ate and drunk politics for the whole of her adult life. The average person would look askance at such a political animal . . . She has the ability and cunning to be leader. I am not sure she has the votes.'

Gillard returned fire: 'Could Tony Abbott have been at the same stage of his political career if he'd been the mother of three children rather than the father of them?' she said. 'The political history of this country has not been that we've had prime minister Janette Howard with non-working John.' It was a sharper, more succinct, and less patronising retort than Abbott's comments.

19

An extra layer of armour

Among the more useful bequests of the ancient Greeks to the western world is the concept of hubris. A modern definition is 'overweening pride or arrogance', which is fine as far as it goes, but it misses an element in the original use of the word: the idea that the person affected by hubris (always a male – this was ancient Greece after all) becomes so vainglorious and lacking in humility as a result of success that he challenges the gods. They waste no time in calling on Nemesis, the goddess of retribution, who always causes the mortal's downfall. The classic definition may have fallen out of use now that relatively few people are familiar with the Greek tragedies, but the psychology is perceptive and accurate. As a description of a successful leader's tendency to overreach, to push that little bit too far with fatal results, hubris is difficult to beat.

During 2005 and 2006 the focus in federal politics was strongly on the industrial relations policy espoused by John Howard's Coalition government. Howard did not want to waste his Senate majority, as he felt the Fraser government had done. He wanted to use his numbers to forge a single national industrial relations system, instead of the existing structure involving both federal and state laws; to override the states and rely on the federal constitutional power to legislate for industrial relations.

By nature and ideological bent Howard was deeply suspicious of the role of unions in bargaining on behalf of workers, favouring closer and more direct relationships between employers and employees. He wanted the power to bargain about wages and conditions to be taken from unions and the Australian Industrial Relations Commission and given to employers, with the open market as the deciding factor.

In 1996, when John Howard first came to office, he had sought to modify the Industrial Relations Reform Act brought in by the Keating government in 1993. Keating's Act had recognised that the 1983 Accord had failed to address the fundamental problem of centralised wage fixing, leaving the Australian economy vulnerable in an increasingly global market in which high levels of productivity and competitive advantage were the keys to survival and growth. Keating's Act aimed to increase the role of enterprise bargaining, provided that certain minimum employment standards, established in awards, were met; to restructure the arrangements for consultation between government, unions and business enterprises; and to encourage the growth of industry unions. It did enshrine the concept of fairness to balance competitiveness, and it included a 'no-disadvantage' rule so that people on an award would not be disadvantaged by conditions agreed to in enterprise bargaining.

At the time, the 1993 Act represented the most far-reaching change to industrial legislation since Federation. Howard's Workplace Relations Act of 1996 extended enterprise bargaining to favour the individual over the collective, and introduced Australian Workplace Agreements (although these were not as important then as they later became). The status of unions was reduced: instead of being parties to an award, they were agents of their membership. And then, in his fourth term, with the Senate under control, Howard set out to complete the total deregulation of the labour market.

The Workplace Relations Amendment (Work Choices) Act greatly diminished the Australian Industrial Relations Commission. (This was something Howard had wanted to do since his stint as treasurer under the Fraser government, when Fraser's request to impose a wage freeze had been rebuffed by the Australian Conciliation and Arbitration Commission at a time of difficulty with inflation.) A new body, the Australian Fair Pay Commission, was established to set minimum wages for juniors, apprentices, piece workers, casual workers and people with disabilities. The Australian Fair Pay and Conditions Standards, established by the new Act, set minimum conditions for types of leave, hours of work, and wages. The Act also required secret ballots for industrial action still protected by the AIRC and gave the minister wide powers to suspend or terminate a bargaining period.

Australian Workplace Agreements between an employer and an employee now became a central feature of the industrial relations landscape, reflecting Howard's ideology that individuals could most effectively bargain for themselves if left alone by government and regulations. A set of complex regulations was attached to the Act to ensure that the individual was free to bargain as long as he or she did not do so collectively, and the no-disadvantage clause disappeared.

The new Act realised Howard's aim of making economic considerations paramount over ethical issues of fairness in the workplace, the cornerstone of industrial relations almost since Federation. (When this became the basis for the churches' criticism of Work-Choices Howard was irritated, saying he did not see how a degree in theology gave anyone the qualifications to comment on such a complex matter.)

The Work Choices Act came into effect in March 2006, with Labor and the minor parties powerless to stop or even modify its provisions. The union movement, whose direct influence had gradually diminished with the transformation of the labour market, knew it was in for the fight of its life. The ACTU, which had been running advertisements against Howard's industrial relations policy since the middle of 2005, decided to work out its own strategy to combat the new law independent of the ALP, since the party still needed to decide how to deal with AWAs. The Opposition debated whether to abolish AWAs altogether or to modify them by applying a new no-disadvantage test, but in the end decided on the former, partly because the unions were so implacably against AWAs. Gillard was not directly concerned in these negotiations, but obviously her union contacts and the centrality of industrial relations to Labor Party policy made her watch developments with some anxiety.

As for the public, Australians might have deserted the union movement as the nature of the workplace changed, but the industrial relations system with its wage determinations and awards was an institution they knew, they had grown up with and whose language they were used to. John Howard had given no indication before the election of his intention to radically alter it, and they found the new set of regulations complex and difficult to understand. The Act came in at 687 pages, plus another 565 of explanatory memoranda. WorkChoices was widely regarded as nasty, brutish and long.

Howard's treatment of the Kyoto Protocol to reduce greenhouse gas emissions also enraged significant sections of the electorate. Originally he had managed to finesse Australia's way through it and avoid any constraints on the domestic economy by negotiating an effective 8 per cent increase in emissions. His government had signed the Protocol in 1998 but would not ratify it, on the grounds that the USA and developing economies had not agreed to reduce greenhouse gas emissions and it would therefore be useless as well as costly for Australia to do so. It was a tricky problem, admittedly, and the coalmining interests that the Howard government bowed to represented one of Australia's most important exports. However, it allowed the ALP to present the Coalition as head-in-the-sand climate-change deniers at a time when much of the population had begun to register the threat of global warming.

Uncharacteristically Howard overrode the electorate's wishes on both industrial relations and environmental issues because his Senate majority allowed him to do so. He had warned his government members against hubris when they discovered they could do more or less as they liked, yet here he was, succumbing to it himself. As far as the depressed Opposition could see, though, Nemesis was a long way away.

Howard dominated the political scene without check or hindrance, and there seemed little, if anything, federal Labor could do about it. Certainly during the first period of Howard's fourth term it made no headway in Parliament.

Angry and frustrated Labor parliamentarians, not for the first time, turned inwards and began squabbling among themselves. The problems had begun with Beazley's shadow Cabinet reshuffle in June 2005. The most prominent members of Beazley's inner circle, whom Latham had called the Roosters, were given three of the most important portfolios. Stephen Conroy became minister for communications, Stephen Smith scored industrial relations and Wayne Swan was shadow treasurer. Lindsay Tanner came back onto the frontbench as shadow minister for finance, and Laurie Ferguson, shadow minister for immigration, was demoted in favour of the Right's Tony Burke. Perhaps Beazley was still trying to heal the Latham wounds but, according to some sources, his decisions irritated and angered a section of the Labor backbenchers, who argued that he had essentially kept the same team instead of bringing in new blood and sending poor performers to the backbench where they belonged.

For Gillard the worst decision Beazley made in the Cabinet reshuffle was to demote Simon Crean from trade to regional development. 'I was very sad to see Simon demoted in the reshuffle . . . I thought that was ill conceived of Kim and said so,' she says. It was well known that Beazley and Crean had never been friends, but Beazley's action looked like an act of spite because Crean had backed Latham.

Discontent with Kim Beazley's leadership grew. There was, ALP people thought, plenty of room for the Leader of the Opposition to hold the government to account. The Coalition had made major errors and miscalculations with WorkChoices and climate change policy, and then there were the revelations, subject to a public inquiry throughout 2006, that the Australian Wheat Board had paid bribes to Iraqi dictator Saddam Hussein to give preference to

Australian wheat. Beazley had a certain paternal forcefulness but somehow what he said did not make much impression on the voting public. The more he spoke – and he was known for his tendency to long-windedness – the more they stopped listening to him. People were used to thinking of him as a pleasant, amiable bloke, but right then what was needed was a killer, and killer instinct just hadn't been built into Beazley.

Indeed, as Julia Gillard has pointed out, Kim Beazley had needed to show three different styles of leadership during the times he had been leader of the Opposition. In 1996, when the ALP endured a bad defeat after thirteen years in government, he had needed to restore a sense of cohesion in a shattered party. In 1998, when the party almost won the federal election, his role had been to channel a renewed sense of purpose and possibility. But from about 2001, when the party's dissensions and rifts – accompanied by all the vitriol and name-calling that the press so enjoyed – were held up to scrutiny, and a gloomy conviction grew that the Howard government would get away with whatever it wanted, a firm leader was needed to guide an unsure, jumpy party. Expecting one person to take on all these roles was a big ask.

Beazley's hands-off view of the party's factional culture, based on his respect for all things to do with the ALP, was also not especially helpful. And so he was unprepared when in February and March 2006 a forest fire broke out in Victoria over preselections. Victorian factions had been notably unstable for years. With Labor in Opposition federally, discipline broke down and rancour resulted. There were disputes in six electorates over preselection ballots.

The most high-profile of these concerned Simon Crean's seat of

Hotham. The national secretary of Crean's own union agreed to dump him in a battle against Martin Pakula, the state secretary of the National Union of Workers. The feelings of many in the ALP, including Gillard, were voiced by Greg Combet, who said, 'Maybe I'm starting to get a bit old fashioned or something but I just think that when you've got someone like Simon Crean, given he has been ACTU President, leader of his union, Leader of the Labor Party, you know, been a minister in a Labor government, he does deserve to be given the respect and dignity of deciding when he's going to pull out himself, I think.'

Crean blamed both Beazley and the Victorian Right powerbroker Stephen Conroy, a close Beazley adviser, for not intervening on his behalf. Crean was especially angry that Beazley, who had expressed support for him in private, had failed to step in. When Crean had originally pledged ritual loyalty to Beazley he had added that the Leader of the Opposition needed to smash the damaging factional culture at the heart of the party. Beazley had not responded to Crean's challenge.

Gillard's view, expressed in March, was that: 'There are things . . . where clearly I've disagreed with [Kim Beazley] and I think he's made errors in terms of [not] being as inclusive as I would have liked [him] to have been. For me the standout there is, you know, the attitude to Simon Crean . . . I certainly think Kim not offering Simon full support in his preselection battle has not been the right judgment call. Not offering that kind of support to Simon risks opening a whole lot of wounds in the federal parliamentary Labor Party and it would be better for all of us, particularly better for Kim, if those wounds weren't reopened . . .'

It was this preselection dispute that called down the wrath of the media, not upon Beazley or Crean, but on the head of one of the latter's most loyal supporters.

Over the previous year Julia Gillard had become a focus of media attention, with newspaper and magazine profiles as well as an increased number of political interviews on TV and radio. In her early days as an MP she had been an earnest and awkward media performer who kept her sense of humour resolutely hidden. But as her visibility and influence within the Labor Party increased so did her public confidence. By this stage she was familiar with media requirements for a brief and incisive comment. Journalists liked her because she thought and spoke clearly, was down to earth and occasionally witty.

A young and personable woman politician, especially if she is highly intelligent and has a sense of humour, is always a candidate for the role of Media Golden Girl. It had happened to Susan Ryan, Carmen Lawrence, Natasha Stott Despoja and Cheryl Kernot, and now it was Gillard's turn. In her case, however, the focus was slightly different, largely because of one photograph, published in the *Sun-Herald* in January 2005. True to the Australian media's love of picturing powerful and influential women in domestic settings, this had shown her sitting at the table in the stark kitchen of her Altona house – with an empty blue fruit bowl much in evidence.

The fuss had been extraordinary. Where were all the little personal kitchen items that made a house a home? How could Julia Gillard live in such a bare, spotless house? (Awful to think of the reaction had the place been messy.) How could this flame-haired leadership aspirant without husband or children possibly relate to the average Australian? Clearly she was not a natural woman . . . And so on.

Gillard had handled it all. On ABC-TV's *Insiders* program on 8 May she had said: 'This has been the most remarked upon lack of clutter ever, and I did sort of busily run around getting rid of dirty coffee cups and stuff before the photographer went in there, which obviously I shouldn't have done. I should have left it ostentatiously around so then people would have said, "Look at that, she can make coffee" . . . No fruit. I think that was the principal flaw. No fruit. I now always have rotting bananas in the bowl just in case.'

It was undoubtedly because of that fruit bowl and all it signified that the producers of ABC-TV's *Australian Story* asked Gillard at the end of 2005 if they could do a profile of her. As producer Belinda Hawkins later explained: 'We'd long been intrigued by the way in which female politicians in Australia seem to get eaten alive once they're regarded as successful . . . The plan was to follow Julia over a period of time during which we would meet her family and explore her Welsh migrant background as well as some of the issues which seemed to dog her, like loyally backing former Labor leaders Simon Crean and Mark Latham, like being single and childless.'

While the program as it evolved in the months before it aired had appealing footage of Gillard's daily life – visiting her parents at Christmas, working in her office, giggling with her assistant while Tony Abbott pontificated at a Parliament House doorstop, chatting with Kim Beazley – Hawkins was worried that it lacked a narrative spine, an event that tied things together, that would create tension and reveal something more. And then Simon Crean's by-election problems erupted. Gillard has since said: 'I had to make a judgment whether to let [the program] wash through or . . . use it to say, "There should be a change here, there are things we should change like the selection of the ministry and the role of factions."' This comment has been seen as disingenuous by some who do not like Gillard – along the lines that she *would* say that, to justify her own love of publicity. But it could also be said to demonstrate an intriguing feature of Gillard the politician: she will not be used by the media, she will use it to make the point she wants.

The *Australian Story* episode went to air the very night that Crean won the rank-and-file vote in Hotham and the contender pulled out of the race. Crean commented on air that Gillard had supported him in public, had said to him what Beazley had said to him only in private, and that he appreciated her courage and leadership in doing so.

Gillard, however, was seen to be by implication publicly criticising her leader. Her comment that 'I genuinely think Kim is trying' was interpreted by some as patronising and a put-down. Her view was obvious: he was not trying hard enough. He had promised a hard-hitting parliamentary attack on the Howard government over the Australian Wheat Board scandal, but it had not materialised. She also went out of her way to praise Kevin Rudd – who had been tagged as her rival for the leadership of the ALP since the days of Latham – for *his* strong handling of the AWB scandal.

The evening after *Australian Story* was broadcast Gillard spoke at the Sydney Institute. Her words were deliberately chosen and immediately taken up by the media. 'Before you can persuade Australians of your credentials to run the country, you have to show that you can run your political party, and to do that we must unshackle our party from the factions,' she said. 'It's time to stop mincing words and to acknowledge that factionalism in the Labor

Party is out of control and destructive. Indeed, we are no longer talking about factionalism. We are talking about fractionalism.'

Certain colleagues and sections of the media swiftly turned on her. Gillard was disconcerted. She hadn't been naïve enough to think that her criticisms of her party would go unnoticed, but she was taken aback by how much of a news event the combination of the ABC-TV program, the by-election challenge to Simon Crean and the Sydney Institute speech became. The reaction made the first two weeks of March 2006 difficult ones for her.

Some in the ALP, such as Carmen Lawrence, criticised her for disloyalty in the course of raising her own profile: 'There's nothing unreasonable about [raising one's own profile] but I think it's important that people who are on the frontbench particularly pull in behind the leader and they aren't making comments that are critical of him or undermining policy.' Lindsay Tanner was considerably briefer, calling Gillard's implied attack on Beazley 'unacceptable'.

Journalists, mostly (although not all) from the conservative press, were even quicker to pounce. Matt Price in the *Australian* thought Gillard had harmed Labor's chances of re-election. Christian Kerr from crikey.com, rarely a man to hold back, said: 'Gillard looked loved, capable and competent. She also appeared to be grossly disloyal. Or opportunistic at best.' And Gillard was caned by Laurie Oakes more than once. In his influential *Bulletin* column he wrote:

> Gillard obviously smells Beazley's vulnerability, and is going flat out to build name recognition. A colleague puts it more bluntly: 'Her strategy is to turn herself into the public's darling.' That may not be enough to make her a viable leadership candidate, but it could force the party to put her into the deputy leadership down the track. Hence

> her double whammy in Labor's horrible week – highlighting Beazley's shortcomings while displaying her own wares on ABC-TV's *Australian Story*, and then putting factionalism up in lights in a Sydney Institute address twenty-four hours later. The resentment generated inside the caucus is palpable.

The criticism was particularly rough in the Murdoch press. Matt Price in the *Australian* on 9 March wrote that 'the once-powerful Gillard' was widely disliked in Caucus, had sold out when she produced a 'hard-line post-*Tampa* immigration policy', was a glutton for publicity, and was now complaining that she had been sidelined under Beazley. In the same paper the following day Michael Costello, Beazley's former chief of staff, called Gillard 'the hypocrisy gold medal winner at the Commonwealth Games level' because she had criticised the factionalism that had benefited her own career, as had Simon Crean, the 'perpetual holder of Olympic gold'. Michael Costello said she had taken every possible opportunity to tear at Beazley, to destabilise him and to promote herself. 'Just like [Cheryl] Kernot did, she presents herself as an aggrieved party, nobly wanting to do not only what is good for the party but hindered by dark and sinister forces.' It is difficult not to see an element of payback here, in the service of Beazley.

Christopher Pearson, again in the *Australian,* wrote that it was hard to see what Gillard really believed, given that her immigration policy had been very similar to Howard's. He added that she didn't put in the hard yards, had a broad, grating voice, and what was more had bought a house in Altona overlooking a petrochemical plant and been the employee of an ambulance-chasing law firm. Janet Albrechtsen gave an impressive display of what could be called *ad feminam* criticism: 'Gillard is single and childless, has the Mark Latham albatross hanging round her neck and has been a strident critic of the US alliance. Add the scary robot voice and you have more than certain defeat at any foreseeable future election . . .'

There was more, much more, from the conservative press. Perhaps the vituperation needs to be set against the facts: firstly that Gillard's *Australian Story* garnered a viewing audience of just over a million, and secondly that early in March an Ipsos Mackay poll found that 32 per cent of viewers backed Gillard to lead the ALP, against only 25 per cent for Beazley. The punters liked her, were interested in her.

The vitriolic press reaction showed that in certain quarters Julia Gillard represented some kind of a threat; that some people felt she had to be cut down before her career advanced any further. The worry that her actions were damaging Labor's re-election chances deserved its own gold medal for hypocrisy, considering its conservative source. Apart from that, though, there was the language used. In dizzying succession, Gillard was portrayed as an ingratiating moppet ('the public's darling'), a slut 'displaying her own wares', and a man-destroying siren à la Kernot who was also the eternal martyr. It would be difficult to find a more comprehensive collection of feminine stereotypes in such a small space. As if this were not enough, Gillard was clearly not a 'true woman' because of her grating voice, her single and childless state, and her unladylike decision to live near a petrochemical plant. And this unnatural female had the gall to complain about problems in her political marriage!

The whole episode did bring up the question of Gillard's loyalty, however – a quality that has been seen both as her most admirable political feature and her greatest liability. Loyalty is one of those key ALP words, but in political terms it can be a complex issue. In the eyes of many colleagues Gillard had broken rank and shown disloyalty to her leader. But Gillard felt Beazley had been disloyal to Crean, who had been his steadfast deputy and supporter, and she owed more to Crean, her friend and patron, than she did to Beazley.

Publicly defending Crean – and her other chief supporter, Mark Latham, before him – had done her very little good within the party, even though she had been careful to express her dismay about Latham's anti-ALP actions. In the criticism she attracted, implicit was the judgement that she should have aired her views only within the party.

It was much easier to attack the high-flying critic than to address the intractable subject she criticised. Gillard's criticism of factionalism was, in fact, less trenchant than that of other ALP politicians, including John Faulkner – but they did not have her high profile, and Faulkner was widely considered the party's moral guardian. Gillard had long regarded factions as at best a necessary evil, and many of her statements show that she actively disliked them. (Michael Costello's view that she 'had criticised the factionalism that had benefited her own career' is certainly not borne out by the history of factional opposition to her.) She had evidently felt that now was the time to bring the issue out into the open, whatever the personal consequences.

Dealing with the reaction cannot have been pleasant. But to reach this level in her career, Gillard had already survived being beaten up by experts. On *Australian Story* she had commented that 'Maybe politics puts an extra layer of . . . armour on the outside because you know what it can be like.' Adverse attention was not really going to bother her. She would have known the old Arab proverb 'The dogs bark, but the caravan passes on'.

27 November 2007: the newly elected prime minister, Kevin Rudd, and his deputy, Julia Gillard, arrive in Canberra to start work after their election victory.

28 November 2008: after announcing the frontbench, Parliament House, Canberra.

Just before the new ministers are sworn in, Government House, Canberra, 3 December 2007. Front row: Julia Gillard and Wayne Swan. Second row: Stephen Smith, Joel Fitzgibbon, Nicola Roxon, Jenny Macklin and Lindsay Tanner.

John and Moira Gillard at home in Adelaide, with a portrait of their famous daughter in the background.

On 11 December 2007 Julia Gillard takes over as Australia's acting PM – the first woman to do so.

Arriving at Kirribilli House, with Tim Mathieson, to celebrate New Year 2008.

A tired but grimly pleased Julia Gillard leaves a doorstop at Parliament House, Canberra, following the passing of the Fair Work Bill through the Senate, 20 March 2009.

The Minister for Education at the coalface: Everton Park State School, Brisbane, May 2009.

20

Nothing for granted

The fact that Labor had been well ahead of the Coalition in the polls since early 2005 pleased the parliamentary party without causing its members to rejoice. They were glumly familiar with doing better than the government through most of the term, only to fall back as election time approached. But it was maddening to be consistently ahead of the government on the two-party-preferred vote and yet not on the other significant indicator: preferred prime minister. On that ranking Howard outpolled Kim Beazley with no trouble whatsoever. In the popular mind the problem was not the ALP but its leader.

On the other side of politics there was also muttering about changing leaders. In May 2007 the media carried a story about an alleged agreement in 2003 that Howard would hand over to his deputy, Peter Costello, some time before the 2007 election. Despite Labor's increasing tensions about Beazley, it was irresistible for it to switch focus to its opponents. On ABC-TV's *Lateline* with Maxine McKew, Julia Gillard had some fun at the expense not only of Howard and Costello but of Christopher Pyne, a Coalition parliamentary secretary, who was also on the program.

GILLARD Christopher has described the Prime Minister and the Treasurer as two grown men. Well . . . they've behaved this week like a mob of kids, and the debate seems to be: It's my turn. No it's not. Yes it is. No it's not . . . We all know that Christopher is desperate for a change of leadership, he'd be measuring up a ministerial office on the strength of it . . . The only thing [Costello] is saying is I've been a good boy. I've worked hard. It's my turn. Well, that's not a set of credentials good enough to try and lead the nation with.

PYNE We're not going to be taking any advice from Julia Gillard . . . The last time [she] had anything to do with changing the leadership of the Labor Party, she gave the Labor Party Mark Latham . . . [And when he was defeated] she didn't have the guts to go into the House and say one nice thing about him.

GILLARD Well, you know, cheap and silly as usual. Good diversion, good spin, but at the end of the day Christopher's got to face up to the fact that there is huge instability in the Liberal Party . . . and his champion, Treasurer Costello, has to work out whether he's got the bottle to challenge, whether he actually stands for something and he's going to lay out that vision, or whether he's going to be content to be the perpetual bridesmaid.

PYNE Well, I think Julia Gillard is the one who lacks the ticker. I mean she came back from Cambodia [actually Vietnam] . . . to run against Kim Beazley for Labor leader . . . She didn't have the bottle to follow through with her challenge against Kim Beazley.

I mean, she's been stalking Jenny Macklin for the deputy leadership of the Labor Party for some years . . .

GILLARD All very cute, Christopher. But we're talking about the prime ministership of the country.

There was a little more toing and froing before Gillard ended the round with a knockout blow:

GILLARD I think that what that means, Maxine, is even a key Costello supporter doesn't think he's got the ticker to go to the back bench and try a challenge: even a key Costello supporter knows in truth he's a very weak man.

Julia Gillard has the great debater's skills of cutting the ground away from her opponent and bringing the debate back to the point she wants to make. This exchange is also a good example of her ability to shrug off personal attacks, to not be distracted by them and – finally – to go in for the kill. There's a touch of the bully here. It's as if she has sized Pyne up and knows she can pick him off as if he were the weak kid in the playground. (All may be fair in political warfare, but it's not just Howard and Costello who are behaving like kids here.) Gillard shows the confidence of someone who had come to know the game and play it hard.

The idea that Costello might take over from Howard did not especially worry the Opposition. The big problem was its own leader. Discontent with Beazley's performance was spreading through the party, from the New South Wales Right party machine – a key source of his support – to levels of the union movement. The criticisms were constant and the same: he was not attacking the government on a broad enough front and not making sufficient political capital out of the ALP's strengths, including its climate change policy, opposition to WorkChoices and rejection of the Iraq war, despite opinion polls sending Labor the message that voters were unhappy about Coalition policies in these areas.

There are various accounts, with different emphases, about what happened next. But the basic facts are reasonably clear.

The ALP had two obvious contenders to replace Kim Beazley: Kevin Rudd and Julia Gillard. However, neither alone had the numbers to win against him, which Beazley knew. As he later said in an interview for Peter Hartcher's book *To the Bitter End*, he had estimated that Gillard, on the Left, had about 40 per cent of the Caucus vote, he had about the same, and Rudd – also mainly from the Right – had the remaining 20 per cent. 'While ever it was split like that I was secure,' he said. 'Because there was a ceiling on Julia's vote – she was not going much above 40 per cent. And whenever Kevin was eliminated [in a leadership ballot] his votes would have gone to me. So when the three of us were interested in the leadership, there was no chance I could be replaced.'

But what would happen if the two leadership aspirants combined forces?

It was a question that increasingly occupied the ALP's powerbrokers as 2006 progressed. Chief among these was the Left's Kim Carr.

Considering the difficult relationship that he and Gillard had had in the past, it seems surprising that he was now increasingly prepared to help her towards leadership of the party. The usual explanation for this is that Carr had come to recognise Gillard's talent and ability since she entered Parliament, but this is probably only part of the story. Gillard was the Left's most recognisable woman – Jenny Macklin, Beazley's deputy, had made very little impression on the voters – and was generally liked and respected in the electorate. She could command a solid bloc of votes in Caucus. And Carr and Gillard, having recognised the pointlessness of holding grudges now that they were both in Parliament, had established a workable professional connection. Moreover Carr, like Gillard, had been appalled by Beazley's hands-off approach to the Victorian preselection fights, and they were both frustrated by his performance. Carr told his political intimates that the future of the Labor movement under Howard's WorkChoices kept him awake at night. Nobody wanted a repeat of 1998, when the ALP had won the popular vote and lost the election. Success in 2007 depended on a solid swing in marginal seats.

Gillard's move against Beazley's leadership has been interpreted as part of her payback for Simon Crean's preselection treatment, but the truth is undoubtedly more complicated. With the ALP up against a government that was felt to be tired, increasingly venal and out of touch, it was absurd that Beazley was holding the party back. Beazley had been given three leadership opportunities to cut through, and he had failed. Gillard's political instincts told her it was time for a change, and her ambition told her she could help bring it about. Under these circumstances sentimentality about the party's leader ran a very poor third.

When Peter Hartcher later asked Gillard who had broached the idea to her of a joint leadership ticket, she replied: 'It's fair to say Kim Carr . . . you didn't have to be on the inside of Labor to work out that if the leadership came into issue that Kevin's name would be there, my name would be there, the question of the combination would be there, and we needed to deal with that . . . Kim was not pressing me to make a particular determination – it was just knowing that I needed to think it through and work it out. And so I did.' The questions she needed to consider, in her own mind, were: 'If Kim Beazley were to resign, what would you do? Would you put your name forward to contest as leader? Would you consider supporting someone else in that situation? Would you consider supporting Kevin in that situation?'

Gillard and Rudd were hardly natural allies – they belonged to different factions, for one thing – but Gillard strongly repudiates media reports that their relationship was ever frosty. They had been on the same parliamentary committees and knew each other reasonably well. Although they seemed to have little in common, she says they thought the same way about things, could always talk together. This is another way of saying that Rudd and Gillard are both highly intelligent, interested in sound processes and outcomes, and strategic thinkers. And both recognised that any rivalry they had felt was now no longer in anybody's interest.

Which one would be leader? From early 2006 powerbrokers on both sides of the ALP considered this question. 'There were people in the middle who would vote for either of us,' Julia Gillard has said. 'By late 2006 the question was how many people in the middle would move to vote for that change.' Members of the Right were much more inclined to vote for Kevin Rudd, who after all was in their faction, than to go for Gillard, who was not, and whom many of them did not even like. It became increasingly clear to Gillard that she did not have sufficient Caucus backing on her own to be leader. She could, however, carry her supporters across to Rudd.

Because the Right needed the bloc of votes that she would bring to the table, Rudd had to be 'sold' to the Left of the party. This was Kim Carr's job, as Gillard's numbers man. A crucial part of Carr's support base was the AMWU, the Australian Manufacturing Workers' Union, and he wanted to know Rudd's views about the future of the manufacturing sector in Australia. When Rudd showed that he was not a free-market purist, that he could see a role for government in the future of the manufacturing industry, Carr was satisfied. Presumably he could see a role not only for the manufacturing industry in a Rudd Labor government, but also for himself.

And so Gillard and Rudd agreed to run on a joint ticket, with Rudd as leader and herself as deputy. Peter Hartcher has praised Gillard for her political maturity in making this decision, and rightly so, but her unblinkered realism was also important. Even if she had succeeded in getting the numbers, Gillard knew that her leadership of the ALP was problematic. She would be the first woman leader of a major federal parliamentary party and she was from the Left, so Beazley supporters would be more likely to undermine her than they would someone else from the Right. A year before a federal election the last thing the ALP needed was to replace an ineffectual leader with one who was actively divisive. Rightly or wrongly the example of Mark Latham was ever before it. And if the ALP should lose the 2007 election with Julia Gillard as leader, she would almost certainly be headed for political oblivion. In any event, of course, the numbers simply did not stack up in Gillard's favour.

Beazley's approval ratings grew worse and worse. By the end of November he was down to 28 per cent. On Friday 1 December 2006 Rudd challenged him to a leadership ballot. Rather than resign, Beazley called for a spill of all leadership positions. It was arranged that the vote would take place on 4 December, and ALP members hit the phones.

An ALP leadership challenge is a great media spectator sport. Much was written about Rudd and Beazley being locked in a titanic political struggle, and there were the usual claims and counter-claims of support and betrayal, with both sides expressing confidence in winning.

When the vote was taken on the Monday morning it was decisive: 49 for Rudd; 39 for Beazley. Gillard's Left votes had combined with a large number from the New South Wales Right. But not everybody on the Left had voted for Rudd, largely because of their dislike for Gillard. Because Rudd had won, Jenny Macklin did not contest the position of deputy leader, so Gillard was elected unopposed.

Beazley conceded defeat with grace and dignity, the more impressively because he had just been informed that his brother had died. There is still a certain amount of ill-feeling among party loyalists who believe Kim Beazley was forced out. Martin Ferguson, formerly a Gillard ally and a strong party loyalist, was outraged by her move against the leader. Their relationship has never really resumed its former cordiality. And Beazley would not have been human if had he not been angry about it himself. In an echo of another Labor leader, Bill Hayden, who was rolled in favour of Bob Hawke in 1983 and famously said that a drover's dog could have won the election, Beazley has said that, given the way the Howard government was travelling, he could easily have been victorious in 2007.

From the moment the triumphant leadership team faced the media, it was clear that Julia Gillard was more than a deputy in the usual ALP sense. She had certainly not been foisted on the leader in a political deal: Rudd could not have ascended to the party leadership without her. Rudd and Gillard were partners from the beginning.

Now the new leaders had to make their mark, and they did not know how long they had before the next election. At first John Howard and his Coalition dismissed the ALP change of leadership, with its rejuvenated Opposition frontbench and stratospheric poll results for Rudd and Gillard: the example of Mark Latham was as obvious to them as it was to the ALP. But Howard had no intention of going to the polls while his opponents' ratings were decisively ahead, and so Rudd and Gillard gained time to get on with the job.

Gillard had handed over the health portfolio to Nicola Roxon and taken on employment, industrial relations and social inclusion. Given the widespread dislike of WorkChoices in the electorate, it was important to push Labor's alternative industrial relations policy. Some in the ALP thought that Rudd needed only to back Beazley's earlier commitment to tear up Australian Workplace Agreements and roll back WorkChoices, but Gillard did not believe that a protest vote, even one reinforced by the ACTU's impressive 'Your Rights at Work' campaign throughout Australia, would necessarily get Labor over the line.

She later said to journalist Christine Jackman: 'My political analysis was different and my national interest analysis was different too . . . The flashpoint was that the average Australian believes in employee rights. But they don't believe in vested interests and they don't believe in union power.' In other words, a union boss dictating employment conditions was just as bad as a corporate boss, and the electorate would not endorse either unions or big business dictating to the prime minister.

Labor's new IR policy, entitled 'Forward with Fairness' and largely drafted by Julia Gillard, was presented to the Labor national conference on 29 April. Briefly, Labor flagged several important changes to the existing Howard system: the abolition of AWAs in favour of systems of enterprise bargaining and common law contracts; the reinstatement of unfair dismissal rights for small-business employees; and minimum wages set not by Howard's government-appointed Fair Pay Commission but by arbitration. There was some grumbling about aspects of the policy – the unions thought there was not enough protection for lower-paid workers, for instance, and elements of the business community wanted to retain AWAs – but the party thought that dissatisfaction on both sides would probably not hurt its credibility in the eyes of the voters.

Labor was still sensitive to any suggestion from the Coalition that it was in thrall to the unions, and so senior Opposition members moved quickly against Dean Mighell, Victorian secretary of the Electrical Trades Union, late in May. Mighell had boasted about obtaining pay rises for workers by threatening strike action, and about getting millions of dollars through pattern bargaining (getting a rise from one employer and using this as a precedent to demand the same or a better deal from other employers). Kevin Rudd jumped on Mighell hard, demanding his resignation and saying ETU funds in support of the ALP would be returned.

Gillard, shadow treasurer Wayne Swan and ALP national secretary Tim Gartrell all joined in the chorus of condemnation. The story had to be killed as fast as possible, but the speed and thoroughness of the counterattack against Mighell showed that Rudd and his team were taking absolutely no chances.

The Coalition unleashed a series of personal attacks on the Opposition, beginning with a famous interview that Senator Bill Heffernan gave to the *Bulletin* of 1 May. In a wide-ranging spray, he said that Gillard was unfit for leadership because she was unmarried and childless. 'I mean, anyone who chooses to remain deliberately barren . . . they've got no idea what life's about,' he said. His comments caused outrage among women voters, and Heffernan was widely ridiculed. So intense and widespread was the feeling against what he had said that all Gillard had to do was make some rather mild remarks about women's right to choose. She had most of the electorate with her. John Howard quickly made Heffernan apologise.

The Coalition personally attacked Kevin Rudd, too. Some of his assertions about his childhood were disputed; and there was a story that his wife, Thérèse Rein, whose success and wealth had already made her the subject of sneering conservative-press comment, had underpaid staff working for her company. And then there was the story of Rudd's 2003 visit to Scores strip club in New York.

Gillard later recalled: 'Kevin said, "There's something we have to deal with in tomorrow's newspapers – it's a big problem for us." He sounded really grim . . . I thought it was some amazing catastrophe. Then when he said, "I was drunk in a bar in New York and it was a strip club", it was so exactly *not* what I thought he was going to say that I just burst out laughing. The whole thing was so absurd. Of all things and of all people!' Rudd took some time to regain his amour-propre after the episode, but Gillard recognised that it would not hurt his popularity. And so it proved.

As the year went on, nothing the Coalition did seemed to work. The Budget gave it a bit of respite from the dismal poll figures, but no bounce. Howard was a prisoner of his own intransigence. He would not ratify Kyoto; his slight softening of WorkChoices, with a 'fairness test' to protect workers on less than $75 000 per annum, did not alleviate public distrust; and the war in Iraq was a big negative – as was the Coalition's treatment of Indian doctor Mohamed Haneef, deported after being wrongly accused of aiding terrorists. So when the government intervened on behalf of Indigenous people in the Northern Territory, the perception within large sections of the electorate was that Howard was doing whatever he thought he could in order to win votes.

Julia Gillard says she felt no personal animosity towards John Howard, then or at any other time. She has described him as 'basically a decent bloke' who 'if he turned up as your neighbour I think you'd be pretty pleased'. She adds that, 'Of course, I don't feel the same way about his policies.'

Throughout the campaign she constantly used phrases that Labor polling had shown were effective against the Coalition: 'mean and tricky' and 'clever politician' to describe Howard, 'desperate' for the government and, most notoriously, 'Australian working families'. The last was used incessantly by Rudd and Swan as well as Gillard (and everybody else, it seemed), and it drove many voters almost to screaming point. 'Thou shalt stay on message' was a political commandment obeyed by Rudd and his team with fanatical diligence.

On 14 August Howard announced the election for 24 November. Labor was ready, with Rudd and Gillard campaigning together under the slogan 'New Leadership'.

All this time Gillard was working hard, apparently everywhere. The difference in her public style was noticeable. Less evident was the apparently relaxed and friendly Julia Gillard the media and electorate thought they were coming to know. Except in her weekly sparring sessions with Tony Abbott on Channel Nine's *Today*, and the occasional doorstop, she was tight, focused, concentrated on getting the message across to voters. Sometimes her delivery sounded flat, almost on automatic pilot. (A lot of the criticism of her voice stems from this period.) There were fewer off-the-cuff remarks and not as much spontaneous wit. Her job was to help beat the Howard government, and she pursued it with great intensity.

Probably because Rudd and Gillard were working so closely together, there was less difference in public style between them during the long 2007 election campaign than possibly at any other time in their association. If Rudd came across as the thoughtful, diligent and capable bureaucrat, Gillard matched him. Election campaigns are not usually played for laughs, especially by the side that perceives itself as the underdog, but there was a certain businesslike and humourless flavour to the whole ALP campaign.

Several books have already been written about the reasons why Howard's Coalition lost and Labor won the 2007 election. All agree that Rudd's strategy – making himself look like a non-threatening alternative to a prime minister who was not widely disliked, positioning Labor as the more fiscally responsible party (not difficult considering the extent of Coalition spending during 2007, although Labor promised only $13 million less), and presenting himself as calm, measured and intelligent – well and truly paid off. But Labor's campaign would have been much less successful without Howard's misjudgement of the public mood, his hubris and the complacency of his ministers.

Julia Gillard is very clear about the reasons for the Coalition's defeat. 'The two things people hated most were the AWAs and the loss of their unfair dismissal rights,' she says. 'Our polling showed that over and over again.'

On election night Gillard, sitting in the Canberra tally room with the Coalition's Senator Nick Minchin and ABC-TV's Kerry O'Brien, watched the figures come in with gratifying clarity. Labor won a uniform national swing of 5.4 per cent and gained twenty-three seats, giving the new Rudd government a majority of seven. It was the third-biggest swing against an incumbent government since 1949.

A huge group of Gillard fans were in the tally room – she had to ask the crowd for 'a bit of shush' at one point. And when it was clear that Labor had won, and that she, Julia Eileen Gillard, had made history at the age of forty-six by becoming Australia's first woman deputy prime minister, she beamed, clearly elated, but did not gush superlatives. She left that to some of her victorious colleagues, and she left the cheering and whooping to the huge crowd of Labor, and Gillard, supporters in the tally room. But she did reach across during a break in transmission to pat Nick Minchin's hand in a gesture that said 'never mind'. He took it graciously.

Very late, after it was all over, two thrilled teenage girls were in a car driving down Commonwealth Avenue when a chauffeur-driven car pulled up beside them at the lights. They saw one occupant, a woman sitting in the back.

The girls gasped. 'It's her!' They wound down their window, called out 'Julia!' and waved frantically. 'Congratulations!'

'Where are you from?' Gillard asked them.

'We've just been in the tally room,' they said. 'Where are you going? To a party?'

Gillard says she might have implied that she intended to follow

Kevin Rudd's advice to go home and have a cuppa, an Iced Vo-Vo and an early night. In fact she was headed to a victory party with her sister Alison, friends from Melbourne and members of her staff. The party involved quite a lot of champagne.

'It was a good night,' she says. 'A very good night.'

21

'An awesome responsibility but a terrific opportunity'

Julia Gillard's long political journey – or at least the first part of it – ended in the yellow drawing-room at Government House, Canberra, on 3 December 2007. Here, wearing a grey trouser suit, and in the presence of Kevin Rudd and his family, she faced Governor-General Michael Jeffery across a small mahogany table while an equerry read, 'Do you, Julia Eileen Gillard, being chosen and summoned by the Governor-General of the Commonwealth of Australia to be a member of the Federal Executive Council, solemnly and sincerely affirm and declare that you will when required advise the Governor-General, or the person for the time being administering the governing of the Commonwealth of Australia, to the best of your judgement and consistent with the good government of the Commonwealth of Australia, and that you will not disclose the confidential deliberations of the Council?'

Gillard's 'I do' was almost inaudible against the locust-like whirring of cameras wielded by a clutch of photographers backed into a corner of the room. She then shook hands with the Governor-General, who congratulated her on being named deputy prime minister and wished her success. The dark-suited Michael Jeffery, tall, white haired and distinguished looking, managed to combine a sense of occasion with warmth and sincerity.

Gillard had had more than a week since the election victory to think about her new positions, to absorb the fact that she was now deputy prime minister – the first woman in Australia's history to be so named – and minister for employment and workplace relations, minister for education and minister for social inclusion. It is probably true to say, however, that as with most huge changes in one's life she would take time to fully come to terms with her enormously increased responsibilities. She was, after all, in charge of an entirely new super-ministry, which in theory dealt with the lives of Australians from the time they started their education until the day they left the workplace.

She and Kevin Rudd had worked out this particular range of responsibilities for her precisely because they were so compatible: the three major portfolios could almost be seen as one machine, with different parts working in unison and slotting into each other. Gillard was also presiding over a huge composite department with more than 6000 people, including junior ministers, parliamentary secretaries and public servants of various grades. In terms of their scope, Gillard's new portfolios were the most wide-ranging and influential in the new Rudd government, excepting Treasury and the prime ministership itself. There could hardly be a clearer statement of Julia Gillard's perceived talent, as well as her predilection for putting up her hand for the toughest jobs.

Like her ALP colleagues, she had to abruptly change gear from shadow minister to senior minister and to come to terms with everything that implied. She already had considerable experience in handling the media; now she had to learn to manage a large staff and to see through Parliament the new programs and major legislation promised during the election campaign.

Behind her she had nine years of being a federal MP, as well as all she had learned as John Brumby's chief of staff. And her struggles to achieve preselection and her time in Opposition had given her a thorough understanding of human behaviour (often in its less attractive forms) and considerable skills in conciliation and persuasion. It remained to be seen what use she would make of these assets.

Julia Gillard and the rest of the Rudd government were very conscious of several facts: keeping election promises was an article of faith for the new government; its first term in office could last no longer than three years, perilously little time to put in place far-reaching changes and see results; and it did not control the Senate. For Gillard this last factor proved especially crucial.

On the day she was sworn in Gillard gave a speech to the Australian Industry Group. It was her first duty as deputy prime minister, and she described her new portfolios' responsibilities. 'It's an awesome responsibility but it's also a terrific opportunity,' she said, 'because it provides the chance to bring together some of the key elements of a new economic reform agenda for the nation . . . In today's world the areas covered by my portfolios – early childhood education and childcare, schooling, training, universities, social inclusion, employment participation and workplace cooperation – are all ultimately about the same thing: productivity.'

The principle that binds these portfolio areas is the concept of social inclusion. Gillard explained the idea to the AIG: 'After seventeen years of economic growth, too many individuals and communities remain caught in an intergenerational cycle of low educational attainment, high unemployment, poor health, high imprisonment rates and child abuse . . . [I]t's going to be my job to bring these people and these communities back within the economic and social mainstream. Simply put, productivity improvement can't be separated from the idea of fairness. Bringing those on the margins of the workforce into full participation in our economy will lift productivity and ease capacity constraints.'

Those excluded from Australian society, then, would be given skills and training to enable them to enter the workforce. There would be new ways of delivering government services, and the introduction of policies tailored to the needs of the most disadvantaged parents, children, neighbourhoods and suburbs, as well as to the needs of employers.

Although a new term in Australian political rhetoric, the idea of social inclusion has been around for some time. It is very familiar, for instance, to those who work with the disadvantaged in society. The phrase first came to prominence during the Labour government of Tony Blair, in a series of policies responding to the deficiencies and the growing costliness of the British welfare state. The Blair government realised it needed to look at social problems in their totality. In the case of poverty, these included unemployment, lack of skills, low incomes, poor health, family breakdown, crime and bad housing.

It is a holistic approach that has informed policy development in all Gillard's portfolios and the Rudd government in general. At its core is the idea that government should be flexible and involve cooperation across different agencies, departments and levels in order to 'join up' the delivery of government services strategically as well as practically. Gillard's social inclusion agenda, anticipated nine years before in her 'equality of opportunity' maiden speech to Parliament, is a good example of the Rudd government's Third Way position. The Rudd government, like similar Centre Left governments, has favoured growth, entrepreneurial activity, enterprise and wealth creation, but also greater social justice, with the government playing an important role in bringing that about. 'Our social inclusion policies . . . will be linked directly to the government's wider economic development and employment participation objectives,' Gillard said to the AIG.

For Rudd and Gillard, with their evident wish to break away from the factional politics that have often stifled the ALP, the attraction of Third Way policies is obvious. And it suits 'big picture' thinkers. As Gillard told the AIG: 'When Kevin Rudd said he wasn't interested in fighting the old battles between Left and Right but wanted a new direction for Australia, he meant it. That's what my approach will be in my new hard-to-announce-in-one-breath-but-easy-to-explain set of portfolios. I'm going to be ignoring the old battles between unions and employers, public and private schools, the trades and universities and welfare and work. Instead I'm going to be measuring policies against the all-important criteria of how effectively they increase national productivity.'

Industrial relations was the most immediate issue Gillard needed to deal with when the Rudd government first came to office because the issue of abolishing WorkChoices had been so central to the ALP's election campaign. During the campaign Gillard, like the trade unions and the ALP in general, had made effective capital out of the fact that the Howard government had had no mandate to introduce WorkChoices and that his softening 'fairness test' had first been costed for advertising effectiveness. After it lost, the Coalition conceded that AWAs were dead and that Labor had a mandate to introduce its own legislation.

Gillard believed that the answer to WorkChoices was not a return to the days of the Hawke–Keating Accord. 'I reckon the Accord was right when we had it. But . . . at some point that kind of solidarity becomes too strained, with people giving up too much,' she has said. 'I think the complex pressures of globalisation and trade [meant that] workplace change had to be tackled at a small enterprise level rather than through great wage movements.

'We had to work out how to base bargaining in smaller units, and I think we got some things right and some things wrong, and then Howard wanted to atomise it to individual bargaining, which is inherently unfair.'

So the task, in abandoning Howard's 'atomised' individual bargaining, was to use the opportunity to achieve a better bargaining and enterprise system than any in the past.

Howard's legislation was a gift to the Rudd government in another respect. Labor's attempts at industrial law reform had always been constrained by its relationship with unions and the labour councils at state and federal levels, as well as by its system of state and national conferences. Howard had got his legislation through by using Section 51 (xx) of the Constitution, known as the corporations power, which gives Commonwealth governments 'the right to legislate with respect to foreign corporations and trading and finance corporations formed within the limits of the Commonwealth'. The unions challenged the constitutionality of this in the High Court but it was upheld. The High Court decision had enormous consequences: by law, the Australian government now had the power to legislate labour-market regulation. This must have been the only High Court decision that Gillard was delighted had gone the Coalition's way.

As well as Gillard's series of wide-ranging commitments made in the lead-up to the 2007 election – to abolish AWAs but respect existing contractual arrangements, to provide national employment standards, to create a fast and simple unfair dismissals system and to simplify and modernise many awards – the Rudd government also wanted to limit the ability of unions to take protected industrial action during periods of bargaining, to restore the unions' authority to enter workplaces when employers breached the law, and to create a new independent umpire.

Gillard's Fair Work Bill was introduced into Parliament on 25 November 2008, a year after the election of the Rudd government and after many months of formulation and consultation. 'Today we deliver the creation of a new workplace relations system,' she announced in her second-reading speech. 'It's a good Bill for employers, for families and for the economy.'

The Fair Work Bill covered an enormous range. At its heart was a response to the Howard government's policies that had reduced the degree of protection given to employees while promoting individual AWAs and had shifted bargaining power decisively to employers and tried to nullify the role of unions.

The Bill introduced ten exacting National Employment Standards intended to put in place a better safety net for all employees, whether outworkers, wage earners or those on high salaries. They covered essential conditions such as weekly hours of work, leave, public holidays, severance pay and the right to request flexible working arrangements.

The principles of collective enterprise bargaining and bargaining in good faith were to be enshrined. When the majority of employees in a workplace chose to bargain collectively the employer would be required to sit at the table with them. Consensus, not confrontation, was to be the rule: an agreement was made when approved by a majority of those to whom it would apply. Unions that represented employees during the negotiations could apply to be covered by the agreement. There was to be 'a right and proper balance between the rights of employees and their union to meet in the workplace and the rights of employers to run their businesses without interference'.

A new body, Fair Work Australia, would be the main organisation to handle industrial disputes as well as to set up, review and adjust awards and wages. Awards would be simpler and more consistent than before and would apply to most employees, unless their AWA or other workplace contract was still in operation, in which case the new award would take over when that expired.

And there were articles in the proposed legislation regarding unfair dismissal. Under the Howard government, employees in businesses with up to 100 workers could be let go for any reason without the right to challenge their dismissal: their tenure of employment was not relevant. The new Bill said that if an employee who had been working for six months in a business employing fifteen or more were dismissed, he or she would have access to unfair dismissal provisions. The same would apply to anyone employed for twelve months in a smaller business.

Gillard's Bill was called 'WorkChoices Lite' by some opponents (often the people who criticised her for rarely uttering the word 'union'). It wasn't. The safety net had been broadened, statutory individual contracts had been abolished and awards had been reinstated. And the Howard government's replacement of the Australian Industrial Relations Commission with the much weaker Australian Fair Pay Commission was reversed, and its powers returned to Fair Work Australia.

But Julia Gillard's assertion that, under the Bill, WorkChoices was 'swept away' was not quite accurate either, as some important aspects of the Coalition's legislation remained. The most significant of these was the retention of the corporations power to establish a single national system, certainly something the Rudd government did not propose to change. Also retained was the ban on industrial action in support of pattern bargaining; the idea of a qualifying period for unfair dismissal provisions; and the power of the minister for workplace relations to intervene in the affairs of unions and employers. Most inflammatory was (and continues to be) the retention of tougher rules in the building and construction industries.

Gillard had expected fireworks, and she was not disappointed. Many unions objected to not being given their former standing. They felt they were under tight legislative control, and some believed that they had been actively discriminated against. Many grumbled at some AWAs being retained until they ran out, and believed that Gillard had consulted employer groups at their expense. There was also disquiet about the prohibition of pattern bargaining, on the grounds that in the past the capacity of unions to campaign for similar outcomes across an industry had helped to achieve major gains for workers. Many unionists also disliked the absence of arbitration, recalling union victories gained through the adversarial system they had always known. The building and construction industries, for which the Howard government had instituted special 'watchdog' provisions, objected that these were being retained by Gillard.

On the other hand some employers, picking up on the clause that gave unions greater rights to enter workplaces, said that the Gillard Bill put the unions back in control. And there was suspicion – from unions and employers alike – about the independence and role of Fair Work Australia. Employers felt their own power to dictate wages and conditions had been seriously undermined, and so did the unions.

Gillard's view, rightly or wrongly, was that if neither side was entirely satisfied with the proposed legislation the balance was probably reasonable. (It is worth noting how often the word 'balance' is used in Gillard's speech to Parliament – an indicator of her desire to conciliate between several parties that, on the face of it, were unlikely to share common goals.) Even though a global economic crisis had appeared out of an apparently cloudless sky, Gillard was determined to nail the industrial relations system.

Having formulated her proposed legislation and presented it to all parties concerned, Gillard faced another series of hurdles: getting it through Parliament.

After months of discussion, Gillard must have known what would be the nature of the opposition to the Fair Work Bill, as well as where it would come from. Sure enough the Bill glided through the House of Representatives along party lines and hit trouble in the Senate, with the Opposition, the Greens, the independent Nick Xenophon and Family First's Steve Fielding lining up against it. For a majority to pass the Bill when the Coalition opposed it, all the others had to be persuaded to change position.

Each had different reasons for declining to support the Bill. Although the Opposition apparently accepted that WorkChoices was dead, it thought Gillard had gone too far in the opposite direction. It said the new laws would give unions too much power and would cost jobs. Gillard had known what the Opposition's position would be, so she did not spend much time trying to talk it around.

The Greens had been using their Senate muscle to take positions on issues outside their original environmental brief. They said the government had broken its promise to 'tear up' WorkChoices and that Gillard's legislation did not give workers sufficient safeguards. Senators Xenophon and Fielding broadly followed the Opposition's lead, wanting more concessions for employers. But Gillard was determined to get the Bill through Parliament in the two-week session scheduled from Tuesday 10 March 2009, before a seven-week break. Parliament would not sit again until the Budget was brought down on 12 May.

A joint-party Senate committee was appointed to inquire into the Bill. The committee took evidence during six days of public hearings, and received 154 submissions. The Opposition and the Greens still pushed for changes. Gillard had to decide how far she was willing to go to meet the conflicting demands, and she remained determined to get the Bill through the Senate in the two-week session.

Gillard made some amendments that she called 'minor' and that

Xenophon, Fielding and the Opposition said were 'significant'. These included changing unions' right-of-entry provisions and making minor adjustments to the bargaining system, the safety net and the role of Fair Work Australia in setting up flexible work arrangements.

Still the Opposition would not commit to the legislation, even if amended: Leader of the Opposition Malcolm Turnbull, who did not oppose abolishing WorkChoices (and who undoubtedly wished the whole issue would disappear), had the hardliners in his party against him, led by Peter Costello who refused to consider dismantling this part of the Howard legacy. The ACTU, emboldened by a survey showing that most workers wanted the new laws passed as soon as possible, kept up the pressure with a TV campaign ('Even at a time like this, they don't want Australians to get back their rights at work . . . the Liberals, putting big business before working people'). However, if Gillard could reach agreement with the Greens and senators Xenophon and Fielding, Coalition support would not be necessary – and she did not in the least mind leaving the Opposition in isolation.

On Monday 16 March, the day before the last sitting week of Parliament began, Gillard and the Greens reached agreement. The Greens were locked in. Now Gillard had to negotiate successfully with Xenophon and Fielding, and time was running out.

Gillard agreed to more minor amendments, most of which concerned unions' workplace rights, but the sticking point was the unfair dismissal laws. Under the Bill these applied to small businesses of more than fifteen people. Xenophon and Fielding argued that a small business should be defined as one employing up to twenty staff rather than fifteen and the threshold should be changed to twenty, and they and the Opposition voted to this effect. The Bill went back to the House of Representatives, where Gillard refused to accept their definition of a small business and the government's majority ensured the amended Bill's defeat.

It seems bizarre that the fate of such a massive and important piece of legislation should depend on something as apparently trivial as the numerical definition of a small business. A more conciliatory minister might well have capitulated. After all, the rest of the Bill had gone through and the number of employees had been reduced from 100 to twenty. But Gillard knew how much the voting public had loathed the existing provisions, she had decided what she considered fair, and she was implacable in her determination to get the Bill through on those terms.

The Bill, with Gillard's amendments only, now moved back to the Senate for the second time. The debate began late in the afternoon of Thursday 19 March and wrangling continued until early the following morning, when Xenophon and Fielding voted with the Coalition to overturn Gillard's definition of a small business. At 2.30 a.m. on Friday the Senate wearily called it a night.

Back went the Bill yet again to the House of Representatives, whose members were not best pleased at having to sit on a Friday. Malcolm Turnbull – a man who has known a thing or two about getting his own way – was particularly irritated. He declared that Gillard was making 'a pathetic political point', and added: 'Why are we *still* here? We're here because of a number. Because the Deputy Prime Minister is so colossally stubborn, so vain, so determined to wring the last bit of political value out of this . . . she's too stubborn, too pig-headed to re-agree to a sensible realistic change to the definition of small business.'

Gillard retorted, 'I can't wait to see the bumper stickers from the Liberal Party for the next election, "Don't vote Labor, they are too stubborn in delivering what they promised".' It was hardly anyone's finest hour in terms of repartee. The House reaffirmed Gillard's amendments for the third time and its MPs thankfully headed for the exits and Canberra airport.

The Senate was due to resume its interrupted sitting early on Friday afternoon, with the threat that the Bill would finally be voted down for the sake of a number. However, before it reconvened, Senator Fielding came to Gillard seeking to break the deadlock. He was already under pressure because his one-man stand against the government's alcopops legislation had cost the Budget $1.6 billion. (As political editor for the *Age* Michelle Grattan observed, the idea of sinking the Fair Work Bill in the same week must have been more than a little frightening for him.)

Gillard and Fielding agreed that the government would introduce the unfair dismissal laws in two phases. Until 1 January 2011 the small-business threshold would be the equivalent of fifteen full-time employees; and from 1 January 2011 fifteen employees, based on a simple headcount.

Gillard went to the Senate with Fielding – she had been present for every minute of the proceedings in both Houses – and watched as debate resumed. There was a certain amount of grumbling on the part of the Opposition, with Senator Eric Abetz echoing Turnbull's words. Senator Chris Evans, government leader in the Senate, shot back, 'It's called keeping your election promises – you wouldn't understand.'

The afternoon was drawing on before the vote was taken. With Senator Fielding supporting the government, it was a tie. A gasp went up from the spectators, and journalists on deadline scrambled for their mobile phones as they sought to find out what this tied vote meant.

But Gillard and the ALP knew. At 4.40 p.m. Senator Joe Ludwig, manager of government business in the Senate, moved that 'the Senate does not insist on the amendments that have been disagreed to'. In other words, no majority vote against the government's Bill had been achieved and so the Senate would accede to the Reps. The Fair Work Bill, with Gillard's amendments, had been passed, to come into effect from 1 July 2009.

There was rejoicing on the government side, with a jubilant Gillard declaring: 'Today . . . we have buried WorkChoices . . . we will now move to the era of fair work!' She hugged her Senate colleagues, who were almost as delighted as she was. Senator Fielding, who was already positioning himself as the man who had buried WorkChoices singlehanded said, a little plaintively, 'I am wondering where my hug from the Deputy Prime Minister is.' Gillard nobly obliged.

In her determination to drive a stake through the heart of WorkChoices, Gillard had needed every bit of her patience, toughness and negotiating skills. She had gone over policy details many, many times, battled to reassure business, and spent countless hours since the election taking the Caucus, union leaders and employers through the details of the complex legislation. And she had had to watch while, at the last, it had almost come to nothing.

As an example of Gillard's brinkmanship, the Fair Work legislation can scarcely be bettered. It was the clearest demonstration yet of her capacity to take an issue right to the wire, and to win.

22

Circling back

'People do not think she is a terribly passionate person but she is, on the issues she really believes in,' says Joan Kirner of Julia Gillard.

Close to Gillard's heart as a minister is her responsibility for education. 'She has always wanted to be minister or shadow minister for education,' says Kirner. 'She is passionate about education, in part because that's how [she] came through . . . Her electorate is a disadvantaged area and she is passionate about enabling kids from all groups to move forward.'

Gillard's commitment to equality of educational opportunity is the thread that runs through her life in politics right back to her student days. But it is yoked to an equal determination to build a strong national economy. Consequently her vision for Australian education is expressed in practical terms, far removed from the language of passion. But she never loses sight of the fact that her educational reforms are intended to work together for a moral purpose. 'Making a difference to disadvantaged children is much more than a question of economics,' she says.

Her portfolio ranges from early childhood to tertiary education. From the start she made it clear what approach she intended to take. One of her first big speeches as minister for education was made on 13 March 2008, when she had been only three months in the job. 'Over the course of the last decade, the issue of human capital has risen dramatically in public policy importance globally,' she said. 'Policy makers now accept that investing wisely in knowledge, skills and innovation is one of the best means available to ensure long term prosperity, leading to both overall economic growth and to better education and work opportunities. Around the world, governments have responded by increasing their policy focus in all areas of education . . . Everywhere, it seems, except here.'

It's a theme she has frequently reiterated, often with graphics, in speeches and interviews: Australia is doing less well than it should, Australia is less competitive than it should be, we must do better. Gillard has constantly followed up the argument that the 'Rudd government's education revolution' – a phrase she seems to have used almost every day since the beginning of the 2007 election campaign – means education outcomes delivering a real and tangible benefit to Australia's economy.

In discussing education, she often speaks about 'service delivery', 'focus', 'efficiency'. This can be disconcerting for people who think in terms of 'learning' or 'qualifications' rather than 'outcomes'. Having inherited a tangled, many-layered system with several levels of bureaucracy, she has needed to cut through with language that is typically unambiguous and managerial.

As are her educational objectives. In April 2008 she announced that a national curriculum, from kindergarten to Year 12, would be developed for all Australian schools. It would be based on a renewed focus on literacy and numeracy, starting with English, maths, science and history. At certain times during their primary education, children all over the country would be given standardised tests. The avowed aims were to lift educational standards, to make life easier for students changing schools across state borders, to increase efficiency and to eliminate bureaucratic duplication. Not everybody has been in favour of this. To some educators it sounds too much like Big Brother. And then there is the question of Gillard's interest in the ideas of Joel Klein.

A former high-profile lawyer and now chancellor of the New York City department of education, which means he is in charge of more than one million students in more than 1420 schools, Joel Klein believes that effective teaching must be performance based, that teachers should be judged on their students' results, and that there should be systems in place to measure and track the impact of teachers on student achievement. Teachers in disadvantaged schools who raise the standards of their students should be given bonuses, and from time to time the work of all teachers should be assessed.

Klein's overriding conviction – that disadvantaged students will never have real educational opportunity unless there is a genuine political commitment to change the way teachers are trained, rewarded and retained – ties in closely with Gillard's social inclusion agenda as well as her pragmatic approach. When she spoke to the principals of Australian primary schools in October 2008 she declared, 'The combination of great classroom instructors, led by professional school leaders, using modern educational facilities to teach the right curriculum, offers the best means to improve outcomes across the nation and overcome the effects of educational disadvantage.'

Her inclination towards Klein's views has attracted a storm of criticism from teachers' organisations and other educational bodies. Demonstrable achievement on the part of teachers, they say, is not the whole educational story. It is not a measure of how, and what, a student learns. They argue that Klein's approach fails to take into account the different needs of students, and so measurable classroom performance cannot be the only indicator of teacher effectiveness. There could also be a tendency for schools to 'cook the books'.

How schools are funded has always been a hot-button issue for Australian governments. The organisation of public education, including funding, is one of the powers delegated to the states. Historically, and partly because of sectarian divisions, the question of extending public funding to private schools has been a problem for Labor administrations. But since 1963, when the federal conservative government made a very popular election promise to fund science laboratories in all the nation's schools, no government has cared to reverse the trend to federal involvement. However, the nature and amount of federal aid to schools remains contentious. Responses to the issue can be seen as ideologically and class based, with Labor governments sporadically trying to reduce or stop funding to the wealthier independent schools and conservative governments increasing funding to private schools in general.

From about the mid-1980s the federal government intervened in broader schools policy and funding despite having no constitutional power to do so. Before John Howard, the funding a private school received was measured against the revenue generated by the parents and other sources; under him the level depended on the capacity of a school's community to support it, as measured by that community's socio-economic status. Gillard has continued that funding model, with a review promised for 2010–11.

Howard was also very keen to establish and support private schools as alternatives to government schools for parents with limited means. On his watch there was accelerated growth in the private sector, particularly of small Christian schools not attached to the Uniting, Anglican or Catholic systems. The educational principle of equity was replaced with the right of parents to choose where to send their children. The government schools lobby said that the main effect of Howard's policy was to increase the disparity in resources between public and private schools.

Gillard is not concerned with changing the mix of public and private schools. Nor does she care about the state aid debate. She says: 'I am not interested in taking resources away from schools . . . What I am interested in is getting additional funding into disadvantaged schools.' Parents have opted for choice, and she is not about to challenge that. She says she is much more concerned with the quality of education that all schools provide, and in making sure it is consistent and adequate.

Australian schools right across the board have been major beneficiaries of the federal stimulatory spending to provide jobs, in response to the global economic crisis. In the Budget of 2009 $47.4 billion was earmarked for spending on schools, and $14.7 billion committed to school infrastructure over the next three years. (In addition $14.4 billion was committed to early childhood education over the following four years.)

All this spending has caused *Sydney Morning Herald* columnist Annabel Crabb to observe:

> That Education Revolution must be down on its knees every day kissing the ground that the GFC [global financial crisis] walks on. Pre-GFC, the Education Revolution was remarkable only for its distinct non-revolutionariness, no matter how stirring the rhetoric of its astute and merciless figurehead, La Gillardine, whose very name causes Coalition hair to stand on end.
>
> Post-GFC, the revolutionary coffers are fully primed with stimulatory spending, and the tumbrils are cheerily loaded with new blackboards, and fresh grouting for tired wet areas.

Working with the vocational education and training sector – post-secondary institutions apart from universities – is central to Gillard's economy-related approach to education. VET has always been a highly sensitive area, especially in times of labour shortages. And the system of state- and territory-based colleges of technical and further education, which cater for more than 70 per cent of VET enrolments, has been problematic and unwieldy for conservative and Labor governments alike.

Just before the 2007 election Andrew Robb, the Coalition's minister for vocational and further education, attacked the TAFE system run by the states and territories, saying it was hampered by bureaucracy and union control. Private training organisations were more efficient in increasing productivity because they could respond more effectively to the needs of the workplace. The Coalition favoured centralised control of vocational education – their conditions for TAFE funding included offering AWAs to employees – and the message to the states and territories was, Change the way you work or you will be marginalised.

Robb's shadow Stephen Smith, however, was committed to the TAFE system and to working cooperatively with state and territory governments. He said Labor proposed setting up Skills Australia, a centralised body of industry, academic and training experts, to advise government on current and future demand for skills and training. He added that vocational training could be provided by either TAFE or private providers, but that the TAFE system needed to be made more flexible.

Both sides of politics, then, favoured centralised government control, more autonomy and flexibility for individual VET institutions and a role for private enterprise.

Gillard as minister for education tackled the subject quickly, promising 450 000 new VET places over four years and continued funding for existing places. In February 2008 she introduced the Skills Australia Bill, setting up a new statutory body to advise the government on workforce development and skills needs. Since the new body bypassed the states and territories and was accountable to the minister, it represented a significant extension of Australian government control over the VET system. Grants under the new legislation would be contestable; that is, they would go direct to the successful provider, whether from the public or private sector.

She came under attack primarily from those who thought she was seeking to undermine the public sector, and so Skills Australia produced a consultation paper. The paper supported 'an expansion of contestability', with national regulation to guarantee quality of vocational education and consultation between employers and training providers, but it also set out a role for the public sector, especially in regional development.

Gillard has maintained the Howard government's centralised

approach to vocational education strategy and extended it. Early in 2009 she announced that Skills Australia would advise the government about the effectiveness of the higher education system in general – universities as well as VET institutions – to meet labour-market needs, and that a body would be set up to improve the connection between the university and VET sectors. And – controversially – Gillard said that Skills Australia would investigate a voucher-like scheme for vocational training, similar to one that the Howard government set up, giving students the power to choose between public and private training providers.

In March 2008 Julia Gillard announced a review of higher education, to be headed by Emeritus Professor Denise Bradley. The *Review of Australian Higher Education Final Report*, handed down in December 2008, recommended major reforms to the financing and regulation of Australian higher education. In clear and urgent language it stated that, for Australia to be more competitive in a global market, the number of citizens with undergraduate qualifications needed to be substantially increased from the current 29 per cent of the population to up to 50 per cent. For this to be achieved, Australia must look to members of groups underrepresented in the system: those disadvantaged by birth, Indigenous people, those with low socio-economic status and people from regional and remote areas of Australia. Greater income support should be given to disadvantaged students, and enrolment targets should be set for students from low socio-economic backgrounds.

The report pointed out that education services were Australia's third-largest export industry, but that the public contribution to higher education had not increased over the previous ten years: governments needed to spend more. This would help reduce the student-to-staff ratio and allow for more permanent academic jobs.

Governments had traditionally monitored the quantity of education through the control of supply, but it was now recommended that education courses should be driven by student demand. The overall responsibility for funding and regulation of tertiary education should be assumed by the federal government, and there should be a national system for accreditation of all higher education providers, whether public or private.

The report was criticised by the so-called Group of Eight, representing the oldest universities in Australia. The group described it as deeply flawed and a 'road map for mediocrity' that failed to acknowledge the principles of excellence, the different goals of different institutions and the importance of university education for its own sake. Its criticisms echoed other concerns about some underlying principles of the Bradley report, and indeed about the report's general approach to education, which seemed similar to Gillard's.

Some critics felt that Gillard's burning desire to ensure that every Australian child will benefit from equality of educational opportunity might mean concentrating too strongly on the negatives. The best way to get rid of inequality, they said, was not necessarily to standardise everything, because that risked creating an environment where individuality and originality – both of which are unpredictable – might be less likely to flourish. Others saw the report as a breath of fresh air; they pointed out that any new regulation always attracted this kind of criticism and that the country needed a great university system, not just several great universities.

Few disagreed, though, that more money needed to be spent on post-secondary education, and in response to the Bradley report the government decided to invest $5.7 billion in higher education and innovation over the next four years. In the VET area $3.8 billion was to be spent over four years to increase the number of apprenticeships and training places.

As far as education spending is concerned, not only for tertiary education but at every level, the global economic crisis certainly supports the adage that it's an ill wind that blows nobody good. Or, more succinctly, that 'crisis' may be a synonym for 'opportunity'. However, changing Australia's various education systems is an even more complex exercise than hammering a new industrial relations order into place. Julia Gillard and Australia will have to wait some time to see if her vision for the education revolution holds true.

By midway through the first term of the Rudd government Julia Gillard might well have felt that a significant amount had been achieved. But it came with a cost. Her own job – running three major portfolios, consulting at all levels and with numerous interest groups, and considering, formulating and sometimes modifying policy, not to mention explaining developments to the public and always being ahead of the Opposition in Parliament – could be extraordinarily demanding.

'I think we have to recognise that whether it's men or whether it's women going into politics, it brings a lifestyle strain,' she has said. Yet despite her extraordinarily heavy load, the hothouse atmosphere of political Canberra and the 'gypsy lifestyle' forced on federal politicians, she seems to have found some balance in her private life.

When she started being seen in public with a new bloke four or so years ago, the media found out about him fairly quickly. In one important respect Tim Mathieson is very different from the other men in Gillard's life: he has nothing to do with her professional world. Gillard's other important relationships – with Michael O'Connor, Bruce Wilson, Craig Emerson – were with men she knew through her job. Tim Mathieson sells hair products.

Mathieson is a few years older than Gillard – in his early fifties, brown-haired and pleasant looking. (Indeed his resemblance to previous men in Gillard's life is a little disconcerting. All are from working-class backgrounds and tallish and well built, with brown hair.) They met in 2004 when he was the chief stylist at the Heading Out hair salon in Melbourne's inner suburb of Fitzroy. They chatted and found, as he says, 'a bit of a nice spark'. Mathieson had knocked around a bit, running hair salons in country Victoria and on the Gold Coast and working in export and home renovation in San Francisco. He was divorced, with an adult son and daughter.

He and Gillard met again on a tram at the end of 2004 and chatted, but Mathieson returned to the country, where he was working; Gillard to Canberra and leadership speculation. A year later Mathieson moved back to Melbourne and called her. After several dates – lunch, the movie *Syriana*, dinner at a Fitzroy pub – they settled into a solid relationship. Mathieson has said: 'It's nice to meet a girl who's grounded. I hate spin and there's no pretence about her in any way.'

Gillard says her relationship with Mathieson has been 'the right thing at the right time'. She has chosen a partner with whom she can relax or, as she says, 'dag out'. It is a very stable, down-to-earth relationship. Mathieson must be not only an archetypal 'nice bloke', but a very confident one, with a solid sense of self to match Gillard's own. She once told a woman friend that men were 'net energy takers'. Clearly Mathieson does not fit into that category. He is interested in politics, but it is not his primary focus.

'I'm sort of a lightweight in that area anyway,' he says. 'She's talking about that with high intellects all day, every day. We just talk about life stuff or joke around. She can switch off.'

But Gillard says Mathieson has perceptive qualities that she lacks. 'He's got a terrific visual sense, he's really good at picking up visual cues. He'll watch one of my colleagues at a press conference and say, "Oh, she's nervous about saying that" or "He looks really comfortable." These are things I don't see – I know them all so well. And he always notices what they wear.'

Gillard and Mathieson live together in her Altona house, and when she has to spend more than a week or so in Canberra he will fly up from Melbourne to join her. He often does the cooking in the townhouse she stays in, not far from Parliament. 'She eats out all week so it's nice for her to come home to something healthy,' he has said. A change from the politician's standard diet of hasty snacks, lavish lunches and late-night pizza must be welcome.

Julia Gillard has always been open – within reason – about private issues, saying she believes voters are entitled to know about the people they elect. She has never shied away from discussing her childlessness, the subject of media comment and discussion over the years. On *Australian Story* in 2006 she said that women's decisions to have children are 'not as mechanical as saying, you know, "I want to have a kid, I'd better find a bloke" . . . If I'd met a man that I was tremendously in love with and the one thing in life he wanted was to have kids, then obviously maybe I might've made a different set of decisions.' (There is no suggestion that she has ever felt a burning desire for children, although she says that, like most women, she has thought about it from time to time.)

She added that for women politicians, constantly in the public eye, the subject of children was a vexed one, regardless of whether their personal circumstances had led to a family or not: 'I think that one of the problems for women is that historically there has been no right answer. If you don't have kids, then people say you can't understand everyone else's life experience, and if you do, then people say who's looking after the kids while you're doing all of this.'

Several years later, soon after Labor came to power, she returned to the subject of women in politics: 'I think women are still making their way into politics. Obviously a lot's changed for women, but there are a few things to change still. There's been more attention on private life questions for me than perhaps male politicians.'

On 11 December 2007, only two weeks after the Rudd Labor government had been elected to office, with Julia Gillard making history as Australia's first woman deputy prime minister, she made history again. She became the first woman acting prime minister of Australia while Kevin Rudd was attending a three-day climate change conference in Bali.

The media coverage was huge. Magazines and newspapers alike had pictures of Gillard sitting seriously at the prime ministerial desk saying she intended to pursue business as usual. When questioned, she deflected any supposition that she might, one day, be prime minister in her own right.

At the same time she recognised her position as a role model. 'I'd like to think that maybe there's a young girl who'll watch the TV today and think to herself, "Maybe I could do that when I grow up." And if one girl thinks that, then I think it's great,' she told the ABC.

'The reaction from women really bowled me over,' she said later. 'I mean, women I didn't know sending me flowers and cards because they were just so delighted.'

A year later Gillard as acting PM had ceased to be the subject of much media comment. By January 2009 she had spent 102 days, one quarter of Kevin Rudd's prime ministership, at his desk while he travelled overseas. There have been the predictable mutterings that Rudd had better watch out: with such a high profile, his deputy could be taking over, and she might be a threat. But as political scientist Nick Economou has bluntly pointed out, 'If Rudd wasn't comfortable about her being in charge, he wouldn't be buggering off overseas.' (And nor would he just send Gillard a simple text message as he heads off, asking her to take over, as she says he does.)

At least one Canberra press gallery journalist has been known to complain that the parliamentary ALP presents a boringly united front at present. No stilettos protrude from Labor parliamentarians' shoulder-blades. Ministers are generally happy and getting on with their portfolios, and being in office is the glue that holds them together. So, too, is the fact that their departments can take advantage of the government's deficit spending in a time of global economic crisis. As deputy leader, Julia Gillard can take some responsibility for this.

Gillard may be pleasant to deal with and efficient, but this is not to be presumed upon. Anyone who is incompetent or lazy will be in no doubt about her displeasure. The view in the bureaucracy is that she has a tongue that could etch glass, and it is not a good idea to get on the wrong side of her.

The bureaucrats, though, are mostly pleased when Gillard is acting PM. She doesn't muck around, they say. 'With Rudd it can be a question of: Who told you about B? Why did you not decide on A? He's got to know where everything comes from. He has to know everything, and it can take a long time to get things through,' says one public service source.

Whereas with Julia Gillard: 'When you give her a document with three recommendations, maybe with "We suggest option B", she'll look at it, study it, think, then make up her own mind, whether she goes for B or not. But once she's made that decision, it's on to the next thing.'

On to the next thing, and the next thing, and the next. Gillard herself says: 'This job, this life, it's relentless. If it were no more than the sum of its parts – the meetings, the amount of work, the travel – it would hollow you out, there's no doubt about it. What gives you the drive to do it is understanding the possibilities it gives. It only matters because it enables you to make changes you believe need to be made.'

Julia up close

The first thing you notice is the handshake. Firm, professional. 'Hi, I'm Julia,' she says. 'Come through.' She is smaller and prettier than she appears on television, with fine, unlined skin and hazel eyes. Her makeup is immaculate and subtle: foundation and blusher, eye shadow and lipstick. Today her hair is in a sleek bob. She is wearing grey trousers and very high-heeled shoes, but not her usual long jacket – she apologises for wearing a cardigan instead.

She is probably not vain: just well aware that, in her business, appearances are important. When I compliment her, the next time I see her, on the navy-pinstriped trouser suit she is wearing with an emerald green blouse, she looks a little surprised and says, 'Yes, people like this one.' She has probably learned about how to dress as part of the job, but her casual manner gives the distinct impression that she would be just as happy to walk around in jeans and an unfussy shirt and flat-heeled shoes. And no makeup.

It is three o'clock on a Friday afternoon in March 2009, not a week when Parliament is sitting, so she is not running quite as fast as usual.

All the same she has already done a couple of TV interviews – the issue this week is the fate of the ABC Learning Centres – and one or two press releases. She shows no sign whatever of being tired; rather she looks cheerful and relaxed.

Her Melbourne office, where I meet her, is large and light, with long windows overlooking Melbourne's Treasury Gardens. It looks like the office of any successful CEO: large desk, comfortable sofas around a coffee table for discussions, anonymous decor. There are very few personal touches – no photographs on the desk, bland paintings – except that on a pillar next to the tidy desk are two drawings with lots of colourful, jagged squiggles. I wonder whose they are. Gillard's niece and nephew, the children of her sister Alison, are now adults. Later I discover that they were done by the child of a staffer. It is pleasant to learn that the deputy prime minister runs an office where children can be told, 'Now, sit down over there and draw Julia a nice picture.'

I mention this to a friend, who scoffs, 'She's just put them up there for show, it's all PR, just fake.' My own view is that Gillard has simply followed the unwritten rule that, if a child draws a picture for you, you will praise it and put it up somewhere it can be admired.

Her personal staff are warm and friendly, with none of the slightly officious proprietary manner that can sometimes be observed in politicians' staffers. And the boss–worker relationship is comfortable enough for an assistant to poke her head round the door and make a comical crying face while pointing at her left wrist: You're running very late, Minister.

Julia Gillard answers questions readily, laughs easily and has a nice line in self-deprecation. When asked about her career choices as a teenager, she says, 'Well, I was told I could do better than being a teacher. [*Pause.*] This sounds wonderful, doesn't it, coming from the minister for education . . .' She is easy to talk to, hiding any natural wariness behind a smiling and relaxed manner. It is obvious that she genuinely likes people. But she gives little away. Under that engaging manner is a reserved person, a woman who is very self-protected.

It took little time to realise that on matters of public record she was not about to change what she had already said. (Once or twice I was amused to find that her responses to my questions were almost word for word.) Asked more personal questions she was forthcoming, answering exactly what she was asked. Only once did I feel I had slipped beneath the surface: when I asked her about her relationship with Bruce Wilson.

'It must have been a painful time for you,' I said.

She shrugged it off with, 'Oh well, these things happen . . .'

When I pushed a bit, quoting some of the more unpleasant tabloid headlines and saying 'That must have impressed you', she flashed 'Not so much', and for a second I saw how that squalid scandal-mongering had hurt her.

She told me that TV journalists and other media representatives had refused to follow up the story after it broke about a week before the 2007 election, and how much she appreciated that.

When I said, 'Sure, it was nice of them, but they knew you were on track to win and they needed to be in your good books,' she looked quite shocked.

'You're a very cynical woman!' she said.

When giving interviews Gillard is always courteous, respectful and friendly. But anyone who regularly watches her being questioned by the ABC's Kerry O'Brien or Tony Jones, or listens to her occasional tussles with Fran Kelly on ABC Radio National, will be well aware that she is not about to let the media run the agenda. She is expert at switching topics and not following interviewers' leads. She says what she wants to, nothing more. At times her consistent staying on message can make her sound rather automaton-like. But, given some interviewers' insistence on repeatedly asking the same question and demanding immediate answers on complex policy matters, that is probably inevitable. She would certainly appreciate the words of US president Barack Obama who, during a recent press conference, refused to answer a question of that kind, adding: 'I know you guys are on a twenty-four-hour news cycle. I'm not.'

Late in May Julia Gillard was the guest of honour at a Melbourne Town Hall lunch during which she gave a speech outlining federal education spending in the 2009 Budget. The points she made about the extra funding available for any Australian child, from primary school through to entry into the workplace, were lucidly illustrated by PowerPoint graphs that she manipulated herself. Her speech was persuasive, absolutely free of Rudd government education revolution rhetoric, and clearly expressed. The audience, comprised mainly of Victorian education bureaucrats, was warm and appreciative.

Afterwards she went upstairs to do a press conference, where she was questioned by journalists. Here the story was slightly different. Because she was not in control of what would be asked, she was slightly stiffer, less natural. She also had to deal with questions that had little bearing on what she had just been talking about. She had to get her points across quickly and so lapsed into boilerplate rhetoric, with criticism of the Opposition thrown in as well. It was a less impressive performance than the lunch speech had been, and a faint undercurrent of frustration could be felt.

It is a politician's truism that you should never believe your own publicity, and Gillard takes this further. 'You never let the media tell you who you are,' she says. (But there are some circumstances in which she is less than comfortable. Having this book written about her is one – she has said she feels rather like a lab rat.)

However, she can be cheerfully forthcoming about 'colour' issues that are not political: food preferences (sushi and anything else that is easy to eat because she is often on the run), what she likes doing in her time off (going for walks, staying home and ordering take-away, watching movies or DVDs) and reading.

'I don't read seriously,' she says apologetically. 'Mysteries, detective novels, stuff like that. Dianne, one of our Commonwealth car drivers, keeps me supplied. I have to have books with storylines you can pick up quickly. Anything complex, or that you have to remember over more than a couple of days, is no good, because I only get to read for about ten minutes before I go to bed.

'I used to read a lot more: Salman Rushdie, Gabriel García Márquez and other South American novelists. And every now and then I think, I really should raise the standard and get back to that. But really, these days I am just too busy.'

Julia Gillard is remarkable because she seems so little different outside the spotlight as under it. Most important of all, she has a solid core of selfhood. She knows who she is.

She has attracted hostility largely, I think, because she plays the political game for what it is. She does not display the vulnerability that people think they expect from women politicians. True, she was teary in Parliament about the Victorian bushfires early in 2009, but there was really something to cry about. In her work she behaves as the job demands: she sees the big picture, she pushes, she goes for results. She keeps her friends close and possibly her enemies closer.

And will she be Australia's first woman prime minister?

It is a question she says irritates her. 'It's only natural that women want to see one of their own in the top job, and if they think it's going to be me, that's great,' she says. 'But you know, after I did that speech in Melbourne Town Hall a woman came up to me and said, "I'm looking forward to your being the next PM." It was nice of her, but I thought, But I've just made a major speech about education – why don't you look at what I'm doing now?'

It is an issue, however, that refuses to go away. As this book was going to press there was another flurry of speculation, with several unnamed Labor colleagues coming forward to say that if something happened to Kevin Rudd, and there was a leadership succession crisis, Julia Gillard would be unopposed. There is said to be consensus among the factions, including the New South Wales Right; unions and employers are 'grudgingly impressed' with Gillard's handling of the industrial relations legislation; and she is no longer a Left warrior – if indeed she ever was – having moved to Labor's centre. Furthermore she is very popular with the public.

The media assumes that if Gillard were given the chance to be prime minister she would jump at it. But is this true? We know she is up to the job, but does that mean she is necessarily up for it?

From the beginning of her career, she has shown herself to be someone who has made the most of opportunities as they occur and been willing to take on the tough jobs. And if Kevin Rudd's health failed, she would obviously take over, at least temporarily.

But as to whether she would want the prime ministership enough to manoeuvre and fight for it with Rudd still PM, the answer appears to be no. It is difficult to believe that if he were politically wounded to the point of becoming a liability and his current stratospheric popularity ratings plummeted, it would be Gillard who delivered the coup de grace. She is no Paul Keating: there is no evidence that for the sake of her own ambition she would be willing to destabilise the party or be prepared to move to the backbench, as he did.

And it is all very well for Gillard's colleagues to tell journalists that she would be unopposed in a future leadership ballot: if it ever came to that point, there might very well be leadership batons in unexpected knapsacks. There is also the question of her support. Gillard has always operated through networks of influence in preference to union blocs or factions. If there should ever be a contest for the leadership, she would undoubtedly take soundings and look at her numbers, but judging from her history she would only put herself forward if she thought she had a real chance of winning.

It's all purely hypothetical at the moment, of course. And given what her career has been, with the struggles she has had to get where she is, it is difficult to believe she does not mean it when she says, 'Anyone who thinks that my being PM is inevitable knows nothing whatever about politics.'

Notes

Our Julia

page

2 'At a shopping centre . . .' Julia Gillard quoted, McGuire, Michael, 'Becoming Julia: The Gillard Story', *Advertiser*, 8 February 2009.

2–3 She can have fun . . . *Rove Live*, Channel Ten, 12 April 2009. The segment was recorded on YouTube, but has been deleted. Gillard has since appeared on the Rove McManus show *Are You Smarter than a 5th Grader?* (aired on Channel Ten, 27 July 2009).

3 'People can be very generous . . .' Gillard quoted, McGuire, op. cit.

3 'There is something about Julia . . .' Frith, Marion, 'Domestic Goddess', *Vive*, 1 August 2008.

5 'As you can probably tell . . .' Julia Gillard, *Counterpoint*, ABC Radio National, 29 September 2004, transcript.

5–6 'Let me share . . .' Julia Gillard, Hansard, House of Representatives, 9 February 2009, at www.aph.gov.au/Hansard/reps/dailys/dr090209.pdf.

6 Former senator Susan Ryan . . . Susan Ryan conversation with Jacqueline Kent, 3 February 2009.

6 'A lot of women . . .' Joan Kirner interview with JK, 18 February 2009.

7 These are qualities . . . Julia Gillard's friend Nicola Roxon, the minister for health, has said of her as a politician, 'She's got everything going for her: she's tough, she's smart, she's funny and she works bloody hard': 'Faces of Julia', *Age*, 21 June 2003.

7 'The kind of image . . .' Gillard quoted, McGuire, op. cit.

7 'Certainly five or ten years ago . . .' ibid.

1 'Australia is my only reality'

8 'Australia is . . . my only reality . . .' Julia Gillard, launch speech, 3 July 2005, at parlinfo.aph.gov.au:80/parlInfo/download/media/pressrel/7QJG6/upload_binary/7qjg63.pdf;fileType%3Dapplication%2Fpdf.
8 'This means the Australian taxpayer . . .' ibid.
9 'I could give you . . .' John Gillard quoted, Valent, Dani, 'Our Julia', *Age*, 18 May 2007.
10 John Gillard spent . . . ibid.
11–12 Barry, the town where . . . When John and Moira Gillard settled there, Barry had a population of about 40 000. See www.barrywales.co.uk.
12–13 For many families . . . Information about Australia's immigration scheme is taken mostly from Hammerton, A., and Thomson, James Alistair, *Ten Pound Poms: Australia's Invisible Migrants*, Manchester University Press, Manchester, 2005.
13 'Oh,' he said . . . Julia Gillard, *Australian Story*, ABC-TV, 6 March 2006, section not broadcast, at www.abc.net.au/austory/content/2006/s1585300.htm.
15–16 Sometimes it was the small differences . . . Gillard launch speech, op. cit.
16 'Our whole thrust . . .' John Gillard quoted, Valent, op. cit.
17 'I had a sense . . .' Julia Gillard quoted, ibid.
17 'One of the many . . .' McGuire, Michael, 'Becoming Julia: The Gillard Story', *Advertiser*, 6 February 2009.
17–18 'I'm not sure . . .' ibid.
18 'Other women would tell her . . .' ibid.
18 'She was a very calm child . . .' Moira Gillard quoted, Hewitt, Jennifer, 'Julia: Her Time', *Weekend Australian Magazine*, 7–8 July 2007.
18 'I've still got friends . . .' Julia Gillard, *Australian Story,* op. cit.

2 'I grew more confident in high school'

19 'I grew more confident . . .' Julia Gillard interview with Jacqueline Kent, 13 March 2009.
19 'Julia was always . . .' Alison Gillard quoted, Hewitt, Jennifer, 'Julia: Her Time', *Weekend Australian Magazine*, July 7–8 2007.
20 'a muted form . . .' Julia Gillard quoted, Valent, Dani, 'Our Julia', *Age,* 18 May 2007.
20 On one occasion they baked . . . *Australian Story*, ABC-TV, 2006, section not broadcast, at www.abc.net.au/austory/content/2006/s1585300.htm.
20 The most important training . . . Gillard interview, op. cit.; Valent, op. cit.
21 When Julia was sixteen . . . *Australian Story*, op. cit.
21 'My parents believed . . .' Julia Gillard, ibid.
22–3 John Gillard was politically . . . ibid.
23 'We grew up . . .' ibid.

23 However, Alison, who does not . . . McGuire, Michael, 'Becoming Julia', *Advertiser*, 6 February 2009.

24 'My reaction was . . .' John Faulkner quoted, 'After 50 Years Gough Tells It Like It Is,' *Age*, 7 November 2002.

24–5 Former senator Robert Ray . . . Richardson, Graham, *Whatever It Takes*, Bantam Books, Sydney, 1994, p. 33.

26 'very vibrant . . .' Gillard interview, op. cit. Marlene Pilowsky died of cancer in 1998.

26 'She would half . . .' ibid.

26 'I started mulling over . . .' ibid.

27 'The thing that amazed . . .' ibid.

27 'He had this heavy accent . . .' ibid.

27–8 For John and Moira . . . ibid.

3 'Student politics is a great way of building up your skills'

29 'Student politics is a great . . .' Julia Gillard, *Australian Story*, ABC-TV, 6 March 2006, section not broadcast, at www.abc.net.au/austory/content/2006/s1585300.htm.

30 At the time, Mandy . . . Julia Gillard interview with Jacqueline Kent, 13 March 2009.

31 The peak body . . . Information about the Australian Union of Students can be found in the National Library of Australia, online catalogue, nos 1077053 and 2412004.

32 when the Liberal Party came to federal office . . . For a sympathetic account of Malcolm Fraser's prime ministership, see Kelly, Paul, 'John Malcolm Fraser', in Grattan, Michelle (ed.), *Australian Prime Ministers*, New Holland, Sydney, 2000.

33 'We thought . . .' Julia Gillard, *Counterpoint*, ABC Radio National, 20 September 2004, transcript.

33 'Probably the first time . . .' Michael O'Connor, *Australian Story*, ABC-TV, 6 March 2006, broadcast section, at www.abc.net.au/austory/content/2006/s1586140.htm.

33 'There were some very public parts . . .' Gillard interview, op. cit.

34 'a lot of hard work . . .' ibid.

34 'I think the fact . . .' ibid.

35 'We all tended to look . . .' ibid.

35 She drove a large, ageing Chrysler . . . It would have been made in South Australia, so the Gillard family were being patriotic. PM Malcolm Fraser had a special stretched version for travel around Adelaide.

35 'She would have been twenty-one . . .' Ken McAlpine interview with Doug Hendrie, February 2009.

35 'I remember sitting down with her . . .' ibid.

36 'When I did Contract Law . . .' Gillard interview, op. cit.

4 'It's like compressing ten years of Parliament into one'

37 'It's like compressing ten years . . .' Julia Gillard, *Australian Story*, ABC-TV, 6 March 2006, section not broadcast, at www.abc.net.au/austory/content/2006/s1585300.htm.

37 'When you come out of it . . .' ibid.

37 Australian Union of Students . . . National Library of Australia, online catalogue, nos 1077053 and 2412004.

38 'A number of other people . . .' Andrew Scott interview with Doug Hendrie, March 2009.

38 'Student politics had been skewed . . .' Gillard, *Australian Story*, op. cit.

38–9 'There was always the big search . . .' Julia Gillard interview with Jacqueline Kent, 13 March 2009.

39 'Some group announced . . .' Andrew Scott interview with JK, 18 February 2009.

39 'AUS used to be . . .' Nick Economou interview with DH, February 2009.

39 Gillard and her AUS executive colleagues . . . Candy Broad is now an ALP member of the Victorian Upper House, and Michael O'Connor is national secretary of the Construction, Forestry, Mining and Energy Union Forestry and Furnishing Products Division.

41 'She had a great sense of humour . . .' Scott interview, 18 February, op. cit.

42 'You didn't really want to be . . .' Michael O'Connor, *Australian Story*, ABC-TV, 6 March 2006, broadcast section, at www.abc.net.au/austory/content/2006/s1586140.htm.

42 'You always feel . . .' Julia Gillard, ibid.

42 'Michael and I . . .' ibid.

42–3 '[F]riends from university . . .' Julia Gillard, Hansard, House of Representatives, 11 November 1998, at www.aph.gov.au/Hansard/reps/dailys/dr111198.pdf.

43 committee called Let's Develop Education . . . Julia Gillard conversation with JK, 8 July 2009.

44 a policy he really wanted to push . . . The Higher Education Contribution Scheme came into being in 1989 under the ALP, with Dawkins as minister. HECS has become an integral part of the Australian higher education system, and total student payments through HECS are now around 20 per cent of the funding available to higher education institutions from the Commonwealth program.

44–5 'Now I'm dealing with . . .' Gillard interview, op. cit.

45 'It's so ironic . . .' ibid.

45 Higher Education Support Amendment . . . *Bills Digest*, 2004–05, no. 187, Parliamentary Library, Parliament of Australia.

46 '[She] gave me the impression . . .' Josh Bornstein interview with DH, February 2009.

46 'Just being in that environment . . .' Gillard conversation, op cit.
47 'You see her now . . .' Bornstein interview, op. cit.
47 'keep going . . .' ibid.

5 Julia the red menace

48 'Scrapping the ANZUS Treaty . . .' Wright, Lincoln, 'Julia Gillard's History as a Radical Student Activist', *Sunday Herald Sun*, 7 October 2007.

48 'obtained access to papers' . . . ibid. The papers of the Socialist Forum, available to anyone who asks, are in Socialist Forum 1984–1998 papers, University of Melbourne Archives, accession no. 102/28, date of transfer 1 May 2002. The papers include formation details, the constitution, and management committee minutes, as well as details of meetings, summer schools and study circles.

49 'The issue isn't just whether . . .' Bolt, Andrew, *Herald Sun*, 23 October 2007.

49 'Labor's deputy leader. . .' ibid.

49 'Are you now . . .' Tony Jones, *Lateline*, ABC-TV, 17 October 2007, transcript.

49–50 The conversation continued . . . Jones and Julia Gillard, ibid.

49 'amalgamated with the Fabian Society . . .' Julia Gillard, ibid. The Fabian Society, which originated in Britain in the 1880s, was originally formed to advance social democratic principles by working within existing social structures, espousing gradual reform rather than revolution. Its intellectual heyday was probably the late nineteenth century up to World War I. The Fabian Society was highly influential in the formation of the British Labour Party, and its principles affected the policies of states emerging from the former British Empire, such as India. Today the British Fabian Society is a think-tank for the Centre Left New Labour movement, and one of fifteen social democratic societies affiliated to the Labour Party. The Australian Fabian Society is similar.

51 1954 Petrov affair . . . Shortly before the 1954 federal election Vladimir Petrov, third secretary of the Soviet Embassy in Canberra, offered to provide evidence of Soviet espionage in exchange for political asylum. He defected in April without telling his wife, Evdokia, who was taken to Sydney airport by two KGB men and put on a plane out of Australia. The crew radioed Darwin, and when the aircraft stopped for refuelling Mrs Petrov was taken off. She decided to defect and join her husband. PM Robert Menzies, up for re-election, announced a royal commission on espionage, citing documents alleged to give evidence of an extensive Soviet spy ring in Australia, and naming two members of staff of ALP leader Dr H. V. Evatt. Labor had been expected to win the 1954 election, but Menzies astutely used the Petrov affair to stir up anti-ALP sentiment. See Manne, Robert, *The Petrov Affair: Politics and Espionage*, Pergamon Press, Sydney, 1987.

51 ALP Split in 1955 . . . During World War II and as a result of pro-Russian (anti-Nazi) sympathy, the Communist Party of Australia built up its strength in the trade union movement, affiliated to the ALP. By 1954 the Catholic wing of the ALP was alarmed at what it saw as increasing Communist power in the trade unions and formed so-called Industrial Groups within the unions to combat this influence. The Victorian branch of the ALP was dominated by Catholics, and their intellectual leader, Melbourne lawyer B. A. Santamaria, headed the Catholic Social Studies Movement (which became known as the Movement), modelled on the European Catholic Action groups. It later became the National Civic Council. In 1954 ALP leader H. V. Evatt denounced the Movement and the Industrial Groups, saying they were trying to take over the ALP. At the 1955 ALP National Conference in Hobart, Santamaria's supporters in the federal and Victorian parliaments were expelled from the ALP, against the constitutional rules. They formed their own party, the Democratic Labor Party, in 1957. The DLP effectively split Labor's vote for almost twenty years. For a full account see Murray, Robert, *The Split: Australian Labor in the Fifties*, Hale & Iremonger edn, Sydney, 1984.

51 'He's getting a bit desperate . . .' Richardson, Graham, *Whatever It Takes*, Bantam Books, Sydney, 1994, p. 128.

52 'Like most things . . .' Julia Gillard interview with Jacqueline Kent, 13 March 2009.

53 'a non-party . . .' This and the quotations that follow from Julia Gillard's articles and other statements about the Socialist Forum are found in Socialist Forum papers, op. cit.

55 In 'Future Directions for the Left' . . . ibid.

58 'Hartley, in his fanaticism . . .' Bob Hawke quoted, Parkinson, Tony, 'Shame, Whitlam, Shame', *Age*, 15 November 2005.

58 'a strident demagogue . . .' Gillard interview, op. cit.

59 'With Kim, there was . . .' Geoff Robinson interview with Doug Hendrie, February 2009.

60 'In hindsight . . .' Frans Timmerman interview with DH, February 2009.

60 'We had been used to . . .' Paul Slape interview with DH, February 2009.

61 'We weren't opposed . . .' ibid.

6 Mixing it with the blokes: 1

63–4 'We tended to sit . . .' Paul Slape interview with Doug Hendrie, February 2009.

64 'They took notice . . .' Julia Gillard interview with Jacqueline Kent, 13 March 2009.

65 'that disreputable firm . . .' Cannon, Michael, *That Disreputable Firm: The Inside Story of Slater & Gordon*, Melbourne University Press, Carlton South, 1998.

65 'If I could live . . .' ibid, p. viii.
65 'Slaters perceives . . .' Peter Gordon interview with Doug Hendrie, March 2009.
67 'On the way to the meeting . . .' Gillard interview, op. cit.
67–8 'After that . . .' ibid.
69–70 Kate Hawkins . . . remembers . . . Kate Hawkins interview with DH, March 2009.
70 'It's quite hard . . .' ibid.
70 'It was a terrible . . .' Gordon interview, op. cit.
70–1 'When I started . . .' Brendan Soraghan interview with DH, April 2009.
71 'In the union movement . . .' Josh Bornstein interview with DH, March 2009.
72 'She had the respect . . .' Hawkins interview, op. cit.
72 'People used language pretty freely . . .' Gordon interview, op. cit.
72–3 'Murphy was flamboyant . . .' Bornstein interview, op. cit.
73 'We enjoyed the odd . . .' ibid.
75 'Just watching . . .' ibid.
75 'She was great . . .' Hawkins interview, op. cit.
76 'I am a complete apostrophe nut . . .' Julia Gillard quoted, McGuire, Michael, 'Becoming Julia', *Advertiser*, 6 February 2009. One or two of Gillard's former colleagues say that the memory of her 'cats' hats' lessons still makes them nervous.
76 'I don't think . . .' Hawkins interview, op. cit.
76 'When Kate and I . . .' Bornstein interview, op. cit.
76–7 'Bernard kept pursuing . . .' ibid.
77 In 1998 . . . The waterfront dispute was primarily between the Maritime Union of Australia, led by Paddy Crumlin, and Patrick Stevedores, with Chris Corrigan as CEO. On the night of 7 April, in the name of improved efficiency on the waterfront and with the support of the Howard government's workplace relations minister, Peter Reith, Corrigan sacked his entire workforce, locked them out and set up new companies to employ a non-unionised workforce trained in Dubai. The case went before the Federal Court, with Justice North finding in favour of the MUA. The finding was challenged and the case ended up in the High Court. The full bench again found, in the MUA's favour, that Patrick had carried out a corporate restructure intended solely to allow the dismissal of their unionised workforce. The MUA and Patrick negotiated a new work agreement, adopted by the company and workers in June 1998.
77 'I picked up the phone . . .' Bornstein interview, op. cit.
77 'Once you become a friend . . .' ibid.
77–8 'She had asked me to go . . .' ibid.
78 'She could get across . . .' Hawkins interview, op. cit.

7 Welcome to first grade

79 Welcome to . . . This story is part of folklore for most Australian football codes.
80 'I lived in a share house . . .' Julia Gillard interview with Jacqueline Kent, 13 March 2009.
80 'She rang me . . .' Brendan Soraghan interview with Doug Hendrie, March 2009.
81 'I knew Lindsay . . .' Gillard interview, op. cit.
82 'I think in part . . .' Andrew Scott interview with DH, March 2009.
83 'There was real bitterness . . .' Andrew McKenzie interview with DH, March 2009.
83–4 'Carr wanted . . .' ibid.
84 'He didn't want her . . .' Darrell Cochrane interview with DH, March 2009.
84 'My supporters were lukewarm . . .' Frans Timmerman interview with DH, March 2009.

8 Mixing it with the blokes: 2

86 By early 1992 . . . Andrew McKenzie interview with Doug Hendrie, February 2009.
87 Peter Gordon believes that people don't remember . . . Peter Gordon interview with DH, March 2009.
88 According to Peter Gordon . . . ibid.
89 'We had commitments . . .' ibid.
89 'I think Brumby . . .' ibid.
90 'Sometimes when you . . .' ibid.
90 'Some people would . . .' ibid.
90 'It was very regimented . . .' Julia Gillard interview with Jacqueline Kent, 21 May 2009.
90 'It was very difficult . . .' ibid.
93 'The story broke . . .' ibid.
94 'Working there . . .' ibid.

9 'Sometimes you can say things happen for a reason'

95 'Sometimes you can say . . .' Julia Gillard interview with Jacqueline Kent, 13 March 2009.
95 'Politics was always . . .' Andrew McKenzie interview with Doug Hendrie, March 2009.
97 'I thought I had . . .' Julia Gillard interview with JK, 21 May 2009.
97 'I was on hold . . .' ibid.
98 'I said I hadn't spent much time . . .' ibid.

98 'It was even worse . . .' ibid.
98 'I knew I had to make a decision . . .' ibid.
99 'John made a good call . . .' McKenzie interview, op. cit.
99–100 'I was coming in as a novice . . .' Gillard interview, 21 May, op. cit.
100 'The chief of staff . . .' McKenzie interview, op. cit.
100 'In the Victorian system . . .' Gillard interview, 21 May, op. cit.
100–1 'It wasn't factional . . .' ibid.
101 'I thought Brumby was . . .' ibid.
101–2 'Kennett had so altered the rules . . .' ibid.
102 'Brumby and his parliamentary colleagues . . .' McKenzie interview, op. cit.
102–3 'In our dark hours . . .' Gillard interview, 21 May, op. cit.
103–4 'He'd been leader . . .' ibid.
104 'I think some of the time . . .' John Brumby, interview, 23 November 2007, at www.premier.vic.gov.au.
104 'I'm not any kind of religious person . . .' Gillard interview, 13 March, op. cit.

10 Getting there

106 'I think there might have been a time . . .' Andrew McKenzie interview with Doug Hendrie, March 2009.
106 'I can't see why they were so against her . . .' Caroline Hogg interview with DH, March 2009.
107 'When Joan Kirner was defeated . . .' Julia Gillard, *Counterpoint,* ABC Radio National, 20 September 2004, transcript.
107 'When I left . . .' Joan Kirner interview with Jacqueline Kent, 17 February 2009.
107–8 'Some were more into . . .' ibid.
108 'It was time for our party . . .' ibid.
108 In January 1994 . . . Others who worked for the 1994 affirmative action rules included Meredith Burgmann and Jan Burnswoods (New South Wales); Judy Spence (Queensland); Carolyn Pickles (SA); Sue Mackay and Fran Bladel (Tasmania); Candy Broad and Kay Setches (Victoria); and Helen Creed (Western Australia).
109 'Then we sat back . . .' Kirner interview, op. cit.
110 The idea to develop . . . Some of the information about EMILY's List Australia has been taken from Lee-Ack, Emily, 'Making a Difference: How EMILY's List Is Working to Achieve Gender Equity in Parliaments', paper presented to the Women's Constitutional Convention, Canberra, 12 June 2002, as well as from Kirner interview, op. cit., and Leonie Morgan interview with JK, 13 March 2009.
110 'We met regularly . . .' Morgan interview, op. cit.
110 'The problem . . .' ibid.
110 'She was one of the first . . .' ibid.

111 EMILY's List Australia . . . In terms of the present representation of women in federal Parliament, the ALP at 37 per cent is well ahead of the Liberal Party (22 per cent) and the National Party (15.4 per cent). The Greens are on 50 per cent. However, the total figure for women parliamentarians across all parties and all Australian parliaments is 30.7 per cent. See 'Composition of Australian Parliaments by Party and Gender as at 30 October 2008', paper by Politics and Public Administration Group, Parliamentary Library, Commonwealth of Australia.

111–12 Victorian federal seat of Lalor . . . See www.politics.net.au/Lalor and apps.aec.gov.au/esearch/LocalitySearchResults.aspx?filter=Lalor&filterby=Electorate.

113 'an instrument for exposing people to . . .' Javes, Sue, 'In So Many Words', *Sydney Morning Herald*, 23 April 2007.

115 'When you're going for a seat . . .' Julia Gillard interview with JK, 13 March 2009.

115 'There were about three hundred . . .' ibid.

117 'If I ever meet anyone tougher . . .' Josh Bornstein interview with DH, March 2009.

117 'I have very clear recollections . . .' Gillard interview, op. cit.

11 New kid on the block

121 'passion and conviction' . . . Julia Gillard, Hansard, House of Representatives, 11 November 1998, at www.aph.gov.au/Hansard/reps/dailys/dr111198.pdf.

121 'a Labor landmark . . .' ibid.

121–2 'As part of Melbourne's industrial west . . .' ibid.

122 'As a community . . .' ibid.

122–3 'Immigrants need courage . . .' ibid.

123 'Around the world now . . .' ibid.

124 'People today . . .' ibid.

124 After she delivered her speech . . . Julia Gillard interview with Jacqueline Kent, 13 March 2009.

125 'I have a really bad sense of direction . . .' ibid.

125 'I had my views about John Howard . . .' ibid.

125 'I knew some of it . . .' ibid.

125–6 'They are the really popular ones . . .' ibid.

126 'They confused me with . . .' ibid.

127 'They were all sitting . . .' ibid.

127 'They were waiting around . . .' ibid.

127–8 Australia's future as a republic . . . The public was asked whether Australia should become a republic with a president appointed by a two-thirds federal parliamentary majority (a bipartisan model previously decided at the Constitutional Convention of February 1998) and whether the constitution should be altered to insert a preamble. About 55 per cent of Australians and all states voted no, so Lalor was not too far from the national average. The referendum was decisively defeated partly because of Australian voters' traditional caution about proposed constitutional change, but also because pro-republicans did not agree on their preferred model, many favouring a directly elected head of state. See www.aph.gov.au/library/intguide/pol/polcon.htm.

12 'We will decide who comes to this country'

131 'We will decide who . . .' John Howard, speech, 10 November 2001, at www.australianpolitics.com.

131 The boat that the *Tampa* . . . Marr, David, and Wilkinson, Marian, *Dark Victory*, Allen & Unwin, Sydney, 2003, gives a detailed and comprehensive outline of events during the *Tampa* crisis and leading up to the 2001 federal election.

132 'There was a profound conviction . . .' Kim Beazley quoted, ibid., p. 99.

134 'on the security issues . . .' Kim Beazley, *Lateline*, ABC-TV, 25 September 2001, transcript.

134 'I always thought we were going to struggle . . .' Julia Gillard interview with Jacqueline Kent, 21 April 2009.

135 Gillard's majority was reduced . . . ibid.

136 'We [had] turned the corner. . .' Tim Gartrell, *Lateline*, ABC-TV, 21 November 2001, transcript.

137 'Labor's idea of generational change . . .' Lynton Crosby, ibid.

137 'Crean is proposing Party reform . . .' Latham, Mark, *The Latham Diaries*, Melbourne University Press, Carlton, 2005, p. 179.

138 'Crean is certainly not afraid . . .' ibid.

138 'Simon also got on well . . .' Gillard interview, op. cit.

139 'I volunteered . . .' ibid.

139 'We were always going to struggle . . .' ibid.

13 'A desire to be practical'

140 'a desire to be practical' . . . When thanking her colleagues from student days during her maiden speech, Julia Gillard said, 'Ours was a radicalism fashioned by a desire to be practical'. See Julia Gillard, Hansard, House of Representatives, 11 November 1998, at www.aph.gov.au/Hansard/reps/dailys/dr111198.pdf.

141 had real potential to split the ALP . . . Some of the information for this chapter is taken from Faulkner, Xandra Madeleine, 'The Spirit of Accommodation', PhD thesis, Department of Politics and Public Policy, Griffith Business School, 2006, chs 7–8. The thesis deals primarily with the role of the ALP factions during this period, with reference to the ALP's responses to Howard's policies.

142 introduced mandatory detention . . . 'UNHCR statistics show that Australia has experienced fewer asylum claims than other industrialised countries, especially the high asylum countries of western Europe. Australia received 5860 claims in 2002, 4300 in 2003 and 3100 in 2004. The UK received 103,080 asylum claims in 2002, 60,050 in 2003 and 40,200 in 2004.': 'The Detention and Removal of Asylum Seekers', e-brief, 5 July 2005, Parliamentary Library, Commonwealth of Australia.

142 Philip Ruddock . . . softened the policy . . . ibid.

146 'a huge learning curve . . .' Julia Gillard interview with Jacqueline Kent, 21 April 2009.

146 'I see my role . . .' Julia Gillard quoted, 'The Wedge Buster', *Workers Online*, 15 March 2002.

146 'I went all over the country. . .' Gillard interview, op. cit.

148 'I actually don't think that the polarisation . . .' Gillard quoted, 'The Wedge Buster', op. cit.

148 'I agree with John Howard's statement . . .' Julia Gillard, *Sunday*, Channel Nine, 14 April 2002, transcript.

150 'He would sashay into . . .' Julia Gillard, Hansard, House of Representatives, 9 June 2003, at www.aph.gov.au/Hansard/reps/dailys/dr050603.pdf.

151 'a cop on the beat' . . . 'Protecting Australia and Protecting the Australian Way: Labor's Policy on Asylum Seekers and Refugees', at www.parlinfo.aph.gov.au/parlinfo/download/library/partypol.

151 'Labor understands that unauthorised boat arrivals . . .' ibid.

153 'Look, I was very proud . . .' Julia Gillard, *Counterpoint*, ABC Radio National, 20 September 2004, transcript.

153 'I wanted to put . . .' Julia Gillard interview with JK, 13 March 2009.

14 The life of the party

155 'the present conservatism . . .' 'Cut the ALP Adrift', paper presented by the CFMEU to a trade union seminar, Melbourne 12 June 2002, at www.greenleft.org.au/2002/495/28152.

156 'We lost because . . .' Tanner, Lindsay, 'The ALP, a Renovator's Nightmare', *Age*, 22 March 2002.

156 national committee of review . . . For the Hawke–Wran report see australianpolitics.com/news/2002/08/02-08-09.shtml.

157 Cunningham . . . by-election . . . See www.aph.gov.au/Library/pubs/rn/2002-03/03rn18.htm.

157 snarling 'junkyard dog' . . . Neil Mitchell, Radio 3AW, 26 April, 2002, transcript.

157 'continued down his well-worn path . . .' Latham, Mark, *The Latham Diaries*, Melbourne University Press, Carlton, 2005, entry for 29 October 2002, p. 201.

158 'Full disclosure by Iraq . . .' John Howard, Hansard, House of Representatives, 4 February 2003, at www.aph.gov.au/Hansard/reps/dailys/dr040203.pdf.
158 'Crean is bleeding . . .' Latham, op. cit, entry for 24 January 2003, pp. 210–11.
159 'There's a lot about being involved . . .' Julia Gillard, *Australian Story*, ABC-TV, 6 March 2006, broadcast section, at www.abc.net.au/austory/content/2006/s1586140.htm.
159 'If it is part of anyone's strategy . . .' Julia Gillard, *Lateline*, ABC-TV, 4 June 2003, transcript.
160 'I believe Simon Crean . . .' ibid.
160–1 'The main interesting point . . .' Alexandra Kirk, *Lateline*, ABC-TV, 2 July 2003, transcript.
161 'She's Smart, Tough . . .' 'Faces of Julia', *Age*, 21 June 2003.
161 'dubbed Elizabeth Taylor . . .' O'Rourke, Jim, *Sun-Herald*, 6 July 2003.
161 'Being involved with a colleague . . .' Julia Gillard, *Australian Story*, op. cit.
162 'Craig and I . . .' ibid.
163 'We are in a terrible position . . .' Latham, op. cit., entry for 11 September 2003, pp. 234, 235.
163 'Excellent news . . .' ibid, entry for 2 June 2003, p. 223.
164 'Obviously there were people . . .' Julia Gillard, quoted in Crabb, Annabel, *Losing It*, Picador, Sydney, 2005, p. 268.
165 'Beazley was fundamentally . . .' ibid.

15 Taking care of business

167 'the new radical centre . . .' Latham, Mark, *Civilising Global Capital: New Thinking for Australian Labor*, Allen & Unwin, Sydney, 1998, p. xxx. See also Blunden, Andy, 'Review: Mark Latham's *Civilising Global Capital*', May 2003, at home.mira.net/~andy/works/latham.htm.
169–70 'The Minister at the table . . .' Julia Gillard, *PM*, ABC Radio National, 7 October 2003, transcript.
172 'Throughout the 1980s . . .' Julia Gillard, speech, Evatt Foundation, 5 September 2003, at www.evatt.org.au.
172–3 'The minister could not be . . .' Julia Gillard, address, Pursuing Opportunity and Prosperity 2003 Economic and Social Outlook Conference, University of Melbourne, 14 November 2003, at www.melbourneinstitute.com.
173 'A good meeting . . .' Latham, Mark, *The Latham Diaries*, Melbourne University Press, Carlton, 2005, entry for 13 February 2004, p. 267.
175 'he straddles the sub-factions . . .' ibid., p. 268.
175 'I like Gillard . . .' ibid.

16 Implosion

176 'a cauldron . . .' Michael Brissenden, *7.30 Report*, ABC-TV, 28 January 2004, transcript.

176–7 '[They comprised] the gay activists . . .' Hearn, Mark, 'Enduring Labor Values: Report of the 43rd ALP Conference 29–31 January 2004', *Labour History*, no. 86, May 2004, at www.historycooperative.org/journals.

177 He spoke . . . ibid. *Plus ça change*: it's interesting to look at some of the subjects that came up for discussion at the forty-third ALP national conference in view of more recent history. Kim Carr said Labor would support strategic intervention; and there was a detailed government procurement policy for protecting Australian manufacturing and jobs and a commitment to establishing a renewable energy target of at least 5 per cent by 2010. Money should be set aside to finance the revival of the Murray–Darling river system and to extend the Great Barrier Reef National Park. There was also a motion that executive pay packages should be approved by shareholder vote, and that tax deductions should be withdrawn for executive packages over $1 million. And Kevin Rudd, shadow foreign affairs spokesman, gave a speech in favour of UN membership, commitment to ANZUS and a more comprehensive engagement with Australia's region.

179 'We have to draft . . .' ibid.

179 'wonderfully penetrating . . .' Dick Morris, *AM*, ABC Radio National, 4 December 2003, transcript.

179 'Howard is like . . .' ibid.

180 Commonwealth contributory superannuation scheme . . . 'On 10 February 2004 the leader of the Opposition, Mark Latham MP, announced that a Labor Government would close down the current superannuation schemes for Federal MPs, judges and the governor-general . . . Mr Latham stated that . . . [these schemes] are well outside the community standard in Australia and have become out of date. They offer superannuation benefits seven times more generous than the current contribution scheme available to the general public. Parliamentary superannuation has become a major source of public dissatisfaction and cynicism in modern politics . . . On 12 February 2004 the Prime Minister, the Hon John Howard MP, announced in response that the the government would close the P[arliamentary] C[ontribution] S[uperannuation] S[cheme] and establish new superannuation arrangements for new Members and Senators elected from the next federal election.': Parliamentary Superannuation Bill 2004, *Bills Digest*, no. 131, 2003–4, Parliamentary Library, Parliament of Australia, at www.aph.gov.au/library.

182 'My numbers are still okay . . .' Latham, Mark, *The Latham Diaries*, Melbourne University Press, Carlton, 2005, entry for 31 July 2004, p. 324.

183 '[The voters] don't . . .' John Utting quoted, ibid.

183 'The electorate is pretty perceptive . . .' ibid.

184 'Forget politics . . .' ibid, entry for 22 August 2004, p. 331.

184 'Let's do the election . . .' ibid.
188 'To the extent that Medicare Gold . . .' Julia Gillard quoted, Crabb, Annabel, 'How Latham Lost the Plot', *Age,* 18 September 2005.
189–90 'In the few days before the policy . . .' Julia Gillard, *Australian Story*, ABC-TV, March 2006, section not broadcast, at www.abc.net.au/austory/content/2006/s1585300.htm.
190 'Politics is not a consideration . . .' Mark Latham, *The World Today*, ABC Radio National, 5 October 2004, transcript.
191 'It's quite clear . . .' CEO Forest Industries Association of Tasmania quoted, 'Labor's Old Growth Forest Gamble', *Age*, 5 October 2004.
191 'If Mark Latham . . .' John Howard quoted, ibid.
191 'Howard was smart enough . . .' Gillard, *Australian Story*, op. cit.
191–2 'I said when . . .' John Howard quoted, 'Howard Trades Trees for Jobs', *Age*, 7 October 2004.
192 '[W]e hope the Labor Party . . .' Michael O'Connor, *PM*, ABC Radio National, 6 October 2004, transcript.
192–3 'Michael [knew] . . .' Gillard, *Australian Story*, op. cit.

17 'Much more than a job'

194–5 'Everybody was shattered . . .' Julia Gillard, *Australian Story*, ABC-TV, March 2006, section not broadcast, at www.abc.net.au/austory/content/2006/s1585300.htm.
195 '[I]n the old days . . .' Latham, Mark, *The Latham Diaries*, Melbourne University Press, Carlton, 2005, entry for 25 October 2004, p. 365.
195 'Gillard is the best . . .' ibid., pp 365–6.
196 'I sat down with Gillard . . .' ibid., entry for 30 November 2004, p. 391.
197 'all the talented Labor women . . .' ibid., entry for 25 October, p. 366.
197–8 'The article said . . .' ibid., 30 November 2004, p. 392.
198 'Mark at that stage . . .' Gillard, *Australian Story*, op. cit.
199 'I've rung you . . .' Chris Evans quoted, Gillard, ibid.
200 'Mark at that stage was holed up . . .' Gillard, ibid.
200–1 'He meant that as . . .' ibid.
201 'I took the view . . .' ibid.
201 'First, the good news . . .' Latham, op. cit., entry for 1 January 2005, p. 405.
201–2 'I knew after the election . . .' Gillard, *Australian Story*, op. cit.
202 'He wanted me to do a rough count . . .' ibid.
202 'In other circumstances . . .' Mungo MacCallum quoted, 'Mark Latham', en.wikipedia.org.
203 'I thought I will get . . .' Gillard, *Australian Story*, op. cit.
204 'As he rang around . . .' ibid.
204 *The Latham Diaries* . . . The story behind their publication is an interesting one. Literary agent Mary Cunnane wrote to Mark Latham, thinking he might

have a book to write about his experience in politics and as ALP leader. She heard nothing for six weeks and then received a letter from him suggesting that they meet. When they did, Latham said that he was indeed thinking of such a book, and that he had kept diaries during his years in politics that could form its basis. When she asked whether other publishers or agents had approached him, to her surprise he said none had. Nevertheless, a number of major publishers subsequently made offers for it, with Melbourne University Press ultimately securing the rights. *The Latham Diaries* reprinted twice and went into paperback, and has been alternately praised and condemned as the political book of the decade. For an interesting perspective on the diaries see 'Labor, Larrikins and the Latham Diaries' at docs.google.com/gview?a=v&q=cache:7Huqd5-x380J:www.uow.edu.au/arts/research/ejournal/archives/nov05/smith-article.pdf+Labor,+Larrikins+and+the+Latham+Diaries&hl=en.

205–6 'I do not keep a diary . . .' Julia Gillard, speech, Going Public Conference sponsored by the Equal Opportunity for Women in the Workplace Agency, 17 September 2005, at webdiary.com.au.

206 'Mark Latham's pin-up girl . . .' Monica Attard, *Sunday Profile*, ABC Local Radio, 25 September 2005, transcript.

206–7 'I don't agree with what Mark . . .' Julia Gillard, ibid.

207 'I'm going to forever have the history . . .' ibid.

207 *Bulletin* columnist Laurie Oakes criticised . . . Oakes, Laurie, 'Power Plays', *Bulletin*, 5 October 2005.

18 The national health

208 'The Howard Government ministers . . .' Tony Abbott, *7.30 Report*, ABC-TV, 13 April 2005, transcript.

210 'If Howard wins . . .' Julia Gillard, *Lateline*, ABC-TV, 12 September 2006, transcript.

210 'The free public hospital . . .' ibid.

211 The controversy over mifepristone or RU 486 . . . For a useful overview of the debate, see 'Therapeutic Goods Amendment (Repeal of Ministerial Responsibility for Approval of RU486) Bill 2005', at www.comlaw.gov.au/comlaw/legislation/bills1.nsf/0/7ACC6C60DDFF4F38CA2570D800799F22/$file/05203b.pdf.

212 'A minister's personal opinions . . .' Gillard, *Lateline*, op. cit.

213 the question of stem cell research . . . For a lucid overview of the debate, see 'The Embryonic Stem Cell Debate and the Lockhart Report Dilemma', at www.drfeelgood.com.au/articles/lockhart.pdf.

214 'so-called therapeutic cloning . . .' 'Abbott Fears Stem-cell Researchers Will Follow Dolly to Clone Humans', *Age*, 3 August 2006.

215 'We don't know whether . . .' Julia Gillard, *The World Today*, ABC Radio National, 30 November 2006, transcript.

215 According to Michelle Grattan . . . Grattan, Michelle, *Age*, 1 October 2003.
216 'Hello. Abbott's out there . . .' Julia Gillard, *Australian Story*, ABC-TV, 6 March 2006, broadcast section, at www.abc.net.au/austory/content/2006/s1586140.htm.
216 'On those rare occasions . . .' Tony Abbott, ibid.
217 'a bit more humanity' . . . Tony Abbott quoted, *Herald Sun*, 5 October 2007.
217 'Could Tony Abbott . . .' Julia Gillard, *The World Today*, ABC Radio National, 6 October 2007, transcript.

19 An extra layer of armour

223 'I was very sad . . .' Julia Gillard, *Australian Story*, ABC-TV, 6 March 2006, section not broadcast, at www.abc.net.au/austory/content/2006/s1585300.htm.
224 Indeed, as Julia Gillard has . . . ibid. Gillard said: 'I think he is aware that he does need to be a different style of leader than perhaps he was able to be in the 96 to 98 period when the sense of having endured a bad defeat together kept people together, the sense that we were close, had almost won the 1998 election, kept people together in the 98–2001 period. But the 2001–04 period had created so many wounds and so damaged the culture I think he knew he was dealing with a whole different federal parliamentary Labor party, a whole different animal.'
225 'Maybe I'm starting . . .' Greg Combet, *PM*, ABC Radio National, 16 February 2006, transcript.
225 'There are things . . .' Gillard, *Australian Story*, op. cit.
227 'This has been the most remarked upon . . .' Julia Gillard, *Insiders*, ABC-TV, 8 May 2005.
227 'We'd long been intrigued . . .' Hawkins, Belinda, in *Australian Story: Off the Record*, ABC Books, Sydney, 2007, p. 55.
227–8 'I had to make a judgment . . .' Julia Gillard, quoted in Crabb, Annabel, *Losing It*, Picador, Sydney, 2005, p. 43.
228 'I genuinely think Kim . . .' Gillard, *Australian Story*, ABC-TV, 6 March 2006, broadcast section, at www.abc.net.au/austory/content/2006/s1586140.htm.
228–9 'Before you can persuade Australians . . .' Julia Gillard, speech, Sydney Institute, 7 March 2006. See Schubert, Misha, and Austin, Paul, 'Gillard Lays Down the Law', *Age*, 8 March 2006.
229 'There's nothing unreasonable . . .' Carmen Lawrence, *Lateline*, ABC-TV, 16 March 2006, transcript.
229 'unacceptable' . . . Lindsay Tanner, ibid.
229 Journalists, mostly . . . A full account of the extent of media hostility to Julia Gillard at this time can be found in Kevin, Tony, 'The Targeting of Julia Gillard', 20 March 2006, at www.tonykevin.com.au.

229 'Gillard looked loved . . .' Christian Kerr quoted, ibid.
229–30 'Gillard obviously . . .' Oakes, Laurie, 'Power Plays', *Bulletin*, 21 March 2006.
230 'the hypocrisy gold . . .' Costello, Michael, *Australian*, 10 March 2006. In *Australian*, 24 March 2006, Costello also wrote: 'She is not about policy. She is about look at me, look at me. Her aim is the celebrity that brings public approval.'
230 Christopher Pearson . . . Pearson, Christopher, 'Something about Julia', *Australian,* 11 March 2006.
231 'Gillard is single and childless . . .' *Australian*, 15 March 2006.
232 'Maybe politics puts . . .' Gillard, *Australian Story*, section not broadcast, op. cit.

20 Nothing for granted

234–5 'Christopher has described . . .' Julia Gillard, *Lateline*, ABC-TV, 6 May 2007, transcript.
236 There are various accounts . . . Several clear accounts have been written by journalists about the Rudd and Gillard strategy in going for the ALP leadership. They include Hartcher, Peter, *To the Bitter End*, Allen & Unwin, Sydney, 2009; Jackman, Christine, *Inside Kevin 07*, Melbourne University Press, Carlton, 2008; Macklin, Robert, *Kevin Rudd: The Biography*, Viking, Melbourne, 2007; and Stuart, Nicholas, *Kevin Rudd: An Unauthorised Biography*, Scribe, Melbourne, 2007.
236 'While ever it was split . . .' Kim Beazley quoted, Hartcher, op. cit., p. 156.
237–8 'It's fair to say Kim Carr . . .' Julia Gillard quoted, ibid., p. 157.
238 'If Kim Beazley were to . . .' Gillard quoted, ibid.
238 'There were people in the middle . . .' Gillard quoted, ibid.
241 'My political analysis . . .' Julia Gillard quoted, Jackman, op. cit., p. 56.
243 'I mean, anyone who chooses . . .' Bill Heffernan quoted, *Bulletin*, 1 May 2007.
243 'Kevin said . . .' Gillard quoted, Hartcher, op. cit., p. 211.
244 'basically a decent bloke . . .' Julia Gillard interview with Jacqueline Kent, 21 May 2009.
245–6 'The two things people hated most . . .' Julia Gillard conversation with JK, 10 July 2009.
247 'It was a good night . . .' Julia Gillard conversation with JK, 1 July 2009.

21 'An awesome responsibility but a terrific opportunity'

248–9 Julia Gillard's long political journey . . . For the swearing-in ceremony, Monday 3 December 2007, see www.abc.net.au/news/video.
250 'It's an awesome responsibility . . .' Julia Gillard, speech, Australian Industry Group, reported in full in *Australian,* 5 December 2007.
251 'After seventeen years . . .' ibid.

252 'Our social inclusion policies . . .' ibid.
252 'When Kevin Rudd said . . .' ibid.
253 'I reckon the Accord . . .' Julia Gillard interview with Jacqueline Kent, 21 May 2009.
254 'Today we deliver . . .' Julia Gillard, Hansard, House of Representatives, 25 November 2008, at www.aph.gov.au/reps/dailys/dr251108.pdf.
255 'a right and proper balance . . .' ibid.
259–62 Gillard agreed to more minor amendments . . . Gillard conversation with JK, 1 July 2009.
260 'a pathetic political point . . .' Malcolm Turnbull, Hansard, House of Representatives,19 March 2009, at www.aph.gov.au/reps/dailys/dr190309.pdf.
261 'I can't wait to see the bumper stickers . . .' Julia Gillard, ibid.
261 As political editor . . . Grattan, Michelle, 'Gillard's Steel Helps Grind Work Choices into Extinction', *Age*, 21 March 2009.
261 'It's called keeping your election promises . . .' Chris Evans, Hansard, Senate, 19 March 2009, at www.aph.gov.au/Hansard/senate/dailys/ds190309.
262 'the Senate does not insist . . .' Joe Ludwig, ibid.
262 no majority vote against . . . 'In the Senate the motion not to insist on those amendments was negatived by equally divided votes, with the effect that the amendments were lost. On this occasion . . . Senator Fielding supported the government on the basis of further undertakings on this subject. The bill then passed without the disputed amendments. The opponents of the bill had the option of locking the bill in the Senate; although there was no motion for a third reading, because the issues in dispute were the subject of amendments rather than requests and the bill had already been read a third time, the passage of the bill could have been prevented by negativing procedural motions following the failure of the amendments to keep majority support . . . but this option was not taken.': Parliament of Australia, Senate, *Procedural Information Bulletin*, no. 230, at www.aph.gov.au/SENATE.
262 'Today . . . we have buried . . .' Julia Gillard quoted, Grattan, op. cit.
262 'I am wondering where my hug . . .' Steve Fielding, Hansard, Senate, 19 March 2009, at www.aph.gov.au/Hansard/senate/dailys/ds190309.

22 Circling back

263 'People do not . . .' Joan Kirner interview with Jacqueline Kent, 18 February 2009.
263 'She has always wanted . . .' ibid.
263 'Making a difference . . .' Julia Gillard conversation with JK, 10 July 2009.
264 'Over the course of the last decade . . .' Julia Gillard, speech, 'A Higher Education Revolution: Creating a Productive, Prosperous, Modern Australia', quoted, *Australian Financial Review*, 13 March 2008.
265 the ideas of Joel Klein . . . See http://bigthink.com/joelklein/ideas.

265 'The combination . . .' Julia Gillard, opening address to the Australian Primary Principals' Association Annual Conference, Sydney, 29 October 2008, at www.alp.org.au/media/1008/speed291.php.

267 'I am not interested in taking resources . . .' Julia Gillard quoted, *Sydney Morning Herald*, 28 May 2008.

267 In the federal Budget . . . The figures for federal investment in education are taken from a press release from Gillard's office: 'Budget 2009–10: Investing in a Fair and Productive Australia', 12 May 2009. It also says: 'In this budget the Rudd government is investing over $4 billion in Job Services Australia to support people who are unemployed. This includes $2.98 million to provide immediate access to employment services for workers made redundant. A $650 million Jobs Fund will help support local jobs and training in regions hardest hit by the global recession . . . The Rudd government will introduce a temporary Training Supplement of $41.60 per fortnight for Newstart and Parenting Payment recipients to encourage those Australians vulnerable to long term unemployment to undertake training.'

268 'That Education Revolution . . .' Crabb, Annabel, *Sydney Morning Herald*, 30 May 2009.

270 a review of higher education . . . *Review of Australian Higher Education Report* (Bradley report), at www.deewr.gov.au/HigherEduation/Review/Pages/ReviewofAustralianHigherEducationReport.aspx.

271 The report was criticised . . . Gill, John, 'Oz Elite Damn Review as "a Road Map to Mediocrity"', *Times Higher Education Supplement*, 26 February 2009.

272 $5.7 million in higher education . . . 'Budget 2009–10', op. cit.

272 'I think we have to recognise . . .' Julia Gillard, *Australian Story*, ABC-TV, 6 March 2006, section not broadcast, at www.abc.net.au/austory/content/2006/s1585300.htm.

273 'It's nice to meet . . .' Tim Mathieson quoted, Valent, Dani, 'Our Julia', *Age*, 18 May 2007.

274 'net energy takers' . . . Julia Gillard quoted, ibid.

274 'I'm sort of . . .' Mathieson quoted, ibid.

274 'He's got a terrific . . .' Julia Gillard interview with JK, 13 March 2009.

274 'She eats out all week so . . .' Mathieson quoted, Valent, op. cit.

274–5 'not as mechanical as saying . . .' Gillard, *Australian Story*, op. cit.

275 'I think that one of the problems for women . . .' Gillard, ibid.

275 'I think women are still making their way . . .' Julia Gillard quoted, 'Julia Gillard Says Today Will Be Business as Usual', *Herald Sun*, 11 December 2007.

276 'I'd like to think that maybe . . .' Julia Gillard, *The World Today*, ABC Radio National, 11 December 2007, transcript.

276 'If Rudd wasn't comfortable about her . . .' Economou, Nick, *Age*, 18 January 2009.

277 'This job, this life . . .' Gillard conversation, op. cit.

Julia up close

280 'Well, I was told . . .' Julia Gillard interview with Jacqueline Kent, 13 March 2009.

280 'Oh well, these things . . .' ibid.

282 'You never let the media . . .' Julia Gillard, *Australian Story*, ABC-TV, 6 March 2006, section not broadcast, at www.abc.net.au/austory/content/2006/s1585300.htm.

282 'I don't read seriously . . .' Julia Gillard interview with JK, 21 May 2009.

283 'It's only natural . . .' ibid.

285 'Anyone who thinks . . .' ibid.

Acknowledgements

This book could not have been completed without the work of two people: journalist Doug Hendrie, who researched and conducted most of the interviews and so played a major role in allowing me to delineate Gillard's career before federal politics, and John Tuchin, whose experience and perspective as a former Commonwealth public servant proved invaluable in interpreting government documents of various kinds.

Thanks also to my agent Mary Cunnane, and Ben Ball and Meredith Rose of Penguin Books. I am especially grateful to Penguin editor Lesley Dunt, the colleague whose focused and unflagging commitment to the project made the job of writing so much easier and more pleasant.

Many people kindly agreed to be interviewed for the book. Firstly I must thank Julia Gillard for several interviews and corrections of fact; and Ben Hubbard, Amanda Lampe and Rachael Purcell on her staff.

My grateful thanks also to interviewees Josh Bornstein, John Buchanan, Mark Burford, Paul Carrick, Darrell Cochrane, Greg Day, Nick Economou, Paul Erickson, Andrew Giles, Peter Gordon, Julie Grainger, Kate Hawkins, Caroline Hogg, Joan Kirner, Andrew McKenzie, Leonie Morgan, Bernard Murphy, Laurie Oakes, Geoff Robinson, Andrew Scott, Paul Slape, Brendan Soraghan, Nick Styant-Browne, Mark Taft, Gayle Tierney, Frans Timmerman,

Laura Tingle, and Lesley Yates. Several people who agreed to be interviewed did not wish to have their comments quoted in the text, which meant the occasional invocation of 'a Labor source'. Having previously considered this phrase as code for 'I made it up', I now realise how unfair that was.

I am also grateful to the staff of the ABC Reference Library, Ultimo; Steve Adams, Chris Bendall, Edna Carew, Andrew Crook and Di Gribble from crikey.com; Beverley Firth; Tom Foley of the National Library of Australia; Candace Gibson; Helen Grasswill and Belinda Hawkins from ABC-TV's *Australian Story*; Anne Hickerton; Marissa Lumasag; David Marr; Kerry Miller; Julianne Schultz; and Junee Waites.

Xandra Madeleine Faulkner's Ph.D. thesis, 'The Spirit of Accommodation: The Influence of the ALP's National Factions on Party Policy 1996–2004', Department of Politics and Public Policy, Griffith University, 2006, gave some very useful signposts. I also wish to thank Mark Latham and Melbourne University Press for permission to use extracts from *The Latham Diaries*, MUP, Carlton, 2005.

To friends and family who continued to express interest despite being told about ALP factional disputes and other arcane matters, I remain grateful. I think you know who you are, but in case you don't: John Tuchin, Telford Conlon, Suzanne Falkiner, Sandy Nash, Christine Draeger, Mardi Kent, Mark Aronson, Duncan Ball, Jill Quin, Dianne Takahashi, Linda Entwistle, Victoria Green, John Pomeroy, Hilary Vallance, Joy Storie and the GRs.

Pictorial sources

The author and publisher are grateful to the following sources for permission to reproduce pictorial material.

First section

The Gillard family at their new home in Adelaide . . . Newspix/News Ltd.
Schoolkid . . . Newspix/News Ltd.
A teenager at Unley High School . . . Newspix/News Ltd.
President of the Australian Union of Students, 1983 . . . Staff/Fairfaxphotos.com.
Members of the Socialist Forum . . . Ray Kennedy/Fairfaxphotos.com.
A partner at Slater and Gordon . . . Ken Irwin/Fairfaxphotos.com.
Protesting against the Liberal government's handling of the 1998 waterfront dispute . . . Angela Wylie/Fairfaxphotos.com.
The newly elected Labor member for Lalor . . . Wayne Taylor/Fairfaxphotos.com.
Photographed at her Melbourne home . . . Craig Sillitoe/Fairfaxphotos.com.

Second section

Julia Gillard and federal Opposition leader Simon Crean . . . Joe Armao/Fairfaxphotos.com.
With Craig Emerson at the National Press Club . . . Newspix/Michael Jones.

Mark Latham and Julia Gillard launch Labor's health policy . . . Newspix/ David Geraghty.

Just back in January 2005 from a holiday in Vietnam . . . Penny Stephens/ Fairfaxphotos.com.

The infamous 'empty fruit bowl' photograph . . . Ken Irwin/Fairfaxphotos.com.

Conflict and consultation . . . Newspix/Kym Smith.

New leadership . . . Andrew Taylor/Fairfaxphotos.com.

Sturt Krygsman's comment . . . Newspix/Sturt Krygsman.

Shortly before the 2007 election . . . ACP Magazines Syndication/James Braund.

Third section

27 November 2007 . . . Newspix/News Ltd.

28 November 2008 . . . Newspix/News Ltd.

Just before the new ministers are sworn in . . . William West/GettyImages

John and Moira Gillard at home . . . Newspix/News Ltd.

On 11 December 2007 . . . Andrew Taylor/Fairfaxphotos.com.

Arriving at Kirribilli House . . . Newspix/Vanessa Hunter.

A tired but grimly pleased Julia Gillard . . . Newspix/Ray Strange.

The Minister for Education at the coalface . . . Newspix/Tim Marsden.

Index

ALSO BY JACQUELINE KENT

An exacting heart: the story of Hephzibah Menuhin

Hephzibah Menuhin had a musical gift most people only dream of. Her refusal to be defined by it led her to reinvent herself not once but twice in her remarkable life.

Born in 1920 in San Francisco she was, like her world-renowned brother Yehudi, a child prodigy, simultaneously thrown into the spotlight at an early age and closeted by a dominating, controlling mother. In the brief spring between the world wars, the Menuhin family travelled extensively, driven by the demands of Yehudi's career. Then Hephzibah, aged seventeen, celebrated as her brother's musical partner and on the brink of greatness in her own right, turned her back on performing. She married Lindsay Nicholas, the Melbourne-born heir to a pharmaceutical fortune, and moved to his sheep property in western Victoria.

Far from playing the conventional wife of a wealthy grazier, Hephzibah threw herself into humanitarian projects in her adopted country. She raised two sons and eventually resumed performing, both solo and with Yehudi, to international acclaim. But after sixteen years that seemed from the outside happy and fulfilled, she met a man who drew her to question what she thought she knew – and to abandon her established life a second time.

What makes a woman walk out on her children? What makes her turn her back on a brilliant artistic career? *An Exacting Heart* reveals the complex and contradictory nature of Hephzibah Menuhin: warm-hearted, humorous, astute, generous, occasionally ruthless and wrong-headed. In portraying the life and times of this fascinating and mercurial woman, Jacqueline Kent examines not only the consequences of possessing great talent, but the costs and rewards of gambling for high emotional stakes.

'An enthralling story' JIM DAVIDSON, *AGE*

'Flawless' PETER ROSE, *AUSTRALIAN BOOK REVIEW*